T0150347

Bouki fait Gombo:
A History of the Slave Community of Habitation Haydel (Whitney Plantation) Louisiana, 1750-1860

IBRAHIMA SECK
DEPARTMENT OF HISTORY
CHEIKH ANTA DIOP UNIVERSITY (UCAD)
DAKAR, SENEGAL

UNO PRESS

Printed in the United States of America

Ibrahima Seck

Bouki fait Gombo: A History of the Slave Community of Habitation Haydel (Whitney Plantation) Louisiana, 1750–1860

ISBN: 978-1-60801-095-0

Library of Congress Control Number: 2013938684

UNO PRESS

University of New Orleans Press

unopress.org

Book and Cover Design: Allison Reu & Kevin Stone

To my departed and sorely missed colleagues
Joseph Caldwell and Joseph Logsdon

CONTENTS

ABBREVIATIONS

SC	St. Charles Parish Court House Archives, Original Acts, Hahnville, LA.
SJ	St. James Parish Court House Archives, Original Acts, Convent, LA.
SJB	St. John the Baptist Court House Archives, Original Acts, Edgard, LA.
SJB-CB	St. John Parish Court House Archives; Conveyance Book, Edgard, LA.
SJB-BR	St. John Parish Colonial Archives; Baton Rouge, State Archives.
SJB-CCR	St. John Parish Clerk of Court Records, 1802-1958, State Archives, Baton Rouge.
MPA	Mississippi Provincial Archives.
NONA	New Orleans Notarial Archives
CHREO	New Orleans, City Hall Real Estate Office

ACKNOWLEDGMENTS

Many individuals and institutions have contributed to the development of this study. I would like to thank them all with a special reference to the Cummings family of New Orleans for devoting much time and resources to the implementation of the site of memory, which is the subject of this monograph. Dr. Gwendolyn Midlo Hall, Professor Emeritus and retiree of Rutgers University, introduced me to this family. The reader will find in the foreword how much I was blessed to encounter this generous lady who has become my spiritual mother. Katie Morlas, a graduate from LSU's History Department, has contributed much to this work by exploring the Sacramental Records of the Archdiocese of New Orleans among other documents. I would also like to acknowledge the support of Deanna Tassin Schexnayder, the daughter of Maurice Tassin, who was the manager of Whitney plantation from the 1940s to the 1970s. Deanna currently holds the position of Associate Director and Senior Research Scientist at the Ray Marshall Center for the Study of Human Resources, a unit of the Lyndon B. Johnson School of Public Affairs at the University of Texas at Austin. Steve Barnes, the grandson of Alfred M. Barnes, also provided valuable firsthand documents and his fond memories of the plantation. Thanks also to Norman Marmillon (Laura Plantation) for sharing his knowledge of the German Coast and precious maps related to this area. We also feel deeply indebted to the descendants of Victor Haydel who shared the memories of their family. I would like to name, among others, Belmont F. Haydel, Sybil Haydel Morial, and Curtis M. Graves. Jay Edwards, a member of the faculty in the Department of Anthropology and Geography of LSU, also brought some valuable direction as the best expert of this site. My thanks also goes to Douglas Chambers of the History Department of the University of Southern Mississippi at Hattiesburg for stepping in and helping tremendously for the editing of this work.

I would also like to express my gratitude to the following institutions and their personnel: the faculty members of UNO History Department, the archivists of St. John the Baptist Parish, St. James Parish, and St. Charles Parish courthouses; the archivists of the Louisiana State Archives in Baton Rouge and those of the New Orleans Public Library and the Historic New Orleans Collection; the Roman Catholic Church of the Archdiocese of New Orleans through Charles Nolan, former editor of the Sacramental Records, and special gratitude to UNO Press and the Midlo Center for New Orleans Studies.

A Wolof proverb advises the lamb to acknowledge the old food that turned him into a ram. Beyond the support of my own country's institutions, the "old food" that nurtured me was composed of several fellowships granted to me through the US Embassy in Dakar, Senegal. The United States Information Agency (USIA) International Visitor Program, sponsored by the Institute of International Education (IIE) allowed me to discover the US South by traveling to Mississippi for the first time in 1989. I was part of a group of nine high school teachers from Africa. The Fulbright Junior Staff Fellowship allowed me to attend a non-degree program at the University of Mississippi at Oxford (Ole Miss) and the University of New Orleans (UNO) during the Academic year of 1995-1996. I was working then on a Doctorate degree at the University Cheikh Anta Diop of Dakar. The Ford Foundation also allowed me to attend the African Humanities Program co-hosted by the University of Ghana (Legon) and Northwestern University (Evanston, Illinois) and co-sponsored by the Council for the Development of Social Science Research in Africa (CODESRIA) back in 1998. I am deeply indebted to the faculty and staff of all the institutions that hosted these different programs of which I was a fortunate participant. They gave me a first-hand experience on the subject of slavery in West Africa and the US South.

Many thanks to people who constantly supported me: Joyce King, Hassimi Maiga, Joyce Marie Jackson and her departed husband, J. Nash Porter. Thanks also to my colleagues at the Gravier street office and at the Sugar Mill in New Orleans, and out there on the site of the plantation: Scott and Christine Zazulak, Larissa Jama, Paul Walther, Robert Slynn, Bill Young, Russell Stagg, Josh Stagg, Denard Roudeze, Nicole White, Jenes de Oliveira Pereira (Jimmy) and his dream team. I also wish to acknowledge the hard work of the staff of UNO Press: the former director Bill Lavender and his successor Abram Himelstein, Allison Reu, George K. Darby, Alex Dimeff, and Jen Hanks. I express a big merci beaucoup to the History department of UCAD (Dakar, Senegal) and to the staff of the West African Research Center in Dakar, Senegal, where half of the time dedicated to this book was spent. Last but not least, I thank my family for their support and patience: my wife Sokhna and my children, Khady Boye, Khady Diouf, Abdoul Aziz, and Cheikh Anta John. The support of my elder brother, Sada Lame, will always be of an inestimable value. When my mother became too weak to work, he withdrew from school, found a job as a night watch, and renounced his salary for many years to make sure I stayed in school and that food would be available at the house. I wish to end this page with a special acknowledgement for my deceased mother, Hawa Lambel Sy, a single parent who worked for many years as a laundress and as a domestic servant. She was not educated, but she knew the meaning of the French word "premier." She wanted me to be always Number One at school. It did happen often, not all the time, but this was her own way of keeping me among the best of my generation. I owe this journey from our cornfield by the Senegal River to the cane fields of the Haydel plantation on the Mississippi River to her.

FOREWORD

It is my pleasure to introduce Dr. Ibrahima Seck's study of the historical background of Whitney Plantation. This exciting book demonstrates the value of looking at Louisiana history, especially the discussion of folklore, foodways, and naming practices from the point of view of a Senegalese historian. He reaches out from a sharply local study of the Haydel/Whitney plantation to an informed discussion of Atlantic history: an extremely difficult thing to pull off. It is well organized and simply and straightforwardly written, avoiding the jargon which weighs down too much scholarly work. The photos and illustrations add a great deal to its value. There is much new research and thought supplied. I met Dr. Seck in 1993 in Dakar, Senegal, where I had been invited to give the keynote address at the initiation of the West African Research Center. Dr. Eileen Julien had initiated and founded this center while she was a Fulbright research scholar there. She had read my book, *Africans in Colonial Louisiana: the Development of Afro-Creole Culture in the Eighteenth Century*, which emphasized the heavily Senegalese origins of the slaves brought to Louisiana, especially during the French period. I also spoke at the Ecole Normale Supérieure, and Dr. Seck was in the audience. He asked me for a copy of my speech. I had a copy on my computer, so I handed him the printout I had used.

That was the beginning of a major transformation of consciousness in Senegal as well as in Dr. Seck's career. Dr. Seck was a high school teacher in Dakar at the time. He went to the University of Dakar and obtained his doctorate in history. He wrote a doctoral dissertation that dealt with the Senegalese influence in Louisiana. He distributed my book to the intellectual community in Dakar. The book as well as the website where my *Louisiana Slave Database* was mounted with a search engine became well known in Senegal. Dr. Seck now teaches in the History Department at the University of Dakar where the students are very interested in the connections between Louisiana and Senegal. In Louisiana, there has been growing interest in Senegal as the mother country of many Afro-Louisianans.

Trips to Senegal and Gorée Island have been organized from Louisiana. Several historical museums and plantations in Louisiana have recognized these ties: the Cabildo in New Orleans, the Laura Plantation, the Afro-American Museums in Donaldsonville and St. Martinville, etc. Urbain Alexandre Diagne, mayor of Gorée Island, and General Mamadou Mansour Seck, Ambassador of Senegal to the United States, attended the initiation of the African-American Museum in St. Martinville in 2000.

Now the Cummings family has opened the new Whitney Plantation Museum to the public after devoting many years and substantial resources to this project. As a trial lawyer, John Cummings knows that one good image is worth a thousand words. He is reproducing many authentic images, including reproduction of the architecture of the past at the Whitney Plantation Museum. With much careful research and thought, Whitney Plantation will engage the wider public in knowledge of slavery and the system of slavery in Louisiana as well as the elements of culture from Senegambia, which played a vital role in the formation of Louisiana Creole culture. He has been wise enough to tap into Dr. Seck's expertise about Senegal and Senegalese history and culture. He could not find a better expert.

Dr. Gwendolyn Midlo Hall

PROLOGUE

One of the most famous historical Louisiana proverbs, which Lafcadio Hearn included in his 1885 collection, *Gombo Zhèbes*, evokes the multicultural reality of plantation slave communities: "Bouki fait gombo, lapin mangé li" (He-Goat makes the gombo, but Rabbit eats it).[1] In other words, this French Creole proverb depicts the master/slave relationship: Bouki–the hyena in Senegalese folktales who does all the work– makes gumbo, Lapin—the folktale ancestor of Br'er Rabbit and Bugs Bunny–eats it. Hearn lived in New Orleans for over a decade, from 1877 to 1888, and in those years he became fascinated with the culture of what is still the most Caribbean of American cities. Indeed New Orleans, historically, and including the old plantation districts up the Mississippi River, such as the German Coast (St. Charles, St. John the Baptist, and part of St. James Parishes), feels so like the Caribbean in large part because of the enduring influence of enslaved Africans and their descendants. From Congo Square to voodoo, and from gumbo to jazz to folktales featuring a character (Bouki) widely known in modern-day Senegal and Gambia in West Africa, we are constantly reminded of particular African influences in the history of Louisiana. That history, however, has often been obscured.

What does an apparently insignificant proverb have to do with the study of a

1 Originally published in Lafcadio Hearn, *Gombo Zhèbes: Little Dictionary of Creole Proverbs, Selected from Six Creole Dialects* (New York, W.H. Coleman, 1885), proverb no.40, p.11; repr. in Lafcadio Hearn, *Inventing New Orleans: Writings of Lafcadio Hearn*, ed., with an introduction, by S. Frederick Starr (Jackson: University Press of Mississippi, 2001), p.205. In *Gombo Zhèbes*, Hearn noted (n1 p.11) that "this proverb is founded upon one of the many amusing Creole animal-fables, all bearing the title: *Compè Bouki épis Compè Lapin* ('Daddy Goat and Daddy Rabbit'). The rabbit always comes out victorious, as in the stories of Uncle Remus." See also Alcée Fortier, "Bits of Louisiana Folklore," *Transactions and Proceedings of the Modern Language Association 3* (1887), pp.100-168; and Alcée Fortier, ed. and trans., *Louisiana Folk-Tales In French Dialect and English Translation*, Memoirs of The American Folk-Lore Society, vol. II (Boston: Houghton, Mifflin and Company, 1895); with selections reprinted in "Trickster Tales in Alcée Fortier's *Louisiana Folk-Tales* (1895): English Translations," *The Southern Quarterly* 46, 4 (2009), pp.88-145.

plantation that has so far remained unknown to the public and tour operators? The response is quite simple. One can think of a gang out there in the fields, during the dog days of August or during the chilly days of December, probably not properly clothed, making sure that enough indigo or sugar would get out of "the indigoteries" or the sugar mills. Think of an overseer walking around with a whip and the master monitoring everything from the far end, under the shade of the rear gallery of the second floor of the big house. Later, the latter would be enjoying a fine meal that may include some okra gumbo cooked by some "apron-girt sambo" while his children were being taken care of by a female slave who spoke to them in Creole, which means a mixture of European (mainly French), African, and native Indian words melted in the crucible of African grammar. Beyond the master, who stands for the rabbit in the above proverb, and the African or Creole slave who stands for Bouki, one should think of the millions of kids today enjoying cartoons featuring Bugs Bunny, the modern rendition of a folktale character that followed the African slaves in the plantations of the U.S. south.

One also should think of how "kingombo," the Bantu word for okra, came to designate a famous Louisiana dish. Or how the African word "okra" itself came to designate the plant that has become a real symbol in Louisiana and in all the southern United States. The history of slavery should not only be the history of deportation and hard labor in the plantations. Beyond these painful memories, we should always dig deep enough to find out how Africans contributed tremendously to the making of Southern culture and American identity. Louisiana was simply "the most significant source of Africanization of the entire culture of the United States,"[2] and the starting point of the most unique cultural productions that are widely associated with the definition of American culture and that have conquered the world, including musical forms such as blues, jazz, and rock & roll.

This study explores the Atlantic slave trade and the historical links between Louisiana and Sub-Saharan Africa through the discussion of slavery on the German Coast and Habitation Haydel, a plantation initiated by a German settler in the middle of the eighteenth century and renamed Whitney Plantation after the Civil War.

---

2 Gwendolyn Midlo Hall, *Africans in Colonial Louisiana: The Development of Afro-Creole Culture in the Eighteenth Century* (Baton Rouge: Louisiana State University Press, 1992), p.157.

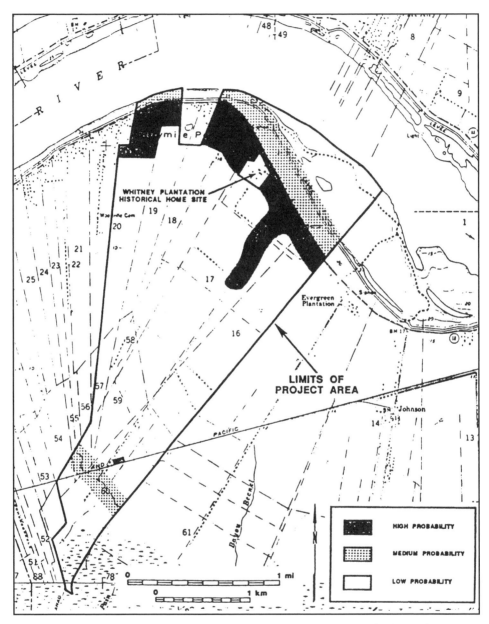

Fig. 1.1. Portion of the 1962 USGS "Lutcher, LA." Quadrangle (7.5' series) showing the Whitney Plantation project area and the probability of archaeological remains existing on the site.

Source: Hunter and als. 1991. Whitney Plantation: Archeology on the German Coast. Cultural Resources Investigations in St. John the Baptist Parish, Louisiana. Volume 1, fig. 4.13, p. 4-29.

CHAPTER ONE

BOUKI FAIT GOMBO
The making of a site of memory

Go on in. You have to go inside.
When you walk in that space, you
can't deny what happened to these people.
You can feel it, touch it, smell it.
—Lt. Governor Mitch Landrieu, after
visiting the site of Whitney Plantation.

The Haydel Plantation, now referred to as Whitney Plantation, is located on the west bank of the Mississippi River, on the historic River Road in St. John the Baptist Parish, between Edgard and Wallace, Louisiana. Ambroise Heidel, a German who immigrated to Louisiana with his mother and siblings in 1721, lived on the original land tract as early as 1752. Jean Jacques Haydel, the younger son of Ambroise, became the owner of the land initially held by his father. In 1803, he claimed a plantation seventeen arpents by forty arpents, located in St. John the Baptist Parish, on the right bank of the river, between Mathias Roussel (upstream), and the plantation of Jacques Haydel and Brothers, the sons of the then late Nicolas Haydel Sr.[1] In 1820, Jean Jacques Haydel Sr. passed on the plantation to his sons, Marcellin and Jean Jacques Jr. Two years later, the heirs purchased the plantation of Jacques Haydel and Brothers, thus extending their property downstream.[2] In

---

1 W. Lowrie, ed., *American State papers, Documents, Legislative and executive, of the Congress of the United States in relation to the public lands*, Vol.2 (Washington, D.C., 1834), p.320. One arpent accounts for about 183 linear feet or 55.7 meters.
2 Abstracts from a copy of the original act passed on 2 December 1822; in SJB-27-1839/ Haydel Francois Marcellin & Jean Jacques: *Inventaire des biens possédés indivisément par eux.*

1840, after the death of Marcellin Haydel, the plantation was auctioned, and Azélie Haydel, his widow, gained total control of the land and ran the plantation until her death in 1860. It eventually became one of the most important sugar plantations in Louisiana.[3] After the Civil War, the plantation was sold to Bradish Johnson, who named the property after his grandson, Harry Whitney.

The first group of German immigrants arrived in Louisiana between 1719 and 1721. This group included farmers who contracted with John Law and the French Company of the West. They settled above New Orleans in the first German Coast (St. Charles Parish). During the 1750s, a second wave of German colonists settled in St. John the Baptist Parish. Later, they carved out the parish of St. James along with the Acadians who found their way to Louisiana after the English expelled them from Canada during the Seven Years' War. The Old Vacherie Road is supposed to be the physical limit between the German Coast and the "Côte des Acadiens" (Acadians' Coast).

Under French rule (1699-1763), the German Coast soon became the main supplier of food to New Orleans through the hard work of the settlers aided by their white indentured servants and African slaves, just like in the early years of the French West Indian colony of Saint Domingue. Wealth and comfort followed later with the massive importation of slaves and the development of the indigo production under Spanish rule (1763-1803).[4] The collapse of the indigo industry at the end of the eighteenth century was soon followed by the birth of the sugar industry, which production skyrocketed with the Louisiana Purchase (1803) and a large influx of slaves, including thousands smuggled from Africa and the Caribbean islands.

The African slaves cleared the land and planted corn, rice, and vegetables. They ran indigo processing facilities and later sugar mills. They built levees to protect dwellings and crops. They also served as sawyers, carpenters, masons, and smiths. They raised horses, oxen, mules, cows, sheep, swine, and poultry. Slaves also served as cooks, handling the demanding task of hulling rice with mortars and pestles. They performed all kinds of duties to make life easy and enjoyable for their masters. African female slaves raised their own children while caring for their masters'. Slaves often escaped and became maroons in the swamps to avoid deadly work and whipping. Those recaptured suffered severe punishment such as branding with a hot iron, mutilation, and, eventually, the death penalty.

It was probably these sad memories that caught up with Mitch Landrieu, former Lieutenant Governor of Louisiana and current mayor of New Orleans, when he

---

3 Joseph K. Menn, *The large slaveholders of Louisiana-1860* (New Orleans: Pelican Publishing Company, 1964).

4 In fact, the Spanish did not take control of the colony until 1769 with the arrival of Alejandro O'Reilly. A first attempt failed in 1766 when Ulloa was expelled by the local officials and planters who opposed the cession of the colony to the Spanish after the defeat of France in the Seven-Year War.

visited the site of Whitney Plantation sometime during the spring of 2008. After sitting for a while inside one of the slave cabins, he confessed to the journalist who interviewed him later that day: "Go on in. You have to go inside. When you walk in that space, you can't deny what happened to these people. You can feel it, touch it, smell it."[5]

Primary sources used in this study are mostly sacramental records and courthouse records. The latter are located in different parishes on the German Coast, the State Archives in Baton Rouge, and Orleans Parish. Throughout the colonial period, the documents encountered are almost exclusively written in French. Although documents were elaborated in Spanish and English, French was still the main language of the official literature before the Civil War. The history of slavery is well documented through manumission cases and trials mostly involving runaway slaves and others accused for murder or minor offenses. Some cases involved masters accused of bad treatment of their slaves. Succession matters provide a clear picture of plantation society and economy by describing landed properties, the slaves attached to them, and, oftentimes, the old and new crops stored in granaries or standing out in the fields. The value of each estate was estimated in *piastres*, a French currency equivalent to the Spanish *peso* and to the American dollar. It was divided into five *livres* or eight "bits" or "rials" (reales).[6]

The Sacramental Records of the Roman Catholic Church of the Archdiocese of New Orleans include marriage, birth, baptism, and death records. Despite the missing data for the early period, they provide the most complete information for genealogy. The free people of color and the baptized slaves are also documented through the Sacramental Records. These documents were accessed indirectly through the nineteen volumes published since 1987. So far, they cover only the period of 1718 to 1831 since volume 20 has been delayed due to Hurricane Katrina and the retirement of Charles E. Nolan, archivist and editor at the Archdiocese for over two decades. The Haydel family is widely recorded in these volumes, but the early transcription of their name (Heidel, Aidle, or Aydelle) can be misleading. Records related to the later period, before and after the Civil War, were accessed directly by Katy Morlas, a graduate of Louisiana State University, who supported this project for some time with her hard work. The writing of the last chapter of this book was made possible partly thanks to her contribution.

Websites have also become a common source of information for researchers around the world. In this regard, Gwendolyn Midlo Hall's comprehensive *Louisiana Slave Database* is the most valuable source used in this study to illustrate the African origins and the ethnic composition of the slave force of the German

---

5 *The New York Times*, 25 May 2008.
6 Jack D.L. Holmes, "Indigo in Colonial Louisiana and the Floridas," *Louisiana History* 8 (1967), p.334, fn.31.

Coast.[7]   Beyond plantation inventories and criminal cases, slaves were also identified in wills, marriage contracts, leases, seizures for debt, mortgages of slaves, and reports of death. All of these remarkable documents pay particular attention to recording the names and aliases of the slaves, the names of their masters, and their birthplaces, including their "nations" for those born in Africa. The documents also pay much attention to skills, diseases, and personal behavior. In the *Louisiana Slave Database*, the vast majority of the slaves whose birthplaces were identified were Africans. Among 38,019 slaves whose birthplaces were recorded, 24,349 (64 percent) were of African birth. Among these, 8,994 (37 percent) indicate specific "nations" while 9,382 (38.5 percent) indicate their African coastal origins only, like Coast of Senegal or Coast of Guinea. Some 5,973 records (25.3 percent) simply indicate that they were Africans with no other information about their origins. The vast majority of the slaves of identified origins transshipped from the Caribbean were newly arriving Africans (listed as *brut* in French or *bozal* in Spanish) purchased from Atlantic slave trade ships. There is a particularly high percentage of identified birthplaces, especially many African "nations" of slaves, recorded in documents dating between 1770 and 1820 in the lower Mississippi Valley parishes: St. Charles, St. John the Baptist, Pointe Coupee, and, to a lesser extent, Orleans.[8]

Firsthand documents include travelers' accounts and newspapers. The diaries used in this study are mostly related to the Colonial period. Three authors, all of them French, provide eyewitness accounts at very crucial times in the history of Louisiana: Le Page du Pratz for the early period, Victor Collot towards the end of the Spanish regime, and Champommier, the tireless "Monsieur Sucre" of Louisiana.

Antoine Simon Le Page Du Pratz (born ca. 1695) arrived in Louisiana on August 25, 1718 when New Orleans "existed only in name," according to his own words. After living on the banks of Bayou St. John for about two years, he left for the Natchez country where he spent eight years. He was lucky enough to leave this settlement just before the massacre of the French colonists by the Natchez Indians in 1729. He was then appointed "intendant" of the King's plantation near New Orleans. His experience gave him a very intimate knowledge of the African slaves and their skills. He returned to France in 1734 and published his book in three volumes in 1758.[9]

By the time of the War of the French Revolution, Georges-Henri-Victor Collot (1750-1805) was appointed governor of Guadeloupe. When the British captured

---

7 Gwendolyn Midlo Hall, *Louisiana Slave Database* (2000), online at http://www.ibiblio.org/laslave/.

8 Hall, *Louisiana Slave Database*: http://ibiblio.org/laslave/AcksandIntro.html (accessed 26 September 2010).

9 Le Page du Pratz, *Histoire de la Louisiane* (Paris: De Bure, 1758).

the island in 1794, Collot was turned over to American authorities in Philadelphia to answer legal charges brought by an American merchant. He was forced to pay bail and remain in the country. Meanwhile, Pierre Adet, French minister to the United States, asked Collot to undertake the delicate task of reconnoitering the interior parts of the country. The French minister worried that the United States might enter the war on the side of Britain, and if they did, France would need accurate intelligence about the Mississippi and Missouri valleys. Collot accepted this responsibility and engaged French military cartographer Joseph Warin, two Canadians voyageurs, and three American boatmen to navigate the waterways in a flat-bottomed boat. The party descended the Mississippi, reaching New Orleans on October 27, 1796. The Spanish authorities promptly arrested them, but Collot was finally released on December 22, 1796. By this time, his companion Warin had died from injuries suffered on the trip. He returned to France where his manuscript was published in 1826.[10] Chapter XXVI of Collot's book is dedicated to the agriculture of Louisiana with a striking account of the collapse of the indigo business and the planters' shift to other crops such as cotton and sugar cane.[11]

P.A. Champommier was a fine observer of the sugar business in Louisiana. Almost all the figures related to the volume of sugar produced on the Haydel plantation come from the data he carefully collected during his visits to the planters at the end of the grinding season. In late March 1847, Eliza Ripley, a fifteen-year-old girl, was on board the riverboat *La Belle Creole* from New Orleans to visit Valcour Aime's plantation in St. James Parish. The narrative of her encounter with Champommier is eloquent enough for the presentation of this man who, over fifteen years from 1844 through the Civil War, dedicated his time to documenting the sugar production in the entire state:

> M. Champomier is on board. Everybody knows *le vieux* Champomier. He mingles with all, conspicuously carries his memorandum book and pencil, and we all know he is "on business bent," getting from any and every available source statistics of the year's crop of sugar. Whether he acted for a corporation, or it was his individual enterprise, I never knew, but he visited the planters, traveled up and down and all around the sugar region, and in the spring compiled and computed and published in a small, paper-covered book (price $5) the name and address of every planter and the amount of sugar made on each individual estate.

10 Excerpts from *American Journeys. Eyewitness accounts of Early American Exploration and Settlement: A Digital Library and Learning Center.* http://www.americanjourneys.org/aj-088a/summary/index.asp (Accessed September 1, 2011).

11 Collot, Georges-Henri-Victor: *Journey in North America, Containing a Survey of the Countries Watered by the Mississippi, Ohio, Missouri, and Other Affluing Rivers* (Paris: Printed for Arthus Bertrand, 1826).

"Champomier's report" was considered as authentic as need be for the planter to know what his neighbor's crop actually amounted to, and the city merchant to adjust his mortgages and loans on a safe basis.[12]

Most of the newspapers cited in this study were found in microfilms in the Louisiana Division of the New Orleans Public Library. New Orleans papers such as *L'Abeille de La Nouvelle Orleans (The New Orleans Bee)* and *The Times-Picayune* are interesting sources for the study of the German Coast. St. John the Baptist Parish was the second permanent settlement in this area. It was started with Karlstein, a little town named after Karl Frederic d'Arensbourg, the leader of the German community for many years. Karlstein was renamed Lucy and became the parish seat until 1848 when it was moved to Edgard. Lucy was also the cradle of journalism in the river parishes, as the printing press for both *Le Meschachébé* and *L'Avant Coureur* newspapers, covering St. John and St. Charles parishes respectively, set up shop there in 1852. *L'Avant Coureur* ceased publication on October 14, 1878, and *Le Meschachébé* continued on into the mid-1940s.[13] This newspaper was published in both French and English. It became a perfect barometer for plantation life, and news of all kinds were also conveyed from the city of New Orleans. This source can be accessed through its microfilmed version housed at the public library in Laplace and at the Hill Memorial Library at LSU.

Last but not least, the oral stories of the former slaves have been used in this study. In the absence of interviews with people who lived on Whitney plantation, a voice is given to them through the testimonies of their fellows taken to court or through the interviews with former slaves conducted by the Louisiana Writers' Project, the local section of the Federal Writers' Project. One of the best interviewers attached to this project was Robert McKinney, an African American "known and trusted by many black Orleanians" and who "understood the psychology of the uneducated Negroes." His interview with Mrs. Elizabeth Ross Hite is considered a "classic" from which most of the oral testimonies used in this study were taken.[14]

There is much literature on the history of the German Coast, but beyond demography and economy, there is no solid emphasis on the slave force, its African background, and certainly not its input in the making of local and regional culture. One of the best references is the book published in 1956 by Helmut Blume in German (*Die Entwicklung der Kulturlandschaft des Mississippideltas in Kolonialer Zeit, unter Besonderer Berücksichtigung der Deutchen Siedlung*). This book was translated, edited, and annotated by Ellen C. Merrill, and published in 1990 by the German-Acadian Coast Historical

---

12 Eliza Ripley, *Social life in Old New Orleans Being Recollections of my Girlhood* (New York and London: Appleton and Company, MCMXII), p.183-184. P.A. Champomier, *Statement of the Sugar Crop Made in Louisiana* (New Orleans: Cook, Young, & Co., 1844, 1845-46, and 1849-50 to 1858-59).

13 Lucy town history: http://www.reocities.com/gee_38/lucy.html. Accessed 10 October 2011.

14 Ronnie W. Clayton, *Mother Wit: The Ex-Slave Narratives of the Louisiana Writers' Project* (New York: Peter Lang Publishing, Inc., 1990), p.4.

and genealogical Society, under the title *The German Coast during the Colonial Era 1722-1803*. The interest of this author was essentially focused on the German colonists, their European origins, and their settlements in Colonial Louisiana. Gwendolyn Midlo Hall encompasses a much wider space in which New Orleans, Pointe Coupée, and Bas du Fleuve (St. Bernard Parish) are given a better focus compared to the German Coast. But the author of *Africans in Colonial Louisiana* (1992) has initiated quite a different approach in which the African slaves and their descendants stand with more agency instead of simply being objects at the mercy of the masters.

Several studies on Whitney Plantation were produced by students related to the School of Architecture at Tulane University in New Orleans or the Department of Geography and Anthropology at Louisiana State University in Baton Rouge.[15] The thesis of Thaddeus Roger Kilpatrick III, produced in 1992 within the Graduate Program in Historic Preservation of the University of Pennsylvania, offers an interesting study of the decorative paintings at Whitney Plantation. He contributed to the writing of specific studies in five volumes, related to the preservation and restoration of the Whitney Plantation, submitted to the Fred B. Kniffen Cultural Resources Laboratory of the Department of Geography and Anthropology of LSU, for the Formosa Plastics Corporation of Louisiana between 1991 and 1992. Jay Edwards, a professor of anthropology and a historian of architecture at Louisiana

---

15 See, Alva B. III. 1982. *Whitney Plantation*. Architectural Thesis. Tulane School of Architecture.

Kilpatrick, Thaddeus Roger III. 1992. A Conservation Study Of The Decorative Paintings At Whitney Plantation, St. John The Baptist Parish, Louisiana. A Thesis in the Graduate Program in Historic Preservation. Presented to the Faculties of the University of Pennsylvania in Partial Fulfillment of the Requirements for the Degree of Master of Science, University of Pennsylvania.

Dillard, Krishnan, Lial, Lessard, and Martin. "Whitney and Evergreen Plantation". In *River Road Preservation and Promotion*. Tulane University, School of Architecture: Preservation Studies, Spring 2005, pp. 28-29.

Roberts, Erika Sabine. *Digging through discarded identity: archaeological investigations around the kitchen and the overseer's house at Whitney plantation, Louisiana*. Thesis Submitted to the Graduate Faculty of the Louisiana State University and Agricultural and Mechanical College in partial fulfillment of the requirements for the degree of Master of Arts in the Department of Geography and Anthropology, May 2005.

State University, was the leading scholar for this project.[16] Two volumes related to archaeology on Whitney Plantation were also submitted to the Formosa Plastics Corporation of Louisiana by Walk, Haydel & Associates in 1991.[17] In all these studies, material culture, especially architecture, is invariably the main topic. So far, no study focused on the institution of slavery on this plantation.

The slaves imported in Louisiana were mostly shipped from three major regions of the coasts of Africa: Senegambia, the bights of Benin and Biafra, and West-Central Africa. The majority of the slave force came from Senegambia throughout the Colonial period especially during the French regime when Louisiana and Senegal were both under the control of the French Company of the West Indies, from 1719 to 1731. Besides providing further details on the mechanisms or *modus operandi* of the slave trade business on African soil, the emphasis on Senegambia is meant to highlight the crucial role played by this region in the making of the Louisiana colony and the shaping of its culture. One important goal of the study of the Haydel/Whitney plantation, which represents the core of this book, is to see to what extent it reflects the patterns of the Atlantic slave trade described above. The nesting of the history of this site of memory in a very wide perspective is also meant to give the reader enough tools for a better understanding of the plantation system through primary sources consisting mainly of inventories. These

16 Jay Edwards, *The Preservation and Restoration of the Whitney Plantation, St. John the Baptist Parish, Louisiana. Volume I: Historic Structures Report.* Department of Geography and Anthropology, Louisiana State University, Baton Rouge, 15 November 1991.

Jon Emerson and Associates. *The Preservation and Restoration of the Whitney Plantation. Volume II: Landscape and Site Planning.* Submitted to the Fred B. Kniffen Cultural Resources Laboratory, Department of Geography and Anthropology (LSU), for the Formosa Plastics Corporation of Louisiana, 15 August 1991.

William Brockway. *The Preservation and Restoration of the Whitney Plantation. Volume III: Specifications for Restoration and Preservation of the Existing Structures and Specifications for the Proposed Visitor's Center.* Submitted to the Fred B. Kniffen Cultural Resources Laboratory, Department of Geography and Anthropology (LSU), for the Formosa Plastics Corporation of Louisiana, 15 November 1991.

Jon Emerson and Associates. *The Preservation and Restoration of the Whitney Plantation. Volume IV: Museum of Louisiana's Creole Culture.* Submitted to the Fred B. Kniffen Cultural Resources Laboratory, Department of Geography and Anthropology (LSU), for the Formosa Plastics Corporation of Louisiana, 1 November 1991.

Kilpatrick T., Mosca M., and Edwards J., *The Preservation and Restoration of the Whitney Plantation. Volume V: Historic paints analyses.* Submitted to the Fred B. Kniffen Cultural Resources Laboratory, Department of Geography and Anthropology (LSU), for the Formosa Plastics Corporation of Louisiana, 5 November 1992.

17 Hunter and als. Whitney Plantation: Archeology on the German Coast. Cultural Resources Investigations in St. John the Baptist Parish, Louisiana. Prepared under contract with Walk, Haydel & Associates, Inc. for the Formosa Plastics Corporation of Louisiana. 2 volumes, 1 November 1991.

documents offer still pictures of the past captured at various occasions such as the death or bankruptcy of the owners, but they remain the primary source of information on slavery. Chapter 2 (The German Coast) and chapter 3 (Atlantic Crossings) are crafted toward the full understanding of the making of the slave society on the German Coast of which Habitation Haydel was a component. The word *creole* is often used here to designate the people and the culture of Lower Louisiana whatever their race or complexion.[18] The racial designation "mulatto" used in this study for individuals born from the mating of Blacks and Whites, no matter the circumstances, must be understood without any pejorative connotation that may lay under it.

The last section of this book addresses important aspects of slave life and culture through the treatment of slaves on the German coast and their resistance to the plantation system, which culminated in the 1811 uprising. Resistance was conducted through marronage (slaves running away) and revolt but also through peaceful and often less suspected means such as music, storytelling, and even food. This chapter is meant to complete the picture of the journey of the enslaved people from Africa to Louisiana. It uncovers some of their contributions to the making of the local culture by looking beyond the hard work in and around the rice fields, indigo vats, and sugar mills. Overall, this book is destined to correct the lack of interpretive African history in plantation tours and tourist areas in New Orleans. It also suggests several topics of research in the field of cultural history and may be useful to teachers of African-American history.

This monograph is a modest contribution to the study of slavery in Louisiana and the German Coast through the dormer windows of Haydel/Whitney Plantation. It focuses on the slaves, badly needed economic agents but dehumanized and inventoried with furniture, tools, animals, and crops. However, there is a ray of light on this absurd world since the slaves were not totally deprived of their identity. Once brought to the colony and sold, the slaves were usually given Christian names or classical names of the Greco-Roman civilization. Some names were inspired by popular French plays of the time. Lindor, probably the most frequent male name in the *Louisiana Slave Database*, is a character in *The Barber of Seville*, a very successful French play by Pierre Beaumarchais, written in 1773 and performed for the first time on February 23, 1775 at the *Comédie-Française* in Paris.[19] Another character in the same play is L'Éveillé. This name was also very popular among the slaves of Louisiana. According to a major genealogy website, Lindor is a surname found mainly in Louisiana within North America. For this source the name remains

18 G. Midlo-Hall, *Africans in Colonial Louisiana* (1992), p.157.

19 The plot involves a Spanish Count, who has fallen in love with a girl called Rosine. To ensure that she really loves him and not just his money, the Count disguises himself as a poor *bachelier* (college student) named Lindor, and attempts to woo her. Lindor is also the name of characters in some other French plays such as *La vie d'une comédienne* (Anicet-Bourgeois & Barrière, 1854) and *Le maître à aimer* (Veber & Delorme, 1907).

unexplained and it speculates on a probable French origin, perhaps a respelling of Linder, an Alsace name of German origin.[20] The name also travelled to Senegal and to the French colonies of Guyana and the Antilles where it has become a family name or a middle name.[21]

Nevertheless, the slaves brought to Louisiana also strongly held onto their African culture and heritage as demonstrated in the retention of African personal names and naming practices.[22] So, it was quite usual for the slaves born in Africa and the Creoles to have at least two names: the Christian name given by the master and the African name they brought with them or which they gave to their children. Nicknames may add to those official names for the purpose of mystical protection. In West African folk beliefs, the more names one carries, the more that person is supposed to be protected from evil spirits and spells cast by human beings. Thus, Sunjata, the founder of the Mali Empire, was "The-man-of-many-names-against-whom-all-spells-have-failed" (*L'homme aux noms multiples contre qui les sortilèges n'ont rien pu*), especially those cast by Sumaworo Kanteh, the powerful king of Soso and his contender for political leadership in the region.[23] Among the Fulbe, the most spread-out people on African soil, each child has a *soomoore*, which means a protective mystical name.[24]

Since many parts of West Africa also had a long history of interaction with Islam, many slaves brought from these regions had Islamic names such as Amar, Alsindor, Aly, Biram (Ibrahim), Mahomet, Omar, Moussa, Baraca, etc. The individuals from Central Africa usually bore Christian names perhaps because of the early Christianization of this area by the Portuguese. The most frequent African names are those typical of the Wolof, Fulbe, Bamana/Mandigo, and Mina/Akan. Other frequent names are those indicating the ethnic or regional origin

---

20 Ancestry.com: http://www.ancestry.com/name-origin?surname=lindor [Accessed October 22, 2013].

21 In French Guyana, Gaston Lindor, a retired professor of music and for many years the leader of the Antilles-Guyane band, was born in 1929 the son of Albert Lindor. One of his albums, "Sénégal 63" (RCA Records Label), was dedicated to the international games "Jeux de l'Amitié" held in Dakar in 1963 [The encyclopedia of music and musicians of Antilles-Guyane: online at http://alrmab.free.fr/glindor.html (Accessed March 24, 2014)]. A famous person bearing this name today in Senegal is Maguette Lindor Ndiaye, a fashion designer and owner of the label Exotic Design. Her husband, Amadou Lindor Ndiaye, is the owner of a luxury car rental in New York City (www.exoticarlimo.com). The latter and many others were named after the late Amadou Lindor Mbaye, a politician and trade unionist from Saalum, Senegal. According to family tradition, this personality got the nickname Lindor from a French friend.

22 An edited list of African names retrieved from the Louisiana Slave Database is posted in the appendix section of this book.

23 Niane D.T. 1960. *Soundjata ou l'épopée mandingue*, Paris: Présence africaine.

24 *Soomoore* (pl. *coomooje*) means literally "wrapper." Table 1 and Table 2 list the *coomooje* of the Western and Eastern Fulbe.

such as Arada/Fon, Senegal (Wolof), Nar (Moor), Bambara (Bamana), Mina, Aoussa (Hawsa), Congo, Tchamba, Igbo, etc. Some names were expressed in French, but they are very reminiscent of naming practices in Africa meant to express the person's temper such as Joly Cœur ("sweet heart" or "the generous one"), Sans Soucy ("without worries"), and Sans Quartier ("without mercy"), often times misspelled Sancartier. The names Sannom or Sans nom ("without name"), for either gender, recalls a custom in West Africa where people avoid giving a name to a child when the mother has lost many others before him/her. Among the Fulbe/Pulaar (Fulani) the child is called "alaa inde" (literally 'does not have a name'). The Wolof use the expressions "Bougouma" ('I don't want') or "Ken Buggul" ('nobody wants'), which are believed to turn away "evil spirits" allegedly responsible for the previous deaths. Bougouman is among the African names listed on *Louisiana Slave Database*. Some had animal names like Bouqui and Golo, respectively the Wolof names for hyena and monkey. Some Creole slaves (born in Louisiana) also had African names. In this case one can easily understand that the slaves also named their children after other fellows on the plantations, the latter acting as godfathers or godmothers.

The *Louisiana Slave Database* reveals traditional naming practices, which one can still find today in Senegambia, among the Fulbe people. In this case, gender and the order in which people were born are taken into consideration (Table 1). For example, the first-born male among these people is nicknamed Hamadi or Sarra. After the 1811 slave revolt on the German Coast, a slave named Sarra, belonging to Mr. Delhomme, was among those who were interrogated at length, judged innocent, and released.[25] The same principles for naming are followed by the Eastern Fulbe (Niger, North Benin, North Nigeria, and North Cameroon). In this case, the seven different sets of names are not related to the seven days of a week. Gender and order of birth remain the only references, with the prefixes Baa and Yaa indicating the gender (Table 2). The comparison of Table 1 and Table 2 shows that both groups of Fulbe share the same names but with differences on the matching of names and order of birth. Dikko is also a popular name among the Fulbe of Fuuta Tooro, but it does not appear in the database.

In Senegambia, children are still being named after some days of the week. Three days are particularly favored if not exclusively chosen for naming babies. The most popular is Aljuma (Friday), the day of the weekly mass gathering for prayers in Muslim countries. The other choices are Altine (Monday) and Alarba (Wednesday). In Louisiana many of the people of African origins were named after the seven days of the week or after the twelve months of the year, either in French or English. Among the Akan, the naming of children depends on gender, the day of the week they are born, the order in which they are born, and the circumstances of birth (Table 3). The Akan people live in modern day Ghana,

---

25 SC-2-1811, "condamnation des Brigands pris dans la dernière insurrection." Procès verbal N°2, 15 January 1811.

Togo, and Côte d'Ivoire. Their naming practices were widely used throughout the African Diaspora in the Americas. They share the same naming traditions with the Mina who were mostly shipped through the Bight of Benin and who became one of the most frequent "nations" documented on the plantations of Louisiana. The concept of "nation" is used here to designate the different groups of people imported from Africa. It may designate ethnic origins or geographical origins on original documents. The notion of "frequency" is determined by the number of times the name of a particular ethnic group or geographical origin is attached to the description of slaves documented in inventories, wills, trials, mortgages, etc. It is a good indicator of the volume of the slave trade from different regions of West Africa since ethnic designations listed in Louisiana documents overwhelmingly involved self-identification by Africans.[26]

---

26 Gwendolyn Midlo Hall 2005. *Slavery and African Ethnicities in the Americas: Restoring the Links.* Chapel Hill: University of North Carolina Press, pp.38-45.

TABLE 1: NAMING PRACTICES AMONG THE FULBE OF SENEGAMBIA AND LOUISIANA VARIANTS

Order of Birth	**Male name** and Louisiana variants	**Female name** and Louisiana variants
First	**Hamadi**/Hamady/Amady/Amadis/ or Sara/Sarah/Sarra	**Sira** or **Dikko**/ Cira /Sihra/Sirie
Second	**Samba**/Sambas/Sembas/Sambo/Sanbat	**Kumba**/Comba/Combas/Coumba/Couba
Third	**Demba**/Dinba/Dimba	**Penda**/Penda/Pinda/Pinder
Fourth	**Yéro**/Yara/Yarra/Yerah	**Takko**/Taco/Taca
Fifth	**Paté**/Pate/Patey/Pati	**Daado**/Dido

TABLE 2: NAMING PRACTICES AMONG THE EASTERN FULBE[27]

Order of Birth	Male Name	Female Name
First	Baadikko	Yaadikko
Second	Baasammbo	Yaatakko
Third	Baayero	Yaakummbo
Fourth	Baapaate	Yaadaado
Fifth	Baademmbo	Yaapenndo
Sixth	Baanjobbo	Yaademmo
Seventh	Baaseebo	Yaaseebo

27 From Dr. Garba Kawu, Kanuri and Fulfulde specialist, The Centre for the Study of Nigerian Languages, Bayero University, Kano, Nigeria; to the internet forum of Tabitalpulaaku International, a transnational association of the Fulbe (jamaa@tabitalpulaaku-international. org). Accessed 31 October 2011.

TABLE 3: NAMING PRACTICES AMONG THE AKAN PEOPLE AND LOUISIANA VARIANTS[28]

Day born Association	Male name and Louisiana Variants	Female name and Louisiana variants	Variants among Akan
Sunday *Kwasíada* Universe	**Kwasí**, Cachy, Cassy, Kissy Kessy, Quachee, Quashe, Quasey, Quash, Quashy, Quasy	**Akósua**, Casiah, Ciba, Kesiah, Kessiah, Kisiah, Kessier, Quasheba	Kwesi, Akwasi, Kosi; Akosi, Akosiwa, Así, Esi
Monday *Edwóada* Peace	**Kwadwó**, Caeadia, Cadian, Codia	**Adjwóà**, Ajoy	Kodjó, Kojo, Jojo; Adjua, Adjoa, Ajwoba
Tuesday *Ebénada* Ocean	**Kwabená**, Comnam, Comeley, Qualmley	**Ábenaa**, Habeny	Komlá, Komlā, Kobby, Ebo, Kobina; Ablá, Ablā, Abena, Abrema
Wednesday *Wukúada* Spider	**Kwakú**, Coicou, Coco, Kako, Kouacou, Kouago, Quako, Quaqou	**Akúà**, Akuba, Ackwa, Akia, Koua	Koku, Kweku, kaku, Kuuku; Akú, Ekua
Thursday *Yáwóada* Earth	**Yaw**, Ya, Yaba	**Yaá**, Aba, Abba, Aya, Yaouas, Yaba, Yebas	Yao, Yaba, Yawo, Yao, Ekow; Ayawa, Baaba, Yaaba, Aba
Friday *Efíada* Fertility	**Kofí**, Coffy, Coefi, Coffee, Coffi, Cophe, Cuffey, Koufe	**Afúa**, Affa, Affy, Fabon	Koffi, Fiifi; Afí, Afía, Afíba Efia
Saturday *Méméneda* God	**Kwámè**, Comina, Cominan, Cocomina, komina, Quamana, Quamina, Quamine	**Ámma**, Ama	Ato, Kwamena, Kwami, Komi; Ame, Ama, Ameyo

---

28 This table is based on a study by Kofi Agyekum: "The Sociolinguistic of Akan Personal Names," *Nordic Journal of African Studies* 15, 2 (2006), p.214.

CHAPTER TWO

THE GERMAN COAST OF LOUISIANA
A founding father called Ambroise Heidel

O, all of you, married men,
If your women have lovers,
Show no hostile mood;
Lest, ill-fate shall upon thee fall;
If in thou anger brews, expect the worst:
To Mississippi thou shall be shipped.
—French popular song (1720s)

French colonization in Louisiana started in May 1699 when Pierre le Moyne Sieur d'Iberville established the colony of Biloxi on the Gulf Coast. The development of the colony was very slow because the colonists were deeply affected by diseases, lack of food, and attacks from the Native Americans. The French did not have human resources willing to develop the new colony, and the royal treasury was bankrupt after the European campaigns of Louis XIV. In 1713, Louisiana was ceded to Antoine Crozat, a rich merchant, for a period of fifteen years. The colony was returned to the French Crown after four years because Crozat did not fulfill his expectations in terms of commerce and mining. In 1717, the colony was ceded to the Company of the West (Compagnie d'Occident) of John Law. At that time, the French population of Louisiana counted only four hundred individuals, men, women, and children.[1]

The Compagnie d'Occident was chartered in August 1717 for a period of

---

1 Gwendolyn Midlo Hall, *Africans in Colonial Louisiana* (1992), p.5. See also Marcel Giraud, *Histoire de la Louisiane Française*, tome 1, *Le Règne de Louis XIV*, 1698-1715 (Paris: P.U.F., 1953), introduction.

twenty-five years by an edict of the King of France. Besides Louisiana, it controlled the fur trade in Canada and tobacco cultivation elsewhere in the French colonies. The Company gained control of Senegal on December 15, 1718, which meant, in theory, the control of the West African coastal trade from Cape Blanc, in modern day Mauritania, to Sierra Leone.[2] On May 27, 1718, in Paris, the board of directors of the Company convened to define the rules to be observed regarding the sale of the slaves that were soon to be sent to the colonies. *L'Aurore*, the first slave ship to arrive in Louisiana from Africa, left Saint-Malo in July 1718. It was soon followed by *Le Duc du Maine*. Before the arrival of the African slave force, finding volunteers for the distant colony of Louisiana proved to be a real challenge. To encourage immigration to Louisiana, the Company granted free land concessions. In order to set a good example, John Law requested under his name a concession, which he planned to populate with German laborers and artisans. Pamphlets describing the riches of Louisiana were printed in many languages, including German, and were distributed in several German states and cantons of Switzerland. Nearly 4,000 German laborers were recruited, but it is doubtful that more than 1,500 of them made it to Louisiana.[3]

The French officials also resorted to penal colonization in order to solve the problem of the scarcity of volunteers for the colony. A royal ordinance issued on November 10, 1718, allowed the deportation to the Americas of *faux sauniers* (non-licensed salt makers), *fraudeurs de tabac* (tobacco smugglers), and so-called vagabonds, deserting soldiers, and young people of all social origins as well as prostitutes held at the Parisian hospital of *La Saltpêtrière*. This policy was planned in 1717 as it was favored on one side by the upsurge of the contraband of salt and tobacco, which were considered royal monopolies, and on the other side by the increase of beggary and of vagrancy in the Parisian region. The deportations consisted at first of a small group of sixty *faux sauniers* whose sentence to the galleys had been commuted into a lifetime exile to Louisiana where, after three years, they were to receive from the Company part of the land they cleared. Simultaneously, the Council of the Marine had begun to send deserters to the colony. In February 1718, more than twenty deserters from Guyenne and the region of Perpignan arrived at Rochefort on their way to Louisiana. Fifteen others soon joined them.[4]

The 1718 royal ordinance was soon reinforced, and judges were instructed to pronounce the deportation of those sentenced to the galleys for vagrancy, including the unemployed found in Paris. For this purpose, a special police force was created in April 1719. Its officers, called *bandouliers du Mississippi* by the commoners (in

---

2 André Delcourt, *La France et les Etablissements Français au Sénégal entre 1713 et 1763* (Dakar, Senegal: Mémoires IFAN, 1952), p.65.

3 Albert J. Robichaux Jr., *German Coast Families, European Origins and Settlement in Colonial Louisiana* (Rayne, LA: Hebert Publications, 1997), p.16.

4 Marcel Giraud, *Histoire de la Louisiane Française*, tome III, *L'Epoque John Law, 1717-1720* (Paris: PUF, 1966), p.252-276.

reference to their backpacks), were quite willing to earn more from the reward the Company paid them for each arrest. They abused the law by arresting persons of all ages, including provincials who came to Paris for their business and laborers falsely accused of beggary, and by robbing their captives or releasing them under the payment of a ransom. Paris, along with the rest of the country, was soon shaken by huge riots and mutinies during which many *bandouliers* were killed or injured by furious mobs.[5] The dangers of deportation eventually inspired Parisian songsters who advised their poor country fellows to keep still and even to pay no mind to the disloyalties of their wives in order to avoid the fate of Quoniam, a *rôtisseur* (grilled meat seller) by trade, deported to Louisiana with the complicity of his wife, as related in the following popular song:

> *O, vous tous, messieurs les maris,*
> *Si vos femmes ont des favoris,*
> *Ne vous mettez martel en tête;*
> *Vous auriez fort méchante fête.*
> *Si vous vous en fâchez, tant pis:*
> *Vous irez à Mississippi.*

> O, all of you, married men,
> If your women have lovers,
> Show no hostile mood;
> Lest, ill-fate shall upon thee fall;
> If in thou anger brews, expect the worst:
> To Mississippi thou shall be shipped.

> *O vous, maris trop austères,*
> *Tremblez toujours,*
> *Si de l'amoureux mystère*
> *Vous traversez les beaux jours.*
> *Il faut être plus commode*
> *Mes chers amis;*
> *Il vaut mieux être à la mode*
> *Que de voir Mississippi.*

> O you, thrifty husbands,
> Tremble always,
> If of the mysterious lover
> You hinder the fun days.
> Be more compromising

---

5 Ibid.

My dear friends;
Better accept the tide of time
Than experience Mississippi ordeal.[6]

Finally, on May 9, 1720, the King of France passed a law forbidding the deportation of French citizens. Peace was restored but, within three years, the Company was able to send more than 7,000 people to Louisiana, including 1,278 deportees, 2,462 indentured servants attached to the large concessions, 302 laborers for the Company, and 977 soldiers. Most of these people obviously died since the general census of the population of the colony of January 1, 1726, listed only 2,228 whites.[7]

The eighteenth-century German settlers of Louisiana arrived in different waves of immigration. The first group arrived between 1719 and 1721 and included such families as the Schexnayders, Edelmeiers, Zweigs, Heidels, Himmels, and many others from Germany, Bohemia, Switzerland, and Hungary. This group was composed mostly of farmers who contracted with John Law and his Company of the West to undertake the cultivation of farms in the wilderness of Louisiana.[8] By the time of their arrival in the colony, the Company of the West was bankrupt, and the Germans were confronted with tremendous difficulties. They finally settled upriver from the newly created town of New Orleans on land formerly occupied by the Taensas Indians.[9] In May 1722, Diron d'Artaguette, Inspector General of the troops of Louisiana, recorded the first description of the German Coast:

> The German families numbering about 330 persons of all sexes and ages are placed 12 leagues above New Orleans on the left bank ascending the river, on very good land where there were formerly Savage fields (Indian fields) easy to cultivate. These Germans are divided into three boroughs on a terrain of great extent that has never been inundated. As these people are very industrious, it is expected that their harvest will be abundant this year and that in the course of time they will succeed in

6 Pierre Heinrich, *La Louisiane sous la Compagnie des Indes (1717-1731)* (New York: Burt Franklin, 1908; repr. 1970), p.36. Translated by Amath Sow, Dakar, Senegal. Unless otherwise indicated, all translations from French to English are by the author.

7 Giraud, *Histoire de la Louisiane Française*, tome III (1966), pp.47-48.

8 Glenn R. Conrad, *Saint-Jean-Baptiste des Allemands, Abstracts of the Civil Records of St. John the Baptist Parish with Genealogy and Index* (1753-1803) (Lafayette, LA: The Center for Louisiana Studies, University of Southwestern Louisiana, 1972), p.IX-X.

9 Robichaux Jr., *German Coast Families* (1997), p.49. For a vivid account of the failures of the Company of the West, see Hall, Africans in Colonial Louisiana (1992), chapter 1 (The chaos of French rule).

making good establishments in the colony.[10]

This was soon confirmed and the *Côte des Allemands* (German Coast), St. Charles Parish at that time, became a precious granary for New Orleans. After official reports to France had requested more German laborers in addition to the usual demands of slaves for land cultivation and soldiers for protection, a second wave of German colonists made it to the country during the 1750s and brought families such as the Kammers, the Jacobs, the Conrads, and many others.[11]

Ambroise Heidel, the ancestor of all the Haydels of Louisiana, reached the colony on March 1, 1721 aboard the ship *Les Deux Frères*. He was listed as Ambroise AIDLE, along with his brother Mathieu and sisters Barbe and Catherine. They were among the forty survivors out of 200 who embarked in Lorient on November 14, 1720.[12] Ambroise was born and baptized in 1702 in Neunkirchen, twelve kilometers from Miltenberg in the Catholic diocese of Wurzburg, Germany.[13] His parents, Johann Adam Heidel and Eva Schnarberg (or Schonberg), apparently moved from Neunkirchen to another village where two daughters, Barbe and Catharina Heidel, were born. From there, the family moved to Lorient, the port of the French Company of the West. In August or September 1720, the father died at this port, probably from the plague that ravaged France that year or simply from the bad conditions of life in the overcrowded outdoor lodgings provided to immigrants. For some reason, the widow of Johann Adam Heidel was separated from the rest of the family and listed on the ship *La Charente*.[14] She probably died shortly after her arrival in Louisiana.

Ambroise Heidel married Marguerite Schoff and fathered three daughters and seven sons: Regina, Marie Françoise, Anne Marie, Jacques, Nicolas, Mathias, Jean Christophe, Jean Georges, Jean, and Jean Jacques. His family was mentioned for the first time in the census of 1724 in the village of Hoffen, on the first German Coast, ten leagues above New Orleans. He had been living there for eighteen months, and he was presented then as "Ambros Heidel, of Neukirchen, Electorate of Mayence, a 22-year old Catholic and a Baker; along with his wife, his brother (Johann Mathias or Mathieu), 18 years old; his brother-in-law, aged 13, crippled." He was also presented as a good worker, very much at ease although his only

---

10 Early Census tables of Louisiana, Hill Memorial Library, Louisiana State University, pp. 19-20. A league (French *lieue*; around 4 kilometers) is an Old Regime unit for the measurement of distance.

11 Ellen C. Merrill, *Germans of Louisiana* (Gretna, LA: Pelican Publishing Company, 2005), p.31. See also Robichaux Jr., *German Coast Families* (1997), p.59; and Conrad, *Saint-Jean-Baptiste des Allemands* (1972), p.X.

12 Deiler 1909, *The settlements of the German Coast of Louisiana and the Creoles of German descent* (Philadelphia, PA: Americana Germanicana Press), p.28.

13 Robichaux Jr., *German Coast Families* (1997), pp.197-200.

14 Deiler, *The settlements of the German Coast of Louisiana* (1909), p.28.

livestock was a pig.[15] Barbe Heidel was married to Jean George Betz, provost of the Germans, who died in August 1727. On January 12, 1728, she was married for the second time to Gaspard Dilly, a native of Alsace, France, and the widower of one Elizabeth Stugle.[16] There is no mention of Catharina Heidel who probably never made it to this country. There is also no mention of Ambroise Heidel's brother after 1727. He probably joined his sister Barbe and her husband Gaspard Dilly (Tilly) in Natchez, Mississippi, where they were probably killed in the massacre of the French colonists in this settlement in 1729.[17]

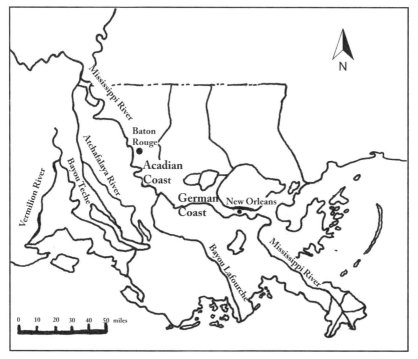

Fig. 2.1. The German and Acadian Coasts of Louisiana.
Map by Allison Reu.

15 Deiler, *The settlements of the German Coast of Louisiana* (1909), p.83.

16 Sacramental Records, vol.1, pp. 20, 82, 139.

17 Robichaux Jr., *German Coast Families* (1997), p.201, footnote 1001.

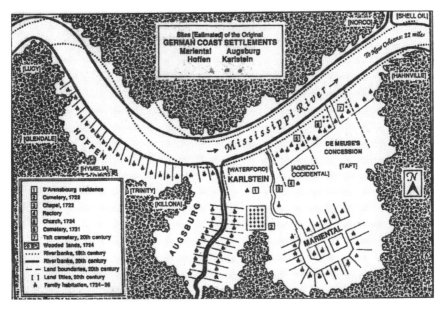

Fig. 2.2. The German Coast settlement in a schematic presentation, circa 1723.
Map by Norman Marmillion, 1990.

The 1731 census recorded Ambroise, his wife, two children (Regina and Marie Françoise), one *engagé* (indentured servant), and three African slaves. The hog was gone but there were two cows. An undated census, probably taken in 1732, shows that he also owned a 15-arpent piece of land on the left bank of the river between Caspar Dups (Toups) and Pierre Brou.[18] Twenty years later he bought a six-arpent piece of land from Widow Bernard Wigner. The farm was located further up the river, between Christophe Houbert and Albert Seychneidre.[19] This is the original tract of land where Ambroise built his wealth when indigo became fully developed on the German Coast. Two of his sons, Mathias and Jean Christophe, found their wives (Magdelaine and Charlotte, respectively) on the neighboring Houbert (Houbre/ Oubre) farm. The exact date of Ambroise Heidel's death is unknown. In the last record in civil documents indicating he was still alive, he was one of the persons who conducted the inventory of the estate of the late Pierre Pommier held on March 20, 1767.[20] Heidel's name is missing in the 1770 census tables of the German Coast.

The arrival of the initial slave population on the German coast

The French colony of Louisiana was constantly affected by severe food shortages until at least 1721. The colonists lived through the most difficult situations when

18 Deiler, *The settlements of the German Coast of Louisiana (1909)*, pp. 83 and 103.
19 SCP-1752-34-125. Land sale: Widow Wigner to Ambroise Heidel. 15 April 1752.
20 Robichaux Jr., *German Coast Families* (1997), p.201.

supplies did not come from Europe or from the Illinois country because of warfare. Sometimes they even resorted to eating grass and shellfish, and many colonists were scattered in small groups in Indian villages, sometimes for long periods before they got established. Soldiers and workers of the French Company were also sent to Indian villages in order to preserve them from starving to death. The worst situation occured between 1719 and 1721, at the time of the French and Spanish war for the control of Pensacola. In March 1721, supplies were totally exhausted at a time when the Indians could not provide the customary help.[21] The Illinois Country was then well established and produced all the wheat in the colony in addition to husbandry of horses, cattle, and pigs. Since transportation was extremely difficult on the Mississippi River, the Company exhorted the colonists to think above all about food crops.[22] Rice was the most suitable crop because it could stand the heavy rainfalls, but none of the colonists had any knowledge of its cultivation. The solution came from the rice growing areas of West Africa.[23]

In 1719, the *Compagnie d'Occident* became *Compagnie Perpétuelle des Indes* (Company of the West Indies) with the incorporation of the domains of the *Compagnie de Chine and Compagnie des Indes Orientales*. It was the ambition of this new company to develop the colony of Louisiana with the importation of slaves mainly from Senegal, the nearest African coast. At its meeting of April 30, 1723 the board of directors decided to send 3,000 African slaves to the French colonies of America, of which 2,000 would be imported from the Concession of Senegal. Among the 3,000 slaves, 570 were destined for Louisiana. In the plan of the Company, 400 slaves were to be distributed to the wealthy owners of concessions; 70 were destined for the needs of the Company itself. Only a hundred slaves were to be sold to the poor colonists and only to those recognized as hard workers and the most attached to the cultivation of land.[24] Only *l'Expedition* and *le Courrier de Bourbon* arrived between 1723 and 1724 with 178 slaves on board. None of them was sold to the German settlers since not a single slave was mentioned there in the censuses taken in 1724 and 1726.[25] The sale of slaves to the colonists was a chronic problem because they could not pay for them in hard currency.[26] But it was also a

---

21 Marcel Giraud, *Histoire de la Louisiane Française*, tome I (1953), pp.130-266. Heinrich, *La Louisiane sous la Compagnie des Indes* (1970), pp.39-48. Hall, *Africans in Colonial Louisiana*, chapter one (The chaos of French rule).

22 Heinrich, *La Louisiane sous la Compagnie des Indes* (1970), pp.31, 49-50.

23 For a general history of this point, see Judith A. Carney, *Black Rice: The African Origins of Rice Cultivation in the Americas* (Cambridge, MA: Harvard University Press, 2001).

24 Décision du Conseil des Indes concernant le commerce d'Asie, d'Afrique et d'Amérique (30 avril 1723); in Elizabeth Donnan, ed., *Documents Illustrative of the History of the Slave Trade to America*, vol.IV, *The Border Colonies and The Southern Colonies* (Washington, D.C.: Carnegie Institution, 1935; repr. New York: Octagon Books, 1969), pp.641-642.

25 See table 5 for the slave population of the German coast and table 2 in Hall, *Africans in Colonial Louisiana* (1992), p.60.

26 Ibid., p.63.

policy of the Company of the West, before its incorporation as the Company of the West Indies, to allow the colonists to pay the price of the slaves either with hard currency or "marchandises de traite" (trade goods) such as tobacco, rice, wheat, and so forth.[27] The sudden appearance of a slave force on the German Coast, between 1726 and 1731 (Table 4), seems to be closely related to the fact that twelve out of the twenty-two slave ships sent from Africa to Louisiana by the Company arrived in the same period of time.[28] This evolution was probably the result of a new policy of the directors who decided on December 19, 1725, in Paris, to provide a bonus of seven *livres* for every slave disembarked, to the captains who made a direct trip from Senegal to Louisiana, exactly the same amount given to those who made the trip from Juda (or Whydah on the Bight of Benin) to the colonies of America.[29]

TABLE 4: EVOLUTION OF THE POPULATION OF THE GERMAN COAST (1722-1737)

Census	Men	Women	Children	Engagés	Slaves	Total
1722	69	79	99			247
1724	51	58	52	0	0	161
1726	48	49	56	0	0	153
1731	67	66	130	18	113	394
1737	75	64	168	?	115	422

Source: calculated from Robichaux's tables: Robichaux Jr., German Coast Families (1997) pp.51, 57, and 58.

In 1731, the Company of the West Indies resorted to giving back the colony of Louisiana to the King of France. According to Gwendolyn Midlo Hall, "[the Company's] ambitious plans were destroyed by a convergence of revolts in Senegambia, at sea, and in Louisiana, where Africans, allied with Indian nations, cooperated in conspiracies and revolts to take over the country."[30] A serious blow came from the Natchez Indians in 1729 when they wiped out the colony of Fort Rosalie in reaction to the decline of their revenue from the trade of deerskins and foodstuff with the French and the promotion by the Company of tobacco

---

27 Ordre que la Compagnie d'Occident veut être observé pour la vente des Nègres qu'elle envoyera à la colonie de la Louisiane. Paris, 27 Mai 1718; in Donnan, ed., *Documents*, IV (1969), pp.638-639.

28 Hall, *Africans in Colonial Louisiana* (1992), table 2, p.60: French Slave-Trade Ships from Africa to Louisiana.

29 Les Directeurs de la Compagnie des Indes au Comte Maurepas, Ministre de la Marine, L.S. Gratification demandée par La Rigaudière pour les Nègres transportés par lui à la Louisiane. Paris, 26 Octobre 1729; in Donnan, ed., *Documents*, IV (1969), p.643.

30 Hall, *Africans in Colonial Louisiana* (1992), p.95.

cultivation around their villages on their most fertile land.[31] In West Africa, the Company also suffered from bad organization and severe competition. As early as March 26, 1693, after a third trip to Senegal where he served as Director General, Sieur de la Courbe wrote a memoir in which he blamed the Company of Senegal for having incompetent directors. Sometimes ships designed to carry slaves were mistakenly sent to Africa to pick up raw goods, and ships designed to carry raw goods were mistakenly sent to pick up slaves. In at least one instance, slave ships left nearly 50,000 cowhides rotting in port because the ships were unable to carry the intended cargo. When raw goods ships were dispatched instead of slave ships, the result was often dangerous overcrowding in "captiveries," the barracoons where slaves waited to be transported. These crowded conditions frequently led to illness and death.[32] Moreover, food was not always easy to find at the trading posts because of permanent political unrest, worsened by natural calamities such as drought and locust invasions. The Company could have thousands of captives waiting to be shipped, but many starved to death.[33]

Foreign competition meant lower profits, and the Company had a hard time recovering the price of the slaves delivered to the Americas. Its monopoly on the French slave trade was also challenged by private ship-owners to whom it had resolved to sell licenses from 1742 with regard to the trade in Senegal. This allowed the planter Joseph Dubreuil of Louisiana and Dalcourt, his partner, to send to Gorée the slave ship *Le Saint-Ursin,* which came back in 1743 with 190 slaves.[34] Three years later, no more than 200 slaves were counted in the entire settlements of the German Coast.[35] The period 1731-1763 can be considered as the "lean years" for the official slave trade in Louisiana because of the withdrawal of the Company of the West Indies and the Seven Years' War, also known as the French and Indian War (1756-1763).

Under Spanish rule, the German Coast witnessed a significant economic expansion related to increased imports of slaves. In the 1769 census ordered by Governor O'Reilly, the slave force on the German Coast had increased over six-fold (640 percent) since 1737. The total number of inhabitants was 2,016 of which 1,268 were white, 8 were free Blacks and mulattoes, and 740 were Black, mulatto,

---

31. Usner, Jr., Daniel H. *Indians, Settlers, & slaves in a frontier exchange economy. The Lower Mississippi Valley before 1783.* Chapel Hill and London: The University of North Carolina Press, 1992, pp. 46 and 66-72.

32 Prosper Cultru, *Premier voyage de Sieur de la Courbe fait à la Coste d'Afrique en 1685* (Paris: Champion & Larose, 1913), p.LII-LIII.

33 Oumar Kane, *La Première Hégémonie Peule. Le Fuuta-Tooro de Koli Tenella à Almaami Abdul* (Paris & Dakar: Karthala-PUD, 2004), chapter XIII, pp.431-456.

34 Hall, *Africans in Colonial Louisiana* (1992), p.140.

35 Helmut Blume, *The German Coast during the Colonial Era 1722-1803* (Destrehan, LA: German-Acadian Coast Historical and Genealogical Society, 1990), p.68.

and Indian slaves. Of the 220 family heads, 66 were Germans.[36] The growth of the population of colonists was partly related to the arrival of the Acadian refugees in 1765. The latter received unsettled or abandoned plots along the river, but the majority was settled on lands above the German Coast, which became *la Côte des Acadiens*. In 1775, the German Coast was divided in two districts, the parish of St. Charles and the parish of St. John the Baptist.[37] But Africans were, by far, the largest group of people introduced into Spanish Louisiana, especially after 1777 when Spain allowed the trade with the French West Indies. In 1782, a royal decree allowed duty-free importation of slaves from friendly or neutral countries.[38] In 1776, the white population (1,005 individuals) of the German Coast still outnumbered the black population (666 individuals), and only 95 of the 216 concessions had slaves. In 1795, the area had 233 concessions and 2,797 slaves.[39]

The Louisiana Purchase and the abolition of the external slave trade

In 1763, France had ceded Louisiana to Spain, but the Spaniards were not able to take effective control of the country until 1769. After the signature of the secret Treaty of San Ildefonso in 1800, the French were getting ready to regain control on the area. In 1803, the colony of Louisiana was sold for $15,000,000 to Thomas Jefferson, acting as the president of the United States. Although this was dictated by Napoleon's need for resources to finance his European campaigns, the connection between the transaction and the Haitian Revolution is also clear. The territory covered then more than 2,000,000 square kilometers (800,000 square miles) of land extending from the Mississippi River to the Rocky Mountains. The Louisiana Purchase, and the new economic boom in the cotton and sugar industries, provoked the Great Migration to the New South. Thousands of planters moved from the Old South to the lower Mississippi River, leaving behind lands impoverished by more than a century of one-crop agriculture. This movement continued until the middle of the nineteenth century and was interrupted only two times: by the War of 1812 against the English and by the Panic of 1819, which was provoked by low prices. The Mississippi area was called then "The Garden of America."[40]

On March 26, 1804, the U.S. Congress adopted legislation organizing the Orleans Territory, which later became the present state of Louisiana. This was the time of the conclusion of the slave revolts in Saint-Domingue, which ended

---

36 Ibid., p.81.
37 Merrill, *Germans of Louisiana* (2005), p.38.
38 Hall, *Africans in Colonial Louisiana* (1992), p.279.
39 Blume, *The German Coast* (1990), pp.86-87.
40 Charles D. Lowery, "The Great Migration to the Mississipi Territory," *Journal of Mississippi History* 30, 3 (1968), p.178.

with the creation of the Republic of Haiti. This revolution played a very important role in the abolition of the Atlantic slave trade since no country, especially not the United States, was willing to experience the fate of Saint-Domingue. In his letter dated May 8, 1804 to President James Madison, Governor Claiborne expressed his concern in these terms:

> The emigration from the West Indies to Louisiana continues great; few vessels arrive from that quarter, but are crowded with passengers, and among them, many slaves. I am inclined to think that, previous to the 1st of October thousands of African negroes will be imported into this province.[41]

In order to prevent revolution in Louisiana, Congress prohibited the introduction of slaves from outside of the United States to this territory, starting October 1, 1804. About two weeks before the vote, Governor Claiborne evoked anger from the planters to whom an unofficial source had revealed the intention of the new American authorities: "This intelligence," he wrote, "has occasioned great agitation in this city and in the adjacent settlements. The African trade has hitherto been lucrative, and the farmers are desirous of increasing the number of their slaves. The prohibiting of the importation of Negroes, therefore, is viewed here as a serious blow at the commercial and agricultural interest of the Province. The admission of Negroes into the State of South Carolina has served to increase the discontent here." In the same letter, Claiborne revealed the suspicions of the planters: "They suppose that Congress must connive at the importation into South Carolina, and many will be made to believe, that it is done with a view to make South Carolina the sole importer for Louisiana."[42] On July 1, 1804, some citizens of New Orleans wrote a petition in which they asked to be allowed to decide for themselves whether to admit slaves or not, since not only did the climate of their territory require "negro labor," but they needed an available supply of slaves to keep the banks of the Mississippi in repair. This petition was read before the Senate on January 4, 1805. In his letters to President Madison dated May 29, June 3, and June 22, 1805, Governor Claiborne did not mention any change in the resentment of the inhabitants of Louisiana.[43] Finally, in March 1807, the U.S. Congress adopted a law forbidding the importation of slaves on the soil of the United States, starting from January 1, 1808.

This ban caused the domestic slave trade to become a very lucrative business between the 1820s and the 1860s. From 1821 to 1841, The Franklin & Armfield Co. became the most famous among the domestic slave trading companies. This

41 William C.C. Claiborne to James Madison, New Orleans, May 8, 1804; in Donnan, ed., *Documents*, IV (1969), p. 662.

42 Ibid.

43 Memorial presented to Congress, 1804, p.18; in Donnan, ed., *Documents*, IV (1969), p.663.

Company was created in 1818 by Isaac Franklin, a native of Tennessee, and his nephew John Armfield, who was a resident of Alexandria, near Washington D.C. From there, he sent cargoes of slaves to Franklin who sold them in New Orleans and upstream toward the Red River and Natchez, Mississippi. In 1833, an observer estimated the annual number of slaves negotiated by the Franklin & Armfield Co. to be between one thousand and two thousand men, women, and children.[44] Other big names of the internal slave trade were the Woolfolk and Slatter families of Maryland, the Hagans of South Carolina. Most interstate traders spent their time buying slaves in the Upper South during the summer when Louisiana was engulfed by the stifling heat that nurtured the vectors of maladies such as malaria and yellow fever. The seasonality of the slave trade was also related to the agricultural calendar. February was the height of the slave-buying season. This was the time when the crops were already harvested both in the Upper and the Lower South and when the buyers had money available to pay for slaves. The duration of the passage to the Lower South lasted seven to eight weeks on foot, with a coverage of twenty miles per day. It took only few days to descend the Mississippi from St. Louis but the shipboard around the Gulf coast from Norfolk to New Orleans lasted about three weeks.[45] Slave stealing also became a major business, involving networks in the North where even free people of color were kidnapped and sold down South. The most famous case was Solomon Northrup, kidnapped in March 1841 in Washington, D.C. and taken to New Orleans where he was sold to a planter from the Red River. He was freed in 1853 after twelve long years in bondage.[46]

The domestic slave trade was partially sustained by the natural growth of the slave population. Delaware, Maryland, Virginia, North Carolina, Kentucky, Tennessee, Missouri, and the District of Columbia were the slave exporting areas. Of all these states, Virginia was the biggest supplier. Captain Richard Drake was told that slave breeding was getting to be the most profitable business in that state and that whole farms were used as nurseries to supply the market with young mulattoes of both sexes. He also made a further observation about a farm near Alexandria: "I counted thirty about to become mothers, and the huts swarmed with pickaninnies of different shades."[47] Slave breeding was also undertaken in Louisiana, according to the testimony of James Roberts, a slave born in Maryland in 1753. Around 1783, he was taken to New Orleans and sold at auction to a planter named Calvin Smith. In the description of the Smith's plantation, he noticed:

44 William Cooper and Thomas Terrill, *The American South, a History*, vol. 1, (New York: MacGraw-Hill, 1991), p. 215.

45 Johnson, Walter. *Soul by soul. Life inside the antebellum slave market.* Cambridge, Massachusetts and London, England: Harvard University Press, 1999, pp.47-50 and 79.

46 Solomon Northrup's fate was related in an autobiography entitled *Twelve years a slave* (London: Sampson Low, Son & Company, 1853).

47 Philip Drake, *Revelations of a slave smuggler: being the autobiography of Capt. Rich`d [i.e. Philip] Drake, an African trader for fifty years, from 1807 to 1857* (1860), p.51.

From fifty to sixty heads of women were kept constantly for breeding. No man was allowed to go there, save white men. From twenty to twenty-five children a year were bred on that plantation. As soon as they are ready for market, they are taken away and sold, as mules or other cattle.[48]

After the Louisiana Purchase, identifications like "nègre américain" and "négresse américaine" became frequent on the German Coast slave inventories to designate those who came from the East Coast of the United States. Some of them were identified according to the state or city of origin; for instance "nègre de Virginie" or "nègre de Baltimore." In 1836, the weekly *Virginia Times* estimated the number of slaves exported from Virginia during the twelve previous months to be forty thousand. The Mississippi valley received the majority of these exports. *The New Orleans Bee*, in its issue from November 18, 1831, reported the import of one thousand and eleven slaves in Louisiana in one month, the majority from Virginia. *The Natchez Courier* estimated the number of slaves exported from the East Coast to the states of Louisiana, Mississippi, Alabama, and Arkansas during the year 1836 to be two hundred and fifty thousand.[49] Although this figure seems to be exaggerated, it is also clear that the internal slave trade, no matter the extent of local slave breeding, was far from satisfying the labor needs of the Mississippi valley. Smuggling of slaves directly from Africa or via the West Indies was widely undertaken.

In fact, the planters of Louisiana ignored the legislation of March 26, 1804 and made arrangements to import an incalculable number of slaves from the African continent. In one of his numerous correspondences with President Madison, Governor Claiborne reported with anxiety that "slaves are daily introduced from Africa, many direct from this unhappy country and others by the way of the West India Islands." The best he could do was to impose controls on slave vessels at Plaquemines in order "to prevent the bringing in of slaves that had been concerned in the insurrection of St. Domingo."[50]

Paul Lachance makes a link between the growth of Louisiana's slave population

48 James Roberts, *The Narrative of James Roberts, a Soldier under Gen. Washington in the Revolutionary War, and under Gen. Jackson at the Battle of New Orleans, in the War of 1812* (Chicago, IL: Printed for the Author 1858), p. 26. Electronic version in *Documenting the American South* (DocSouth), a digital publishing initiative sponsored by the University Library at the University of North Carolina at Chapel Hill: http://docsouth.unc.edu/neh/roberts/roberts.html (accessed on Sept. 17, 2010).
49 Documents of the British and Foreign Anti-Slavery Society presented to the General Anti-Slavery Convention held in London, June, 1840; in Theodore D. Weld, ed., *Slavery and the internal slave Trade in the United States* (New York: Arno Press & The New York Times, 1969), pp.12-13.
50 Governor William C.C. Claiborne to James Madison, New Orleans July 12, 1804; in Donnan, ed., *Documents*, IV (1969), p. 663.

during the early American period with the arrival of thousands of slaves pushed out of Saint-Domingue by the Haitian Revolution. Several thousand refugees found asylum in the Territory when Congress decided, on June 18, 1809 to allow them in the country for humanitarian reasons and not to apply the March 1807 law against the slaves who accompanied them. It was reported that 9,059 refugees from Saint-Domingue arrived in Louisiana between May 1809 and January 1810, including 3,012 free blacks (*gens de couleur libres*) and 3,226 slaves. A total close to 5,000 slaves from Saint-Domingue were finally allowed into the country.[51]

In the southern United States, the natural environment was more than favorable to smugglers, especially in Louisiana with its lush wilderness, swamps, and bayous. The island of Barataria was the main way by which smugglers of various nationalities introduced slaves into Louisiana. Among the pirates of Barataria, the celebrated Lafitte brothers (Jean and Pierre) were probably the most successful.[52] William M. Johnson and George Bradish, two sea captains from Nova Scotia, became partners of the Lafitte brothers, selling the slaves delivered to them up and down the Mississippi River.[53] Slaves were also smuggled from Texas and Florida. According to Richard Drake, "the Spanish possessions were thriving on this inland exchange of Negroes and mulattoes; Florida was a sort of nursery for slave-breeders, and many American citizens grew rich by trafficking in Guinea Negroes and smuggling them continually, in small parties, through the southern United States." Between 1810 and 1860, the slave force of Louisiana multiplied by ten. It almost doubled between 1810 and 1820. Several decades after the 1807 law, Louisiana still had

many African-born people in its slave population. On the German Coast, the slave force grew rapidly. Between 1785 and 1860, the number of slaves in St. Charles Parish more than tripled. In St. John the Baptist Parish, the number of slaves

---

51 Paul F. Lachance, "The Foreign French," in Arnold Hirsch and Joseph Logsdon, eds, *Creole New Orleans, Race and Americanization*: Baton Rouge: Louisiana State University Press, 1992. This is being challenged by new scholarship. For example, Rebecca J. Scott questions if the slaves brought in from Saint-Domingue by way of Cuba in 1809-1810 were really legally slaves at all because all French slaves were freed in 1794 and a bit earlier by the French governors of St. Domingue [Rebecca J. Scott and Jean M. Hébrard 2012, *Freedom Papers: An Atlantic Odyssey in the Age of Emancipation*, Harvard University Press].

52 Stanley Faye, "Privateers of Guadeloupe and their Establishment in Barataria," *Louisiana Historical Quarterly* 23, 1 (1940), pp. 431-433.

53 Stephen Whitney Lindsay, *Bradish Johnson 1811-1892*, online article accessed 5 December 2013 (http://stevelindsay.net/DickeyLindsay/BRADISH_JOHNSON_AND_ME.pdf). According to this author, Captain Johnson and Captain Bradish purchased in 1795 a large plot of land on the Mississippi Delta forty miles south of New Orleans. On it they founded a plantation that they called "Magnolia". They proceeded to grow sugar cane there, refining it in one of the first sugar refineries built in Louisiana. Captain Johnson had four sons. Bradish Johnson, the owner of Whitney Plantation between 1867 and 1880, was the third of them. He was born in 1811 in New Orleans and was named after his father's partner.

multiplied almost by eight during the same period of time (Table 6).

TABLE 5: THE RACIAL COMPOSITION OF
THE POPULATION OF LOUISIANA: 1810-1860

Year	Slaves	Free colored	Whites	Total
1810	34,660	7,585	34,311	76,556
1820	69,064	10,476	73,383	152,923
1830	109,588	16,710	89,441	215,739
1840	168,452	25,502	158,457	352,411
1850	244,809	17,462	255,491	517,762
1860	331,726	18,647	357,456	707,829

Source: R. Miller and D. Smith, Dictionary of Afro-American Slavery (New York: Greenwood Press, 1988), p.414.

TABLE 6: SLAVE AND FREE POPULATION ON THE GERMAN COAST
UNDER SPANISH AND AMERICAN RULE

	St. Charles			St. John		
	White	Black		White	Black	
		Free	Slaves		Free	Slaves
1785	561	69	1,273	714	5	581
1810	820	150	2,321	1,402	70	1,518
1820	727	148	2,987	1,532	113	2,209
1830	871	158	4,118	1,980	204	3,493
1840	874	104	3,722	2,141	191	3,444
1850	867	121	4,132	2,586	191	4,540
1860	938	177	4,182	3,037	299	4,594

Source: Blume, *The German Coast* (1990), p.142; for the 1785-1850 period. U.S. Census data (1860).

CHAPTER THREE

ATLANTIC CROSSINGS
AFRICAN ETHNICITIES IN LOUISIANA

In the deepest of the night,
King sends out roaring drums announcing:
Run for your life,
Slavery doom shall be on whoever sees morrow!
— Wolof (Senegal) folksong

On the German Coast, like elsewhere in Louisiana, the slave force came from all major slave harbors of Africa. Senegambia, the Bight of Benin, the Bight of Biafra, and Central Africa were the most important suppliers among these slave harbors.

Greater Senegambia

Geographically, Boubacar Barry defines Senegambia as part of the tropical zone, wide open to the Atlantic Ocean, between the Sahara Desert and the tropical forests of Guinea. The main waterways here are the Senegal and the Gambia Rivers, whose sources are located in the Fuuta Jalon Mountains of Guinea. The Gambia River is the main route of transportation into the hinterland and divides the region in two parts: Northern Senegambia and Southern Senegambia.[1] Millet (*Pennisetum typhoides*) and different varieties of sorghum (Guinea corn) were the principal food crops in the savanna grasslands and the Sahel. In Arabic, "Sahel" means "shore", a word that describes the transition-like attribute of this ecological

1 Barry 1998, *Senegambia and the Atlantic slave trade* (Cambridge: Cambridge University Press), pp.3-5.

zone, between the desert and the wooded savannas further south. The terrain of the Sahel is mostly flat and covered by drought-resistant grasses, thorny shrubs, and acacia trees, or gum trees such as *Acacia senegal*. Gum arabic was obtained by incisions on the bark of the acacia trees and the sap was collected when dry. It was essential to the European textile industries because of its use in the processing of fabrics. Beside slaves, it became the main product fetched by the trading companies to the extent of producing a gum war, which involved the French, the British, and the Dutch early in the eighteenth century.[2]

Northern Senegambia was the site of many kingdoms where Islam became the principal religion besides the traditional practices. Political unrest and natural contingencies such as drought pushed many people toward southern Senegambia. This region, also called the Upper Guinea Coast, comprised the area reaching from the Gambia River, down to the forests of Guinea in the south. All along the coastal side, from Casamance to Sierra Leone, a myriad of streams colonized by thick mangrove swamps pour into the Atlantic Ocean. This region, called "Rivières du Sud" (Southern Rivers) by French sailors or "Rios de Guinea" by the Spanish and the Portuguese, became a refuge for people such as the Jola, Balanta, Baňun, Manjak, Mankaň, Papel, Baga, Nalu, Landuman, Susu, Temne, Kisi, Toma, and others. Through the centuries, they established egalitarian societies where life was centered on villages led by councils of elders. Rice was (and still is) the principal crop in this region where heavy rains last six to ten months every year. Moving eastward from the Atlantic coast, the mangrove swamps transitioned into vegetation composed of a mixture of savanna-like grasses and rainforest. In this area, Fulbe ("Fulani") and Mandingo migrants created respectively the kingdoms of Fuuta Jalon and Kaabu, which became strong slaving powers. The hill country bordering the Fuuta Jalon Mountains to the north also became a refuge for the Basari and the Koňagi.

At the beginning of the 1600s, slaves destined to the trans-Atlantic trade came mostly from Senegambia. This region, which already had a long history of providing slaves to the trans-Saharan trade, began to play a pivotal role as a gateway to the Western world. The 1696 Letters Patent of the King of France called it arbitrarily "Concession of Senegal," from Cape Blanc on the coast of Mauritania down to the mouth of the Sierra Leone River.[3] The French sailors called the coast of Mauritania and its hinterland "Barbarie," a name that reveals the limits of their geographical knowledge of Africa of that time. The two main outposts there were Arguin and Portendick, where Europeans traded with the Moors who brought to them gum arabic and slaves. In 1727, at the conclusion of the "Gum War" with the Treaty of The Hague, the French ousted the Dutch from the area. Arguin and Portendick

---

2 Barry 1998, *Senegambia and the Atlantic slave trade*, pp.69.
3 André Delcourt, *La France et les Etablissements Français au Sénégal entre 1713 et 1763* (Dakar: Mémoires IFAN, 1952), p.65.

Fig. 3.1. Greater Senegambia in the eighteenth century.
Map by Allison Reu.

became dependences linked to Saint-Louis, Senegal.[4]

From the mid-1700s through the first two decades of the nineteenth century, the history of European presence in Senegambia was, above all, the history of French and English competition for the control of the trade. Saint-Louis, the first permanent European establishment at the mouth of the Senegal River, was founded in 1659 by French sailor Louis Caulier on a small island in the middle of the river where it was well protected against the assault of the ocean waves.[5] A fort was built there and named in honor of King Louis XIV. This island was part

---

4 Barry 1998, *Senegambia and the Atlantic slave trade*, pp.73.
5 Delcourt 1952, *La France et les Etablissements Français au Sénégal*, p.91.

of Waalo, a Wolof Kingdom called Senghâna by the Arab traders. The Portuguese called it Senega and, later, the French and the English started using the name Senegal. Fort Saint-Louis soon became the main base for the peopling and the exploitation of the French colonies. There was the residence of the Director General of the French Concession of Senegal and the general *entrepôt* of supplies and trade goods. From there the French had control of the entrance of the Senegal River.

The trade upriver was done with a flotilla of flatboats and gunboats since the deep-sea ships could not safely navigate beyond the fort. During the low water season, trade was hardly undertaken beyond the trading post of Podor. Millet, hides, and gum arabic were traded at such places as Escale du Désert, Escale du Coq, and Escale du Terrier Rouge. During the rainy season, from June to November, when the river rose high enough to allow navigation further inland, the traders went upriver to the country of Gajaaga, better known as Galam. This spot was the real business center of the Concession with ivory, gold, and slaves as main products of the trade. According to Saugnier, "Galam is the place of good business (...). One can get from this nation a lot of slaves brought there by caravans from various regions of Africa."[6] Beyond Galam the entire Upper-Senegal-Niger region was integrated to the trade with St. Louis. This city would have been the biggest center of the slave trade in Africa were it not for navigational difficulties on the Senegal River and competition from the English, who diverted many of the caravans originally bound for Galam toward the Gambia River.

The trade of Galam reached its climax between 1720 and 1750. In his *Memoir on the trade of Senegal* (1752), Pruneau de Pommegorge, a former commissioner of the Company, asserted that riverboats engaged in the trade made two, or even three times the round trip to Galam before the end of the rainy season and each could bring eighty to one hundred and twenty captives.[7] The captives were designated under the generic name "Bambara" although not all of them were natives of Ségou and Kaarta, two kingdoms located in the territory of nowadays Mali and constantly torn by fratricidal wars in the eighteenth century. Many found their way to Louisiana where they were extensively listed on plantation inventories along with the Mandingos, who belong to the larger Mande group along with the Bambara. The domain of this group is located on the Jolibaa River (Niger), from Lake Debo in the North to the source of the Tinkiso River in the south. The group is composed of the Northern Mande (Bozo, Soninke, Jula), the central Mande (Kagoro, Banmana or Bambara, Xaasonke, Foulanke, Malinke or Mandingo), and the Southern Mande (Jallonke, Samo, Samorho, Sia, etc.). The original settlements of the Bambara were located further south on the right bank of the Niger River,

---

6 Saugnier, *Relations de plusieurs voyages à la côte d'Afrique, à Maroc, au Sénégal, à Gorée, à Galam, etc,* (Paris: Roux et Compagnie, 1792), p.182.
7 Pruneau de Pommegorge, *Mémoire sur le commerce du Sénégal* 1752; quoted in A. Bathily, *Les portes de l'or* (1989), p.258.

near the town of Siguiri in present day Guinée Conakry. They left this area apparently to escape from the domination of the emperors of Mali who had adopted Islam. The arrival of the Bambara in the interior delta of the Niger River affected the Senufo. Many were absorbed, but the majority of them migrated south to the Sikasso region and Northern Côte d'Ivoire.[8] The Bambara and the Mandingo carry the same surnames (Coulibaly, Diarra, Traoré, Doumbia, Keïta, Koné, Konaté, etc.), they speak mutually intelligible languages, and they have in common the Komo secret society designed for the initiation of the youth.[9] The Senufo share this cult with them along with some surnames and a related language. Nevertheless only the Bambara and the Mandingo were visible in Louisiana official documents along with the Susu. This may indicate the fact that the other components of the Mande people had chosen to identify themselves with the larger groups.[10]

Up to 1742, the trade of Senegal was a monopoly of the French Company of the West Indies. Gorée Island was the principal *entrepôt* where both merchandise and slaves were safely stored before being shipped away. On July 3, 1761, the importance of Senegal and Gorée in the Atlantic slave trade was highlighted in a message to the King of France, in which the officials of the Company denied assertions that portrayed the Concession of Senegal as a burden for France: "Senegal is the key of the slave trade; on one hand, it provides the only slaves who are usable in Louisiana, Guinea being too distant; on the other hand, it serves as a relay for vessels bound to Guinea (…)"[11] Guinea meant here the coastal line beyond Sierra Leone down to Central Africa. The "relay" evoked in the message is nothing else but Gorée. The strategic advantages of the island are mentioned in another account written by Pelletan de Caplon, a former director of the French Company of Senegal. According to Pelletan, all along the coast, from the harbor of Mogador in Morocco down to the Gold Coast, sandbars impeded the landing of even the smallest boats. Nowhere were they able to careen or to lay the boat on its side in order to mend a leak, unless they entered the mouths of the rivers with the help of local pilots familiar with the waterways. Being protected by the

---

8 Delafosse M. 1972, *Haut-Sénégal-Niger*, tome 1, Maisonneuve et Larose, Paris, pp. 252-300. According to oral tradition, their strong willingness to safeguard their independence and ancestral beliefs gave them the name *ban-ma-na* (*refusal of a master*), which means "those-who-refused-to-surrender." Banmana was misspelled Bambara by the French.

9 Cissoko S.M. 1971, *Histoire de l'Afrique occidentale. Moyen Age et Temps modernes, VIIe siècle-1850*, Paris, Présence Africaine, p. 234. Delafosse 1972, pp. 410-411.

10 A large discussion of the meaning of the concept on "nation" in the African Diaspora can be found in what can be considered as the "Bambara controversy" which opposed Gwendolyn Midlo Hall to another historian. See Peter Caron 1997. Of a nation which the others don't understand: Bambara slaves and African ethnicity in Louisiana, 1718-60; in David Eltis & David Richardson, *Routes to slavery. Direction, ethnicity and mortality in the Transatlantic slave trade*. London-Portland: Frank Cass, pp.98-121. Also see Gwendolyn Midlo Hall 2005. *Slavery and African Ethnicities in the Americas: Restoring the Links*, pp.22-54].

11 *Mémoire of the Compagnie des Indes* (3 July 1761); quoted in Delcourt 1952, p.23.

long tip of the Cap-Vert peninsula and within the distance of a league from the continent, Gorée Island offered an excellent mooring for the vessels as well as facilities for taking on water and wood.[12] Moreover, Gorée was protected from the attacks of the local chiefs by water. Surrounded by reefs and rocks, except on its eastern side, Gorée was easily defensible against attacks by European competitors. The Portuguese, the Dutch, the French, and the English successively occupied the island. The Dutch settled on Gorée in 1617. Sixty years later, French naval officer Maréchal d'Estrée captured the island and the biggest portion of the slaves traded by the French in Senegambia embarked from there. The "middle passage" to the Americas lasted about one month off the coast of Senegal. Beyond southern Senegambia, the crossing of the ocean to Louisiana would have lasted much longer with a certainty of higher death rates.

Although Senegambia exported slaves across the Sahara desert many centuries before the beginning of the Atlantic slave trade, the exploitation of a pre-existing slave market was far from being able to satisfy the huge demand of the Americas. Since slaves were obtained mainly through wars, the only reliable solution to this problem was to generate permanent warfare between nations. From Senegal to Angola and Mozambique, African rulers were methodically played against each other by the European trading companies. Political successions were turned into civil wars in which the European companies supported the candidates whom they would later use as indispensable allies for the slave trade. The slave traders also soon understood that war was not enough by itself. Putting the African warlords in the middle of an enslaving business would prove to be more efficient. Addiction to European commodities was the bait used in their strategy, in which alcohol and firearms played a key role. Firearms were in high demand in the process of empire building. Wine and hard liquor were used in negotiations in order to obtain the best terms of trade and ultimately became basic items of the same trade.[13]

In time of peace, farmers were kidnapped in their fields by mercenaries, who were usually royal slaves called *jaami Buur* in Wolof. The *jaami Buur* were linked to the local elites and armed by the European companies. In his confessions, Philip Drake spoke of one Captain Fraley who was engaged in extensive operations on the Gambia River. He owned a fleet of Bristol and Liverpool vessels, which he supplied with human cargo from his factories on the African coast. Captain Fraley obtained his slaves by barter, but he also organized hunting parties on his private account, to operate with various African kings. One Captain Fisher also told Philip Drake that: "he had been upon many hunts on the small rivers, which emptied into the Gambia. It was customary for parties of sailors and coast blacks to lie in wait

---

12 Pelletan de Caplon, *Mémoire sur la colonie du Sénégal, par le citoyen Pelletan, ancien administrateur et ancien directeur de la Compagnie du Sénégal* (Paris, An X [1802]), p.93-94.
13 Gwendolyn Midlo Hall, *Slavery and African Ethnicities in the Americas: Restoring the Links* (Chapel Hill: University of North Carolina Press, 2005), p.16-18.

near the streams and little villages, and seize the stragglers by twos and threes, when they were fishing or cultivating their patches of corn. Sometimes an attack was made by night on the huts, and as many seized as could be conveniently managed in the boats."[14]

A typical warlord in eighteenth-century Senegal was Lat Sukabe Faal, King of the Wolof Kingdoms of Kajoor and Bawol for over two decades between 1698 and 1720. Contemporary witnesses described his army as being capable of bringing back from a single campaign nearly two thousand captives, including men, women, and children.[15] Villages were usually raided at night. Dwellings were set on fire to increase confusion. Elderly people, and sometimes children, were killed and their bodies left to rot under the sun, becoming prey to vultures and hyenas. The strong ones were caught, shackled, and walked to the coast, carrying trade goods such as elephant tusks on their heads. Many died of exhaustion on their way to the coast or from starvation while awaiting slave ships in dungeons. Sad memories of these raids are still being conveyed in modern day Senegal through songs:[16]

Nga bay sab gerté
Dugub ji ne gaňň
Buur teg ci loxo
Ne la jël naa ko!

You reap your peanut,
Millet is plentiful,
King comes in, claws out…
"My hand is on this food."

Ngèèn tëdd ba guddi
Buur tëgg ndëndam
Ni jog lèèn
Fii ku fi fanaan di jaam!

In the deepest of the night,
King sends out roaring drums announcing:
Run for your life,
Slavery doom shall be on whoever sees morrow!

The large estuary of the Gambia allowed vessels to go deep inside the course of

---

14 Philip Drake, *Revelations of a slave smuggler* (1860), p.98.
15 A detailed description of this warlord is given by Boubacar Barry, *Senegambia and the Atlantic slave trade* (1998), pp.81-85.
16 Wolof folksong; translated by Amath Sow, Dakar, Senegal.

the river whatever the season. Slaves and gold could be traded there at a cheaper rate. Both banks of the river were controlled by principalities built by the Mandingo traders. The English possessed a fort on James Island, not far from the mouth of the river, which they conquered in 1661 from the Dutch. During the Seven Year War (1756-1763), the English occupied Gorée and Saint-Louis as early as 1758. A treaty of peace was signed in 1763. The French gave up Saint-Louis but kept Gorée Island under their control. On November 1, 1765, a decree of the King of England created the Province of Senegambia with Saint-Louis as its capital. The appointment of Charles O'Hara as governor of the Province resulted in the upsurge of the slave trade. During ten years, from 1766 to 1776, Charles O'Hara committed himself to financing the raids of the Moorish emirates on the Wolof kingdoms of Waalo and Kajoor. The English governor himself participated in the depredation of the Wolof villages situated on the two banks of the river. He was recalled in 1776 as a result of petitions signed by the British merchants and the population of Saint-Louis accusing him of brutality and clandestine trade of gold and slaves. Some of the slaves were sent to Jamaica and put to work on O'Hara's own plantation.[17] Others were probably sent to South Carolina and Louisiana.

The Fulbe of Fuuta Tooro were also victims of the depredations of the Moors, who usually kept the children, whom they turned into domestic servants, herdsmen, and field hands for the exploitation of palm groves in the desert and gum trees on the Sahel dry lands. The adults were taken to the coast and sold to the European traders. Retaliation also allowed the Wolof and the Fulbe to capture their enemies whom they sold into slavery. The Wolof, the Moors, and the Fulbe were among the most frequent ethnicities on Louisiana plantations where they were respectively referred to as Senegal, Nard, and Poullard.[18] *Nard* is the Wolof name for Moors. The Fulbe of Fuuta Tooro refer to themselves as *Haal Pulaar* (Pulaar speakers). "Senegal" and "Poullard" have been retained as family names in southwest Louisiana. Through Ancestry.com, Poullard is presented as a "*pejorative derivative of Old French "poule" (chicken)*." This explanation is a simple reproduction of the definition given by George W. Cable back in the 19th century.[19]

The American Revolution allowed the French to reconquer Northern Senegambia. In 1779, an expedition led by French officer Lauzun expelled the English from Saint-Louis and conquered Fort James. This fort was taken back by the English four years later according to the Treaty of Paris (1783). The French trade in Senegal was totally ruined after the 1789 Revolution. The blockade imposed by the British navy during the wars of the French Revolution resulted

---

17 Barry, *Senegambia and the Atlantic slave trade* (1998), pp.112 and 134.

18 Gwendolyn Midlo Hall, *Louisiana Slave Database*, online at http://www.ibiblio.org/laslave.

19 Ancestry.com: http://www.ancestry.com/name-origin?surname=poullard [accessed October 24, 2013]. George W. Cable, *Creoles and Cajuns. Stories of Old Louisiana*, Arlin Turner ed., New York, 1959, p. 372.

in the breakthrough of American traders who handled most of the trade formerly carried out by the French.[20] The American presence in Senegal increased during the Napoleonic wars and the occupation of the country by the British from 1800 to 1817. There is explicit evidence of a slave trading link between Louisiana and Senegal at that time. In 1803, a few months before the prohibition of the external slave trade into the Orleans territory, three vessels arrived in New Orleans with 463 slaves on board. Jean François Merieult, a Louisiana French Creole, whose house is now the headquarters of the Historic New Orleans Collection, organized these voyages. The vessels were named *Sally*, *L'Africain*, and *La Confiance*, and the captains were respectively Peter Farmuel, John Louis Sacray, and Augustus Buibert.[21]

To the south of the Gambia River, the slave trade was carried out on every estuary, from the Casamance River to the Sierra Leone River. New scholarship has demonstrated that the stateless societies so characteristic of this region actively participated in the Atlantic trade as they were forced to produce captives to procure the materials and weaponry needed to defend against and resist the very trade they were feeding.[22] The French were established in Bissau, Boulama, and Cacheu, but they could not sustain the competition with the Afro-Portuguese, who were well-established in the region and had woven very strong ties with local chiefs. The pioneers of Portuguese colonization, the Lançados, and their descendants had also colonized the Cape Verde Archipelago. Rio Pongo (Fatala River) and Rio Nunez, inshore outlets of the territory known today under the name of Guinea Conakry, were also large slave trading areas as early as the fifteenth century. The dominant populations there were the Mande-speaking Susu on the Rio Pongo, the Landuman on the Rio Nunez, and the Baga. In the eighteenth century, numerous companies and even individuals had gained control of the islands at the mouths of these rivers. The most famous among these traders was Miles Barber from London, established on one of the Los Islands off the mouth of Rio Nunez. His principal partners were French but also, toward the end of the century, a constantly increasing number of ship-owners from the United States of America. The Southern Rivers provided about ten percent of the total volume of the trans-Atlantic slave trade with the birth and the backing of the theocratic state of Fuuta Jallon. Under the guise of "jihad" (holy war), the predatory expeditions of the Fulbe were extended far beyond

---

20 Pelletan de Caplon, *Mémoire sur la colonie du Sénégal* (1802), p.93.

21 Gilbert Leonard to Governor William Claiborne, New Orleans, January 25, 1804; in Donnan, ed., *Documents*, IV (1969), p.661. For details about these voyages including all slaves sold from each of them, see Hall, *Louisiana Slave Database* (work from SPSS, doctype 25, year 1803). See also Douglas B. Chambers, "Slave trade merchants of Spanish New Orleans, 1763-1803: Clarifying the colonial slave trade to Louisiana in Atlantic perspective," *Atlantic Studies* 5, 3 (2008), pp.335-346.

22 Walter Hawthorne 2003. *Planting Rice and Harvesting Slaves: Transformations Along the Guinea-Bissau Coast, 1400-1900* (Portsmouth, NH: Heinemann).

the Jalonke and Pulli populations who did not convert to Islam. The Bambara, Mandingo, Kisi, Basari, and Koñagi were among their victims.[23]

The Fulbe of Fuuta Jallon were themselves victims of this chaotic situation. The most famous among them was Abdul Rahman Barry, a son of Ibrahima Sori, king of Fuuta Jallon. In 1788, he was captured during a war against the neighboring Mandingo kingdom of Kaabu and sold to the coast. He was then taken to the Caribbean island of Dominica and from there to New Orleans, where he was sold to Thomas Foster, a planter established in Natchez, Mississippi. According to Gwendolyn Midlo Hall's calculation, Abdul Rahman might have arrived in Dominica in 1789 on the ship *Africa*, operated by Captain John Nevin and owned by John Barnes of London. It left the Gambia in 1788 and arrived in Dominica on April 28, 1789. The ship began selling slaves in New Orleans on September 16, 1789. Abdul Rahman Barry spent forty years in bondage in Natchez, where he was referred to as Prince.[24]

In the beginning of the sixteenth century, the estuary of the Sierra Leone River was already a relay for the Portuguese vessels engaged in trade with Africa and the Indies. This area was well known to the Lançados who went far in the neighboring rivers to the lands of the Bulom, the Temne, and the Limba and even farther inland to the territories of the Loko, the Susu, and the Fulbe. The slaves were sold to slave ships along the coast. During the 1670s, the Royal Africa Company had established an outpost on Bence Island, at the mouth of the Sierra Leone River. This establishment became an active center for the slave trade and home to a growing population of Afro-English descent. A party led by Afro-Portuguese destroyed it in 1728. Private traders of British origin then controlled the fort on Bence Island until its capture in 1779 by the French. The slave trade developed again when the island was returned to the English after the 1783 Treaty of Paris. The French traders were still present, but most of the slaves were sent to North America and to the islands of Grenada, St. Christopher, and Jamaica where the English traders who controlled Bence Island had their own plantations. To the south of the estuary of the Sierra Leone River, on the Sherbro River, an Anglo-African community also existed. In the beginning of the eighteenth century the slave trade was very active there, as well as along the coast of what became Liberia, from Cabo Monte (Cape Mount) to Cape Palmas.[25] This region was known as the

23 Thomas, *The Slave Trade* (1997), p.341; Barry, *Senegambia and the Atlantic slave trade* (1998), p.98.

24 Terry Alford, *Prince among slaves* (New York: Oxford University Press, 1977); Hall, *Louisiana Slave Database*, voyage no.88808.

25 Thomas, *The Slave Trade* (1997), pp.342-343. This is confirmed by new scholarship on the history of the British Province of Senegambia. See Brown, Christopher Leslie. *Moral Capital: Foundations of British Abolitionism* (Chapel Hill, NC: University of North Carolina Press, 2006) and Paul E. Lovejoy, Forgotten Colony in Africa: The British Province of Senegambia (1765-83), in *Slavery, Abolition and the Transition to Colonialism in Sierra Leone*, Paul E. Love-

Côte de Malaguette (Pepper Coast) or *Côte des graines* (the Grain Coast).

The captives sold from the Southern Rivers played a very important role in the development of rice cultivation in the southern United States, notably in South Carolina and Louisiana. The slaves of the Côte de Malaguette were called Bouriquis, Miserables, Mesurades, or Cangas in French Saint-Domingue.[26] The Canga were among the most frequent ethnicities on Louisiana plantations, along with the Kisi. Many Temne and Susu (Soso) were also listed on slave inventories along the German Coast of Louisiana.[27]

In the first decade of the nineteenth century, several European nations (and the U.S.), which had entered the Industrial Revolution, had decided to abandon the Atlantic slave trade and to fight against its continuation. But England was alone to fight against the "illegitimate trade" from its basis of Freetown, which had been founded in 1787 by philanthropists sustained by the British government.[28] During the first half of the nineteenth century, the Southern Rivers region became a major place for the clandestine slave trade in greater Senegambia. From 1818 to 1848, many traders, of French origin mostly, were convicted of smuggling slaves apparently destined for the lower Mississippi River Valley, via Martinique, Guadeloupe, and Cuba. In 1848, the French authorities of the Second Republic officially abolished slavery in the territories under their control. Some of the freed slaves were soon recruited by the French colonial army or regrouped in the so-called "villages de liberté" (freedom villages) where they became a reservoir of labor. Senegambia had provided the majority of the slaves imported into the Americas from the fifteenth century through the seventeenth century. This region still exported large numbers of slaves during the eighteenth and nineteenth centuries but never on the same scale as other regions of Africa such as the Bights of Benin and Biafra or Central Africa.

The Lower Guinea Coast: From the Ivory Coast to the Bight of Biafra

The Ivory Coast, from Cape Palmas to Cape Three Points, was named so because of the quantity of ivory traded there. From Cape Three Points to the mouth of the Volta River lies the Gold Coast where the Europeans maintained in the eighteenth century no less than a hundred trading posts, the biggest of them being

---

joy and Suzanne Schwarz, eds. The Harriet Tubman Series on the African Diaspora. Africa World Press (forthcoming).

26 M.L.E. Moreau de Saint-Méry, *Description physique et topographique de la partie française de l'Isle de Saint-Domingue*, 2 vols, [Philadelphia, PA, 1797-1798], New Edition by B. Maurel et E. Taillemitte (Paris: Société de l'Histoire des Colonies Françaises et Librairie Larose, 1958), p.49.

27 Hall, *Louisiana Slave Database*.

28 Barry, *Senegambia and the Atlantic slave trade* (1998), pp.133-134.

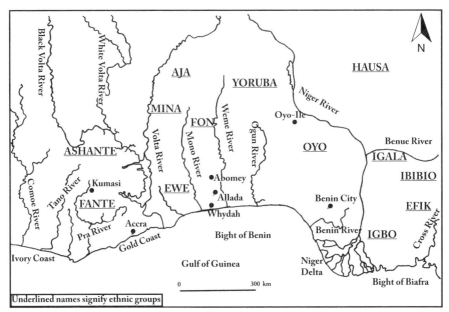

Fig. 3.2. The Lower Guinea Coast in the eighteenth century.
Map by Allison Reu.

Elmina. Very few slaves from the Ivory Coast and the Gold Coast were taken to
the Mississippi River, except the Mina, who were among one of the most populous
ethnicities of Louisiana. The Mina belong to the Ewe ethno-linguistic group and
their traditional domain is centered on the Mono River, encompassing eastern
Ghana, the territory of modern Togo, and the west of modern Benin.[29]

It is likely that most of the Mina transported to Louisiana were shipped from the
Bight of Benin, also known as the Slave Coast. This region ran from the estuary of
the Volta River to the kingdom of Benin and the western Niger River Delta. In the
eighteenth century, this section of the coast became a very active slave trading zone.
In the beginning of the century, Agaja, king of Danhome (Abomey), undertook a
series of conquests toward the ocean in order to gain a direct hold on the Atlantic
trade. It was a tradition among the kings of Danhome to have animals, such as
the chameleon, the lion, or the shark as heraldic signs. By choosing a ship as his
emblem, Agaja's views toward the coast were quite clear. After having conquered
the kingdoms of Oueme and Allada, King Agaja gained control of the coast with
the conquest of Popo and Ouidah. This town was (and still is) a great sanctuary
of *vodun* (voodoo). It became the main outlet of the slave trade and the legacy of
the past is still visible in the case of Ganvié, a village where people are still living
in stilt-dwellings built on the water, which once protected them against the slave
hunters.

---

29 Kofi Awoonor, *Guardians of the sacred word-Ewe poetry* (New York: Nok Publishers Ltd.,
1974), p.13.

The Portuguese were the first to have commercial relations with the Bight of Benin. But, until the seventeenth century, the slave trade was not developed in this zone, and Europeans were never able to build fortresses there comparable to those of the Gold Coast. The local rulers, chiefly the King of Danhome, destroyed the modest European fortifications and held their ships at a distance off the coast. From the 1780s, Porto-Novo (Jaquin) and Badagry, on the eastern part of the Slave Coast, saw a considerable development as well as the Island of Onim on which the city of Lagos was constructed. These trading posts were under the control of the Yoruba Kingdom of Oyo, which became their main supplier of slaves until the end of the century when Oyo began to decline. The Kingdom of Benin was opposed to the slave trade for a long time, but it became deeply involved in the eighteenth century. About two million slaves were exported from the Slave Coast between 1640 and 1870, and they were mostly carried by ships owned by the Portuguese and the Brazilians (900,000), followed by the English (360,000), the French (280,000), the Dutch (110,0000), with smaller numbers carried by the Spaniards, and the North Americans.[30]

The captives of the Slave Coast, as listed by Moreau de Saint-Méry, are identifiable in the local ethnography: "*Socos* (Sehue), *Cotocolis*, *Popos*, *Aradas*, *Maïs* (Mahi), *Fida* (Pedah), *Fond* (Fon), *Aoussas* (Hawsa), and *Nagos* (Yoruba)."[31] The Fon, also called Aja, created polities such as Allada, or Ardra, Popo, Ouidah, and Danhome. Yorubaland, farther inland, reaches to the north to the territory of the Hawsa. The Fon/Aja/Arada, the Yoruba/Nago, and the Hawsa were among the eighteen most frequent ethnicities on Louisiana plantations.[32] With the Fon came the fundamentals of "vodun," retained in Louisiana as voodoo. The word means "spirit" and is used to designate any kind of deity that human beings call upon to solve their problems. The equivalent is "tuur" among the Wolof, "pangol" among the Sereer, and "orisha" among the Yoruba. Voodoo was seen in the mythogenic city of New Orleans as mere superstition and witchcraft, and the metropolitan police constantly harassed worshippers throughout the nineteenth century. Strange stories were built up by outsiders' imagination and are still conveyed by tour guides in the French Quarter where "voodoo" remains to this day an object of fascination and a source of revenue.

The Bight of Biafra, centered on the Niger Delta and the Cross River of southeastern Nigeria, became a significant exporter of slaves from the 1700s. It dominated the trans-Atlantic slave trade, along with the Bight of Benin, until its effective end beyond the mid-nineteenth century. At least 4,500 captives were exported every year from the Bight of Biafra between 1711 and 1733. In the eighteenth century, the English dominated the trade, and the principal trading

---

30 Thomas, *The Slave Trade* (1997), p.360.
31 Moreau de Saint-Méry, *Description physique et topographique* (1958), p.50.
32 See Hall, *Slavery and African Ethnicities in the Americas* (2005), Table 2.4, pp.43-44.

posts were Bonny, Old Calabar (Iboku, Duke Town), and New Calabar (Elem Kalabari). A great number of slaves from this part of Africa were sold into North America.[33] In Louisiana, slaves from this coast were listed as Edo, Ibo (Igbo), Ibibio, and Calabar. They were among the most frequent ethnicities listed on official documents.[34] According to Moreau de Saint-Méry, many planters of the French West Indies were reluctant to buy the Igbo since they had the tendency of committing suicide en masse, believing that this allowed them to return home. Thus developed the Creole saying "Ibos pend' cor à yo" (The Ibo hang themselves). This could be prevented, Moreau de Saint-Méry wrote, by cutting off the head, or simply the nose or the ears of the first who commits suicide and having those body parts posted on a pole. This punishment was thought to work because none of them wanted to face the dishonor of going home mutilated.[35] "Igbo" has evolved into a family name (Ebow) in southwest Louisiana. One of the bearers of this name is Josephine Ebow (spouse Cormier), the owner of Josephine's Creole restaurant in Saint-Martinville (Petit Paris), a few miles from Lafayette on Bayou Teche. This family name is less popular than Senegal and Poullard.

West-Central Africa and the East Coast

Beyond the Niger Delta, past the Cameroon and the Gabon Rivers, ran the great coast of Loango, Congo, and Angola. The biggest slave harbor of West-Central Africa was Mayumba, followed by those of Malimba and Cabinda in the Kingdom of Loango. The trade was open to all the foreign traders and the *Maloango* (the Kings of Loango) appointed a special representative, the Mafouk, to deal with the trade. The French were their favorite customers although the Dutch had established trading posts at Mayumba and Loango in the sixteenth century. The Dutch began to ask for slaves in the 1640s, and thirty years later, human cargo supplanted natural products like copper, ivory, and red wood. In 1670, the Dutch Company of the West Indies traded 3,000 slaves in one year from the harbor of Loango. The global volume of the trade in Loango was about 20,000 slaves every year with probable peaks of 40,000 to 80,000 between 1765 and 1790. Kongo, to the south of Loango, was a kingdom on the decline after having played a premier role in the slave trade during the seventeenth century. A large population of Afro-Portuguese mulattos lived there. To the south of Kongo, the Kingdom of Angola provided three-quarters of the slaves imported into Brazil and eventually two-thirds of the slaves imported into Mexico. Luanda, an island located on the estuary of the Cuanza River, was the main harbor. The English appointed a Governor at Cabinda and built a fort there, but the Portuguese governors of Angola destroyed

---

33 Thomas, *The Slave Trade* (1997), p.362.
34 Hall, *Louisiana Slave Database*.
35 Moreau de Saint-Méry, *Description physique et topographique* (1958), p.51.

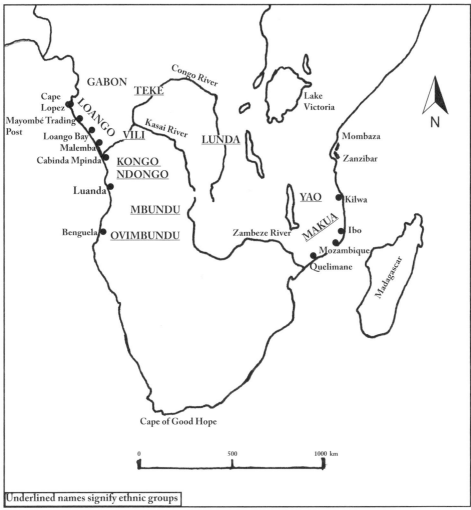

Fig. 3.3. West Central Africa and the South-East Coast in the eighteenth century.
Map by Allison Reu.

the fort. Nevertheless, the English colonies, including those of North America, received every year one out of every five slaves exported from this part of Africa in the eighteenth century.[36]

At the Congress of Vienna (1815), the British pressured Spain, Portugal, France, and the Netherlands to agree to abolish the slave trade, but Spain and Portugal were permitted a few years of continued slaving to replenish labor supplies. In 1817, Great Britain and Spain signed a treaty prohibiting the slave trade. Spain agreed to end the slave trade north of the equator immediately and south of the equator by 1820. British naval vessels were given the right to search suspected slavers. Still, loopholes in the treaty undercut its goals. A later source estimated that in some months, as many as sixty vessels landed slave cargoes in Cuba, and the number

36 Thomas, *The Slave Trade* (1997), p.365-368.

of slaves actually transported to this island per annum reached 60,000.[37] Many of these Africans, mostly from the Congo-Angola region, ended their journey in the U.S. South, since a slave purchased for $300 to $500 in Cuba could command a price of $600 to $1,000 on American soil.[38] New Orleans, the most attractive slave market of the Western hemisphere, was the normal destination of these slaves smuggled through the platform of Cuba.

According to Moreau de Saint-Méry, the most common and the most appreciated slaves on the island of St. Domingue (Haiti) were those of the coast of Congo and Angola. They were designated under the generic name of Congo among whom the French distinguished the true Congo or *Francs Congo* to the center, the *Mayombes* to the north, and the *Malimbes*, the *Mousombes*, and the *Mondongues*, who were captured from the East and taken to the coast of Congo.[39] The term "Congo" was also the generic name under which the slaves from Central Africa were designated in Louisiana and certainly the most frequent reference for slaves recorded on official documents. These slaves were most heavily clustered on plantations in Orleans Parish and, after 1803, in St. Charles Parish. They were less prominent farther up the Mississippi River, where Africans from Senegambia and the Bight of Benin predominated. The proportion of "Congo" listed in official documents spiked between 1800 and 1820 along with the boom of the sugar industry.[40]

The Congo basin was also linked to the east coast where Arab traders had settled as early as the ninth century. This encounter between the East African coast and the Arab world yielded a hybrid society using Swahili as a *lingua franca*. Patterns of the slave trade in this area can be well depicted through the late career of Hamed bin Mohammed bin Juma bin Rajab el Murjebi, better known as Tippu Tip, the most famous Afro-Arab trader of the area. He was born in Zanzibar and, at the age eighteen, became a dealer in slaves and ivory, trading between the interior and coastal towns. By 1880, he had built a large commercial empire between the Upper Congo, Lake Tanganyika, and Bagamoyo on the coast. The slaves were transferred to Zanzibar for sale to foreign merchants.[41] Slaves from the east coast were mostly sold in the Middle East, but some ended up in the Western Hemisphere. For Moreau de Saint-Méry, although the Coast of Angola was the boundary-mark of the slave trade destined to the French colonies of America, a few slaves were

---

37 Drake, *Revelations of a slave smuggler* (1860), p.98. These numbers are obviously exaggerated. This book was published just before the Civil War and was apparently meant to support abolitionist propaganda.

38 Weld, ed., *Slavery and the Internal Slave Trade* (1969), p.249.

39 Moreau de St.-Méry, *Description physique et topographique* (1958), p.52.

40 Hall, *Slavery and African Ethnicities in the Americas* (2005), p.160. See also fig. 3.4. and fig. 3.5.

41 Heinrich Brode, *Tippu Tip, the history of his career in Zanzibar and Central Africa*, ed. by Mark Wilson (Zanzibar, Tanzania: Gallery Publications, 2000; originally published in 1903).

imported from Monomotapa (Zimbabwe), Mozambique, and Madagascar.[42] Slaves from the east coast called Makwa were exported to Louisiana where they stood among the eighteen most frequent African ethnicities.[43] Also called Mirazi, their homeland runs along the banks of the Rovuma River, the current boundaryline between Mozambique and Tanzania.

The Africans on the German Coast

The distribution of African-born slaves in St. Charles and St. John the Baptist parishes (Fig. 3.4. and Fig. 3.5.) reflects perfectly the patterns of the slave trade between Africa and Louisiana prior to 1820. The enslaved Africans documented in said parishes came mostly through four major regions: Senegambia (Sierra Leone included), the Bight of Benin, the Bight of Biafra, and Central Africa. The same distribution is confirmed on Habitation Haydel through official documents, mostly succession inventories, dating from 1819 to 1860 (table 8). Fourteen African ethnic or coastal names were documented among the fifty-eight individuals clearly identifiable as African born, including Congo, Mandingo, Kiamba (Chamba), Bambara, Soso (Susu), Kanga, Poullard, Mina, Igbo, Senegal, Nard, Temne, and Edo. The birthplace of one African slave was Guinea, a rather imprecise place since this name could designate any portion of the west coast of Africa. But according to patterns of the slave trade to Louisiana, his origin would likely be Senegambia. On January 15, 1801, the inventory of the property of late Jean Christophe Haydel listed sixteen arpents of land and fifty-eight slaves.[44] Among the latter, eight had *Guinea* as their birthplace, including a male slave called Mass. This may be the diminutive of Massamba, a name very popular among the Wolof of Senegambia, as it is among the people of the Congo River basin.

Out of the fifty-eight Africans clearly identified on Habitation Haydel from 1819 to 1860 (table 8), twenty-eight came from Senegambia (48.2 percent), sixteen from Central Africa (27.5 percent), and thirteen from the bights of Benin and Biafra (22.3 percent). The 1818 inventory of the estate of late Mathias Roussel Père (table 9), immediate upriver neighbor of Habitation Haydel, listed fourteen slaves born in Africa, half of them from Senegambia. The records of this property are also valuable references since it became part of Whitney Plantation in 1919. Among the slaves who lived on the Haydel and Roussel plantations, a sizeable number was composed of people of African and Indian descent called *Grifs,* meaning those born in Louisiana, and *Caracoli,* if their birthplace was in the French West Indies.

---

42 Moreau de St.-Méry, *Description physique et topographique* (1958), p.54.

43 Hall, *Louisiana Slave Database*; *Slavery and African Ethnicities in the Americas* (2005), Table 2.4, pp.43-44.

44 Jean Christophe Haydel was the owner of the plantation known today as Evergreen plantation. Jean Jacques Haydel, his younger brother and next-door neighbor, was the owner of the future Whitney Plantation.

The 1819 inventory of Habitation Haydel (table 10) listed sixty-one slaves, nineteen of them born in Africa, including twelve from Senegambia (63.1 percent), four from the Bight of Benin (21 percent), and three from Central Africa (15.7 percent).[45] In the case of Senegambia, this distribution of African-born slaves is closer to the calculations done from the Du Bois database, which estimates 60.8 percent of the slave population of Louisiana came from Senegambia.[46]

Besides the Congos, the vast majority of the slaves listed on Habitation Haydel belonged to the Mande group (Mandingo or Malinke, Bambara, and Susu). The Mande people contributed very deep cultural influences to the culture of Louisiana including masking, which eventually led to the resilient tradition of the Mardi Gras Indians of New Orleans. In this city, "Congo" became synonymous with "Africa" like "Guinen" (Guinea) in Saint-Domingue (Haiti). "Congo Square" or "Place du Congo" (now Louis Armstrong Park), the most symbolic place for Afro-Creole culture in New Orleans, was named so by the folks who, every Sunday afternoon, used to dance there in circles representing different African nations. Jazz came mostly from the fusion of these circles and the assimilation of some European musical forms. Vachel Lindsay (1879-1931), the celebrated poet from Springfield, Illinois, was acquainted with Louisiana at least through his knowledge of the writings of authors such as George W. Cable. In his most famous poem ("The Congo"), which uses syncopated jazz rhythms, Mumbo Jumbo (Maama Jombo), a Mandingo mask, is referred to as "the God of the Congo":

> *Be careful what you do*
> *Or Mumbo Jumbo, God of the Congo*
> *{…}*
> *And all the other gods of the Congo*
> *Mumbo Jumbo will hoo-doo you*
> *Mumbo Jumbo will hoo-doo you*
> *Mumbo Jumbo will hoo-doo you.*[47]

---

45 See table 7.
46 David Eltis, Stephen Behrendt, David Richardson, and Herbert S. Klein, *The Trans-Atlantic Slave Trade: A Database on CD-ROM* (Cambridge: Cambridge University Press, 1999); quoted by Michael A. Gomez, *Black Crescent. The experience and legacy of African Muslims in the Americas* (New York: Cambridge University Press, 2005), p.162.
47 Excerpts from Poemhunter.com, "The Congo": http://www.poemhunter.com/poem/the-congo-a-study-of-the-negro-race/ (accessed 17 September 2010).

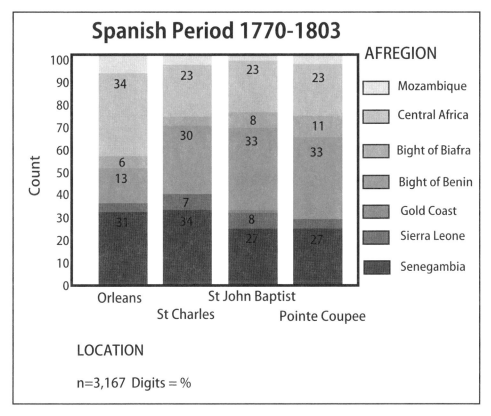

Fig. 3.4. African origins of Louisiana slaves: Spanish Period.
Source: Gwendolyn Midlo Hall, Louisiana slave database.

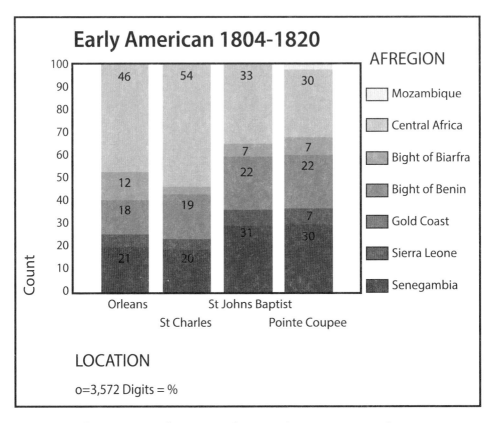

Fig. 3.5 African origins of Louisiana slaves: Early American Period.
Source: Gwendolyn Midlo Hall, Louisiana slave database.

TABLE 7: EIGHTEEN MOST FREQUENT AFRICAN ETHNICITIES IN LOUISIANA (1719-1820).

Ethnicities	Gender		Total
	Male	Female	
Greater Senegambia			**2,756**
Bamana/Bambara	413	53	466
Mandinga	617	305	922
Nard/Moor	101	35	136
Poullard/Fulbe	160	50	210
Senegal/Wolof	363	234	597
Kisi	51	35	86
Kanga	210	129	339
Bight of Benin			**1,777**
Chamba	276	139	415
Mina	430	198	628
Fon/Arada	126	117	243
Hausa	122	11	133
Nago/Yoruba	247	111	358
Bight of Biafra			**819**
Edo	38	28	66
Igbo	287	237	524
Ibibio/Moko	61	21	82
Calabar	88	59	147
West-Central Africa			**2,988**
Congo	2,064	924	2,988
East Coast			**102**
Makwa	67	35	102
Total	**5,721**	**2,721**	**8,442**

Source: Gwendolyn Midlo Hall, Slavery and African Ethnicities in the Americas (2005), Table 2.4, pp.43-44.

TABLE 8: AFRICAN NATIONS AND AFRO-INDIANS LISTED ON HABITATION HAYDEL (1819-1860).

Nation	Number of Individuals	Region of Origin	Observations
Congo	16	Central Africa	
Madingo	11	Senegambia	
Grif	9	Louisiana	African and Indian
Kiamba (Chamba)	7	Bight of Benin	
Bambara	4	Senegambia	
Soso (Susu)	4	Senegambia	
Canga	3	Senegambia	
Poullard/Fulbe	3	Senegambia	
Mina	3	Bight of Benin	
Igbo	2	Bight of Biafra	
Senegal/Wolof	1	Senegambia	
Nard/Moor	1	Senegambia	
Temne	1	Senegambia	
Guinea	1	?	Imprecise location
Edo	1	Bight of Biafra	
Caracoli	1	French Antilles	African and Indian
Total African born: 58			
Total Senegambia	28	48.2%	
Total Central Africa	16	27.5%	
Total Bight of Benin	10	17.2%	
Total Bight of Biafra	3	5.1%	
Total Guinea	1	1.7%	

TABLE 9: INVENTORY OF THE ESTATE OF
LATE MATHIAS ROUSSEL PÈRE. 19 OCTOBER 1818 [SJB-48-1818]

Name	Origin	Qualification	Born ca.	Observations
Polydore	Poulard		1758	Hernia
Dick	Soso		1758	
Yéro	Poulard		1768	
Coacou	Mina		1768	
Samba	Poulard		1768	
Codio	Mina	Domestic	1783	
Charles	East Coast		1778	
Thom	Ybo (Igbo)		1783	
Valentin	Kiamba		1778	
Justin	Bambara		1778	Epileptic
Moussa	Mandingo		1778	
Jean Pierre	Congo		1788	
Toussaint	Creole	Cart man	1788	
Benc	Mandingo		1793	
Isidore	Creole	Cart man	1793	
Jean Louis	Creole	Cart man	1793	
Pierrot	Creole	Cart man	1793	
Célestin	Creole	Cart man	1793	
Gabriel	Creole	Domestic	1798	
Guiermimy	Congo		1806	
William	East Coast		1803	
Adam	Creole		1811	Orphan
Clemence	Creole	Domestic	1788	
Magdelaine	Creole	Domestic	1786	+ son Louis (9)
Françoise	Kiamba		1768	
Marie	Caracoliene	Cook	1758	Afro-Indian from the Antilles
Marie	Acadienne	Domestic, Spinner	1798	+ daughter Marie Ève (3)
Babet	Griffonne	Domestic	1801	Young female Grif
Poly	Creole	Domestic	1798	+ sons Adam (2) & Firmin (8m.)
Thérèze	Creole	Domestic	1804	

TABLE 10: AFRICANS LISTED ON HABITATION HAYDEL (1819)

Name and Age	Nation	Observations
Sam, 60	Soso	Blind
Honoré, 30	Canga	Recovered from hernia
Bernard, 50	Kiamba	Fits of madness
Adonis, 50	Bambara	
Sophie, 35	Congo	
Barnabe, 30	Bambara	
Lucas, 35	Soso	
Hector, 50	Soso	
Michel, 30	Canga	
Valere, 25	Canga	
Achile, 22	Mandingo	
Philipe,	Timiny (Temne)	
Isidore, 20	Congo	"teigne" (tinea)
Gabriel, 25	Congo	
Raphael, 60	Kiamba	
Lubin, 50	Mandingo	Hernia
Mars, 60	Kiamba	
Augustin, 50	Kiamba	
Alexandre, 30	Bambara	Sickly

Source: Inventory of the community of J.J. Haydel Père and late Marie Madelaine Bosonnier [SJB-116-1819].

CHAPTER FOUR

HABITATION HAYDEL
They called him Godfather of the Church

*The so-called German Coast furnishes
a lot of rice to the city, many vegetables,
corn, milk products, but very little indigo
and sugar. This is because the inhabitants
do not have enough Negroes at their disposal
although they are the best workers in the colony.*
—Redon de Ressac (1763)

Indigo generation: The first Louisiana-born Haydels

The German settlements stretched in a narrow belt along the Mississippi River where the natural levees, created by the annual flooding accompanied by deposition of alluvial sand and silts, made a favored location for dwellings and cultivation.[1] The planters' homes, storehouses, and slave quarters were located near the river. They had to be built on posts and piers because the frequent flooding did not allow houses to be erected directly on the ground. Wide galleries protected the inhabitants from the summer heat. Every colonist owned one or more pirogues in which produce was transported to New Orleans. Each plantation had its dock for loading and unloading, including a cypress or oak post sunk into the ground where larger boats were tied up.[2] The location of a plantation was determined by

1 Jay D. Edwards and Nicolas Pecquet du Bellay de Verton, *A Creole Lexicon, Architecture, Landscape, People* (Baton Rouge: Louisiana State University Press, 2004), p.124.
2 Helmut Blume, *The German Coast during the Colonial Era 1722-1803* (Destrehan, LA: German-Acadian Coast Historical and Genealogical Society, 1990), pp.76-78.

its distance from New Orleans, its position on the Mississippi River (left or right bank), and neighboring pieces of property.[3] The latter were designated in official documents as being "above" (upstream) or "below" (downstream) the piece of land to be sold. Land was distributed in arpents measured on front footage along the waterways.[4] Most of the early plantations in the area were six arpents wide and property lines went far back from the river into the *cyprières* (cypress swamps), the *lataniers* (dwarf palmetto groves), and woodlands. The customary depth (*profondeur ordinaire*) was forty arpents. Land grants more than forty arpents in length were occasionally consigned during the Spanish period in recognition of the work accomplished by certain inhabitants.[5] But this was only possible in locations where the natural levees were sufficiently high to provide arable fields more than three miles deep behind the river.[6]

The most difficult tasks were the clearing of the land, the building of artificial levees for protection against floods, and the digging of drainage canals. An official report sent to France on October 10, 1731, stated that a single settler, if he did not get sick, could prepare only one arpent of land for planting in a whole year. Another report from Governor Périer to the French officials assured that the land could only be worked by those who have a slave force, since the labor to build levees was so difficult.[7] The building of levees was necessary to keep the muddy waters of the Mississippi River from destroying crops and dwellings. Each farmer had to build levees on the riverfront of his property and permanent maintenance was necessary, especially at places such as the Bonnet Carré bend, a few miles below Whitney Plantation, where breaches (*crevasses* in French) would bring devastating floods. The "Bonnet Crevasse" became a nightmare for planters of that vicinity. During the last two decades of the antebellum period, floods occurred three times: in August 1844, in December 1850, and in May 1859.[8] The cultivated land was also easily flooded by the heavy sub-tropical rains, which favored rice cultivation. But, for most of the crops, well-drained soil was needed. Thus, there was the necessity to dig deep canals, which drained flood waters off into the cypress swamps.

The German colonists planted corn, rice, and vegetables on their small plots. Rice required more work and, above all, special skills for the preparation of the land, the planting of the seeds, the control of water, the hulling of the grain, and its preparation for food. The French Company quite early encouraged the development of rice cultivation in Louisiana. Among the instructions to Herpin, captain of *l'Aurore*, the first slave ship sent to Louisiana from the African coast,

---

3 The distance was calculated in lieues (leagues). One lieue equals 2.8 miles.

4 One arpent is equal to 183 linear feet or 55.7 meters.

5 Blume, *The German Coast* (1990), p.107.

6 Edwards and du Bellay de Verton, *A Creole Lexicon* (2004), p.124.

7 Blume, *The German Coast* (1990), p.30.

8 Joseph K. Menn, *The large slave holders of Louisiana-1860* (New Orleans: Pelican Publishing Company, 1964), p.359.

was the obligation to acquire rice and slaves who know how to cultivate it: "In the different places where the aforesaid Sir Herpin will trade Negroes, he will make sure to buy a number of slaves who know how to cultivate rice, he will also buy three or four barrels of rice suited for seedlings, which he will deliver upon his arrival in the colony to the director of the Company."[9] In 1720, rice was produced along the Mississippi river, and Louisiana soon began to export rice to the French Antilles.[10]

The history of the slave trade is not merely the history of a deportation into the Americas of able-bodied people who could tolerate the tropical climate. It was also a transfer of technology and know-how experienced for many centuries on African soil. In Senegambia, the region of rice cultivation runs from Saalum, at the center-west of Senegal, down to Sierra Leone. The Casamance region, the land of the Diola (Joola) and many other ethnicities, is the center of gravity of this rice kingdom. In his memoir on the colony of Senegal, Pelletan de Caplon, former director of the local French company, could not specify the number of slaves one could trade there; but he knew that one can get from this river a great quantity of very good quality rice.[11] In his monumental work, Paul Pélissier considers rice cultivation and the Joola peasant synonymous: "to eat for a Diola doesn't have any sense other than eating rice ... being rich means to dispose of rice fields and abundant rice granaries that are source of prestige and ease... Next to the dead that one buries, is carefully placed a provision of this precious viaticum; there is no sacrifice to the Boekins (spirits) that doesn't include, with the traditional palm wine, an offering of rice."[12] *Oryza glaberrima* was the main species of local rice and had been domesticated in the Niger River Valley since the second millennium before our era, according to R. Portères.[13] Other varieties of rice were introduced from Asia by the European navigators in the coastal region, from Saalum to Sierra Leone, where populations not only consumed certain varieties of rice but also possessed techniques of cultivation capable of producing the new ones. Corn developed on a larger scale from the Gold Coast to the Slave Coast, where people

---

9 "Instructions pour le Sr Herpin Commandant du Vaisseau l'Aurore destiné pour la Traitte des Nègres à la Coste de Guynée, 4 juillet 1718"; in Elizabeth Donnan, ed. *Documents Illustrative of the History of the Slave Trade to America*, vol.IV, *The Border Colonies and The Southern Colonies* (Washington, D.C.: Carnegie Institution, 1935; repr. New York: Octagon Books, 1969), p.636.

10 Gwendolyn Midlo Hall, *Africans in Colonial Louisiana, the Development of Afro-Creole Culture in Eighteenth Century Louisiana* (Baton Rouge: Louisiana State University Press, 1992), p.122; Pierre Heinrich, *La Louisiane sous la Compagnie des Indes* (1717-1731) (New York: Burt Franklin, 1908 ; repr. 1970), p.48.

11 Pelletan de Caplon, *Mémoire sur la colonie du Sénégal,* p.38.

12 Paul Pélissier, *Les paysans du Sénégal* (Saint-Yrieux, France: Fabrègue, 1966).

13 Portères R., "Géographie alimentaire, berceaux agricoles et migrations des plantes cultivées en Afrique intertropicale," *Société de biogéographie*, no. 239 (1951), p. 18.

were devoted from immemorial times to root crops like yams.[14] In Juda (Bight of Benin), Captain Herpin was not expected to find any rice, but from there he had to buy "le mahy dont il croira avoir besoin pour la nourriture de ses nègres" ("the corn which he would need for the nourishment of his Negroes").[15]

The farmers of the German Coast produced rice using the expertise of their African slaves. They also produced other food crops which, along with rice, solved the essential problem of food supply for New Orleans. Their settlements eventually bore the name of "jardin de la Capitale" (garden of the Capitol) as surplus was regularly shipped, mostly on pirogues, to the market in the city. This is documented in a 1763 report:

> These people are very industrious, dedicating themselves very much to the cultivation of rice and Indian corn. The principal occupation [of the Germans] is gardening, the cultivation of rice, and the raising and fattening of cattle. The so-called German Coast furnishes a lot of rice to the city, many vegetables, corn, milk products, but very little indigo and sugar. This is because the inhabitants do not have enough Negroes at their disposal although they are the best workers in the colony.[16]

It is not quite certain that sugar was ever produced on the German Coast before the end of the eighteenth century, but indigo became a major crop in that area in the 1770s. This plant belongs to the legume genus *Indigofera*, a subtropical shrub that grows to be around four to six feet tall. The species *Indigofera tinctoria* has always been the most valuable indigo species traded. It was originally domesticated in India and has been widely distributed and naturalized all over the tropics. It is the leaves that yield the fade-resistant blue dye, indigo, which became the "king of dye" early in history. India supplied blue dye to the ancient Middle East and the Greco-Roman world. The ancient Greeks acknowledged the central role played by India in reference to the product as the Indian dye, *indikon*. In sub-Saharan Africa, indigo grows wild almost everywhere, and Africans have used indigo for centuries as a symbol of wealth and fertility. Indigo-dyed cotton cloth excavated from caves in the Dogon country in Mali dates to the eleventh century, and many of the designs are still used by modern West Africans. Most dyers are women among the Yoruba, the Malinke, the Dogon, and the Soninke. Among the Hausa of Northern Nigeria, where the export trade in prestige textiles was highly organized, the trade was controlled by women until the advent of Islamic rule around 1807. Then male dyers working at communal dye pits became the basis of the wealth of the ancient

---

14 Pélissier, *Les paysans du Sénégal* (1966), p.713.
15 "Instructions pour le Sieur Herpin…"; in Donnan, ed., *Documents*, IV (1969), p.637.
16 Redon de Ressac, Plan pour rendre la Louisiane la plus riche et la plus puissante de toutes les colonies francaises, 19 August 1763. Quoted in Blume, *The German Coast* (1990), p.67.

city of Kano. Dyeing is also performed by men among the Mossi of Burkina-Faso and Northern Ghana.[17]

To this day, and despite the decline of natural indigo in the textile industry, West African farmers quite religiously spare the indigo plants they find in their fields because of their medicinal value, especially for the cure of the ailments of the genitals. In Northern Senegambia, indigo (*boru* in the Pulaar language) still grows wild in extended groves (*boruuje*) on the natural levees built by the Senegal River and beyond. In this area, like elsewhere in sub-Saharan Africa including Madagascar, the primary ingredients are dried balls of indigo leaves crushed in mortars with pestles.[18] The dry indigo is soaked in pots called *canaris* in West African French, where it ferments in an alkali solution made with ashes. Cloth has to be dipped repeatedly in the fermented dye, exposed briefly to the air, and then reimmersed. The number of dippings and the strength and freshness of the dye determines the intensity of the resulting color. After the dyed cloth has dried, it is customary to beat the fabric repeatedly with wooden beaters, which both presses the fabric and imparts a shiny glaze.[19] Every individual from the Sahel and savanna grasslands areas of West Africa would be likely to know these basic principles since dyeing has not been reserved to any special "caste," such as blacksmithing, weaving, woodworking, leatherworking, and both free and enslaved people could have performed the trade.

The trade of indigo from Asia was controlled by the Portuguese in the middle of the sixteenth century. Their main competitors—the Spanish—took indigo plants from Asia to their new colonies in Central America where indigenous varieties of indigo also existed. Soon hundreds of commercial indigo establishments emerged, particularly in El Salvador and Guatemala. In the seventeenth and eighteenth centuries, Central American indigo was exported in huge quantities to Spain, Peru, and Mexico. Spain re-exported indigo to Britain and the Netherlands with extra duties. Later, the French and the British were able to set up successful indigo industries in their Caribbean and North American colonies. The English gained their first West Indian indigo-producing colony in 1655 when they captured

17 "The devil's blue dye: indigo and slavery"; an essay contributed by Jean M. West for Slavery in America Educational Outreach Team: www.slaveryinamerica.org/history/hs_es_indigo. htm (accessed 17 September 2010). Also see the following selected bibliography: Rita Bolland, *Tellem Textiles. Archaeological finds from burial caves in Mali's Bandiagara Cliff* (Amsterdam: Royal Tropical Institute, 1991); Judith A. Byfield, *The bluest hands: a social and economic history of women dyers in Abeokuta (Nigeria), 1890-1940* (Portsmouth, NH: Heinemann, 2002); Nast 2005, *Concubines and Power: Five Hundred Years in a Northern Nigerian Palace* (Minneapolis: University of Minnesota Press); Andrew F. Clark, "Environmental decline and ecological response in the upper Senegal valley, West Africa, from the late nineteenth century to World War I," *Journal of African History* 36, 2 (1995), p.197-218.
18 Beauvais-Raseau, *Art de l'Indigotier* (Paris: L.F. Delatour, 1770), pp.14-15.
19 Adire African Textile, online at www.adire.clara.net (accessed 17 September 2010).

Jamaica, but by 1740, sugar had replaced indigo as the main crop of this colony. This was also the beginning of the indigo boom in South Carolina. The Dutch set up their indigo industries in Java. The global indigo market was characterized by strong competition confronting suppliers from the Philippines, Java, India, Mauritius, Egypt, Venezuela, Brazil, Guatemala, Saint-Domingue, and South Carolina.[20]

In the Western Hemisphere, female slaves were mostly involved in the raising of the crops. Men undertook the process of extraction, which involved much more labor and was made all the more difficult by the strong odor that emanated from the tanks of rotting indigo. As part of their preparation, the leaves of indigo had to go through a process of fermentation and then oxidation to yield the blue dye. Traditionally, fermentation was carried out naturally by bacteria. The harvested plants were packed into a higher vat or "steeper" (*trempoire* in French) and covered with water. After a few hours, the leaves became saturated and fermentation began. The pressure of the rotten leaves could be so high that planks had to be placed on top of the vat to keep the plants in. This process could take up to a day and a half to complete but had to be finely timed since long fermentation would ruin the product. The dark blue liquid was siphoned into the middle vat or "beater" (*batterie*) at a lower level, leaving the plants behind. The liquid was then stirred continuously for several hours because it needed oxygen from the air to stimulate oxidation. The addition of limewater hastened the process. The solution was left to rest in the lower vat (*reposoir*), allowing for the sedimentation of the indigo at the bottom of the tank. Then the water was drained, and the indigo was dried and cut into cubes or made into balls.[21]

20 Pierre-Paul Darrac and Willem Van Schendel, *Global Blue: Indigo and Espionage in Colonial Bengal* (Dhaka, India: University Press Limited, 2006), pp. 11-17. See also Anne Mattson, *Indigo in the Early Modern World*, online at http://www.lib.umn.edu/bell/tradeproducts/indigo (Accessed 17 September 2010).

21 Plant Cultures. Exploring plants and people: http://www.plantcultures.org/plants/indigo_history.html (Accessed 17 September 2010). Also the source of the comments of figure 4.5.

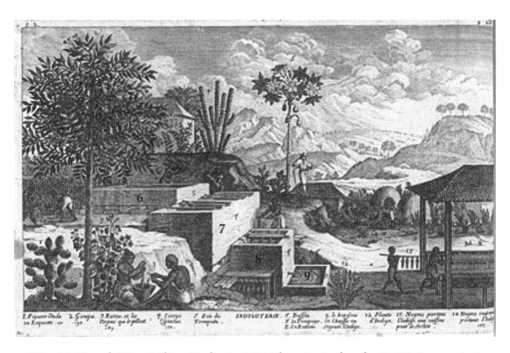

Fig. 4.1. French West Indies: "Indigoterie" with water tank or basin (6), "trempoire" (7), "batterie" (8), and "reposoir" (9). Source: Jean Baptiste DuTertre, Histoire Générale des Antilles Habitées par les François, Paris, 1667, vol. 2, p. 107.

Fig. 4.2 Indigo Plant.
Source: M. de Beauvais-Raseau, Art de l'Indigotier. Paris: L.F. Delatour, 1770, Plate 3.

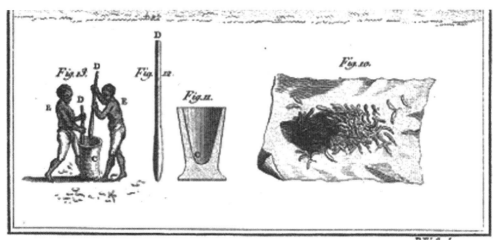

Fig. 4.3. French West Indies: Indigo seeds being removed from pods with mortar and pestle. Source: M. de Beauvais-Raseau, *Art de l'Indigotier*. Paris: L.F. Delatour, 1770, Plate 3.

Fig. 4.4. French West Indies: Seeds being sown into drills made with a drill plow or into holes dug with hoes. For both illustrations, the author shows men handling the tools and women handling the seeds, which are sown directly into the field. Germination starts after three days.
Source: Beauvais-Raseau, *Art de l'Indigotier*. Paris: L.F. Delatour, 1770, plate 4.

Fig. 4.5. French West Indies: Harvesting of indigo field.
Source: M. de Beauvais-Raseau, *Art de l'Indigotier.* Paris: L.F. Delatour, 1770, plate 4. Branches are harvested when the plants are about four to five months old and flowering. The plants can continue to be harvested like this at three to four months intervals three times a year. The total life span of a crop can be two to three years.

Fig. 4.6. French West Indies: "indigoterie simple" with "trempoire" (A), "batterie" (B), and "reposoir"(C). On the background: well (right) and shed (left) where indigo is dried and stored.
Source: M. de Beauvais-Raseau, *Art de l'Indigotier.* Paris: L.F. Delatour, 1770, Plate 2.

Indigo grew wild in Louisiana, but neither the early settlers nor the Indians knew how to process it. As early as 1709, it was reported that there was wild indigo, which could yield dye of the best quality (*indigo franc*), according to a man from the islands who had grown some in Louisiana.[22] Although officials and some settlers did experiments quite early, the cultivation of indigo did not start in this country until the 1720s. The importations of seeds from Saint-Domingue and of a substantial slave force from Africa were the key to the establishment of a meaningful indigo industry in the colony. This was explained in Article Seven of the minutes of the Council of Louisiana at its meeting on January 7, 1723:

> Proposal of the Council: The Council at the request of the inhabitants having sent a vessel to the Cape (Cap François/Saint-Domingue) to get indigo seed, it hopes that they are preparing the land properly in order to be able to cultivate this product and not to make the voyage of the said vessel fruitless (…).
>
> Reply of the Inhabitants: There are few inhabitants in a position to undertake the culture of indigo for which a sufficient number of negroes is needed, otherwise it must not be thought of. This article can be accepted for the present only by those who have forces enough to work at a business that deserves that attention should be paid to it. It is for the gentlemen of the Company to hasten its cultivation by a prompt dispatch of Negroes.[23]

On 6 September 1723, Jacques de La Chaise, one of the two commissioners sent to organize a new government in New Orleans and regulate slavery through the Code Noir, wrote to the directors of the Company of the West Indies in France insisting on the need for a slave force:

> Everybody, Gentlemen, is asking for negroes in order to be able to have work done on preparing land to plant indigo for next year when the colony expects to send you some returns. It grows marvelously here and in spite of the floods that lasted until the beginning of July it has grown perfectly well. Everybody is keeping what he has in order to have seed. However several tests of it have been made. It proved to be very fine and copper-colored. Mr. De Bienville, who is the only one who has been able to make any because he had himself and Mr. De La Tour three quarts of seed, is sending you, Gentlemen, sixty pounds of it by the Galatée (…). As for that which Mr. De La Tour had planted, it was entirely destroyed

---

22 Memoir on Louisiana by Mandeville, MPA, vol. 2, p.50.
23 Minutes of the Council, 7 January 1723. MPA, vol. 2, pp. 285-286.

by the flood which overflowed his land from the rear.[24]

In 1723, *L'Expédition* and *Le Courrier de Bourbon* landed 178 slaves directly from Africa. The next year, and despite the early difficulties, the planters of Louisiana produced three thousand pounds of indigo. Joseph Dubreuil was one of the most successful planters. Documents reveal him selling indigo to the Company of the West Indies in 1724. A native of Dijon, France, Dubreuil was then the richest man in the colony, where he settled in 1718. His fortune was built on his extraordinary methods of tapping into the know-how of African slaves.[25] In 1725, the planters of Louisiana exported excellent quality indigo destined for the market in France but the shipment was lost at sea with the sinking of the *Bellone*. Nougaret evaluated the total loss to 60,000 *livres* worth of raw indigo (*indigo crû*). According to this eighteenth-century author, indigo cultivation was abandoned in 1727 because of the wars against the Indians and the Company's preference for tobacco. But indigo production resumed in 1737.[26]

At the beginning of the 1730s, it was gradually recognized through experience that the Lower Mississippi Delta was not especially suited for tobacco cultivation. The widespread replacement of indigo with sugar in the West Indies encouraged the planters of Louisiana to gradually shift to indigo production. They probably benefited from the expertise of new settlers from the French islands where the thriving sugar business was taking most of the available land. Since good land was not unlimited there and after most of it was given away to the vast concessions, the new plantations had to take over the small holdings. Some dispossessed small farmers retreated to marginal areas and most of them left.[27] But the expansion of indigo in Louisiana could not be accomplished quickly because the planters still had to deal with the lack of slaves. By 1731, the Company of the West Indies had sent twenty-two slave ships directly from Africa to Louisiana. All but one of the slavers came from Senegambia and the Bight of Benin, two regions of West Africa where people already had a strong tradition in indigo processing.[28] By 1738, some 70,000 pounds of indigo were produced by fifteen planters near New Orleans, mostly in the Chapitoulas area.[29] The data collected by Helmut Blume shows that indigo cultivation really took off in

24 De La Chaise to the Directors of the Company of the Indies, 6 September 1723, MPA, vol. 2, pp. 321-322.

25 Hall, *Africans in Colonial Louisiana* (1992), pp.60, 124 and 137; Henry P. Dart "The career of Dubreuil in French Louisiana," *Louisiana Historical Quarterly* 18 (1935), pp.291-331.

26 Pierre J.B. Nougaret, *Voyages Intéressans dans différentes colonies françaises, espagnoles, anglaises, etc.* (Londres-Paris, 1788), pp.271-272.

27 Robert Louis Stein, *The French sugar business in the eighteenth century* (Baton Rouge: Louisiana State University Press, 1988), p.42.

28 Hall, *Africans in Colonial Louisiana* (1992), table 2, p.60: French Slave-Trade Ships from Africa to Louisiana.

29 Miller Surrey, *The commerce of Louisiana during the French Régime, 1699-1763* (Doctoral dissertation, University of Columbia, Faculty of Political Science, New York 1916), p.192.

1743, the very year *Le St. Ursin*, a ship chartered by Joseph Dubreuil and his associate came back from Goree Island with 190 slaves that were used mainly on Dubreuil's plantation.[30] Indigo became the chief export of Louisiana in the 1750s, representing 20 percent of the total value of its trade with France. By 1754, forty-seven planters in the country produced 82,000 pounds of indigo. Between 1756 and 1762, the production increased steadily, with the value of the crop of 1760 reaching 1,350,000 *livres*, but exports declined toward the end of the Seven Years' War as shown on the statistical data provided by Villiers du Terrage[31]:

1756..270,000 livres (pounds)
1757...475,000 "
1758...540,000 "
1759...891,000 "
1760...1,350,000 "
1762...410,000 "

After the war, Louisiana became a Spanish colony, and this was the time when large numbers of slaves were introduced in the country. The production of indigo rose again from 200,000 pounds in 1775 to range between 400,000 and 500,000 pounds in 1793.[32] But a natural disaster and international competition soon ruined the efforts of the planters. According to Victor Collot, Louisiana indigo was preferable to that of Georgia and the Carolinas but very inferior in quality to that of Guatemala and the Antilles. However, Louisiana planters also had to face stiff competition from India, which furnished European markets with large quantities of indigo of the highest quality. Collot also mentioned natural contingencies as a major factor to the collapse of indigo production in Louisiana:

> The harvests (…) are very precarious because this plant requires a dry soil; while the indigos planted in Lower Louisiana, which is overflowed almost every year, often perish before they ripen. Independently of the variety of accidents which render the cultivation of this plant very hazardous in the country where the indigo grows, the root of that of Louisiana is liable to be pricked by a small worm, which, from the extreme humidity of the ground, abounds in this part and destroys the plant. The harvests have been known to fail two or three years successively; this misfortune happened in 1794, and no indigo was made on any plantation.[33]

30 Blume, *The German Coast* (1990), pp.51-57; Hall, *Africans in Colonial Louisiana* (1992), p.60.
31 Surrey, *The commerce of Louisiana* (1916), pp. 214-215; Villiers du Terrage, *Les dernières années de la Louisiane française* (Paris: E. Guilmoto, 1903), pp.147-148.
32 Jack D.L. Holmes, "Indigo in Colonial Louisiana and the Floridas," *Louisiana History* 8 (1967), p.340.
33 Collot 1826. *A journey in North America*, vol. 2 (Paris: Arthus Bertrand), p.166.

Indigo became a significant part of the landscape of the German Coast in the 1770s, but some planters were apparently very successful in the indigo business before this time. So was the case of Ambroise Haydel. The last census of St. John the Baptist Parish, which included his name, was taken on June 25, 1766. This source also indicates that his property had grown then to 11 ½ arpents and his labor force to twenty slaves. On March 31, 1774, his widow and children sold the farm, along with its indigo processing facilities (*indigotterie*), to Louis Girard Pellerin. The sale was cancelled, and the farm was finally sold to Antoine Albert on May 6, 1776. The property was bounded above by the farm of Jean Jacques Haydel and below by the farm of Nicolas Haydel.[34] Jean Jacques Haydel (the youngest son of Ambroise) bought his initial land on April 27, 1766 from the succession of Antoine Schaafe, his maternal uncle.[35] He also bought back the farm of his father from the community of Antoine Albert and his deceased wife.[36] This is confirmed by later configuration of land ownership. When Nicolas Haydel died in 1777, he left a farm bounded above by the farm of Antoine Albert and below by the farm of his brother Mathias Haydel. When Nicolas's wife died in 1803, the same piece of land was bounded above by Jean Jacques Haydel.[37] In 1822, the latter's children bought Nicolas Haydel's farm, thus expanding the property downstream toward the future Evergreen Plantation, owned then by Magdelaine Haydel.[38] This lady was the daughter of Jean Christophe Haydel and Charlotte Oubre (Huber). Her father died in 1800, leaving to his three children (Jean Georges, Françoise, and Magdelaine herself) a labor force of sixty-five slaves and sixteen arpents of land. Remnants of the indigo industry were still visible on the plantation, which had been turned into a sugar-producing unit.[39] Jean Christophe Haydel's wealth was built on the indigo business. The main house standing today on Evergreen Plantation was erected by him around 1790 on the portion of land later inherited by Magdelaine. The latter was married to Pierre Becnel, Sr. After her death in 1830, her grandson, Pierre Clidament Becnel, assumed ownership of the plantation and commissioned John Carver to remodel the big house in the classical revival style.[40]

34 SJB-BR-18-1774 (Widow Ambroise Haydel & children to Louis Girard Pellerin; and SJB-BR-19-1776 (Widow Ambroise Haydel and children to Antoine Albert).
35 Conrad 1792: p.9 and Robichaux 1997, p.201, footnote 1002.
36 SJB-29-1776. Inventory of the community of the late Antoine Albert and Geneviève Leroux. Nov. 14-15, 1776.
37 SJB-14-1777: Inventory of the estate of late Nicolas Haydel and his widow Perinne Leroux. 11 March 1777. SJB-26-1803/Inventaire de tous les biens meubles et immeubles de la défunte Veuve Nicolas Haydel. 6 May 1803.
38 Abstracts from the copy of the original deed of sale passed on 2 December 1822. Cf. SJB-27-1839/*Haydel Francois Marcellin & Jean Jacques: Inventaire des biens possédés indivisément par eux.*
39 SJB-3-1801/ Acte de Partage des biens du défunt Christophe Haydel entre ses héritiers et qui sert a constater la propriété de ce qu'ils ont eu. 15 January 1801.
40 Dillard & als. 2005, River Road Preservation, Tulane University, School of Architecture; Preservation Studies, spring 2005, p.29.

Mathias Haydel (1733-1800), the oldest son of Ambroise, was married to Magdelaine Oubre (Huber). His wife died in April 1776 and left behind nine children, including Alphonse, the father of Marie Azélie Haydel. This lady was the last member of the Haydel family to own what is called today Whitney Plantation. The inventory of the community of Mathias and his deceased wife mentioned, besides the moveable goods, seven slaves, and a farm six arpents wide and forty arpents deep. The food crops included corn, rice, and *fèves* (peas). Indigo was planted on fourteen arpents of land. The plantation had its own processing facilities (*batteries à indigo*) with two sets of vats. The inventory also mentioned 640 livres (pounds) of indigo worth one piastre per pound.[41] This farm was sold in 1788 to Jean Christophe Haydel and became part of the future Evergreen Plantation. On March 1791, Mathias signed a contract with a certain Mr. Fortier of St. Charles Parish. He would manage the Fortier Plantation for that year and would keep one-sixth of the income generated from the sale of the indigo, half of the entire rice crop, and half of the surplus of corn after deduction of the provisions of the slaves for a year.[42] In this parish, Mathias Haydel also owned a thirteen-arpent indigo plantation equipped with three sets of brick vats and one set of vats made with wood. This plantation was sold in 1797 in the middle of the indigo crisis.[43]

By 1800, many regions of the Western Hemisphere either abandoned indigo production or reduced international trade because of unfavorable political and economic environments or because of natural contingencies. After the American Revolution, the British lost their control over North American indigo. Indigo was almost completely phased out of South Carolina by 1798 because of competition from India and the loss of Britain's protective tariffs. In French Saint-Domingue (Haiti), indigo cultivation was destroyed by the 1790s' slave revolts along with the sugar business, which had relegated it to a second-class product. Central American indigo trade collapsed by the turn of the nineteenth century because of war between Spain and Britain in 1798 and locust attacks in 1801.[44] According to Collot, the European markets were inundated with the high quality indigo from India and the low price of the indigo of Louisiana could not indemnify the planters for their expenses and the frequent failure of their harvests. By the time of his trip to Louisiana in 1796, he was able to witness directly the extent of the disaster in this area:

---

41 SJB-10-1776/ Inventaire des biens de Mathias Haydel et défunte Magdelaine Ouvre sa femme. May 1, 1776.
42 SJB-3-1788/Haydel Mathias ; Vente d'habitation à Christophe Haydel; SCP-1791-1046/ Marché entre Vgene (?) Fortier et François Mathis Haydel. 28 March 1791.
43 SCP-1797-399/Vente judiciaire de tous les biens de Mathias Haydel à sa réquisition. January 17, 1797.
44 Darrac and Van Schendel, *Global Blue* (2006), pp. 11-17. Anne Mattson: Indigo in the Early Modern World: http://www.lib.umn.edu/bell/tradeproducts/indigo (Accessed 17 September 2010).

I saw the indigo works in ruins and the planters reduced to growing maize and yams, sawing planks with mills which they had built, and framing timber for houses, which they send to the Havannah and the Islands, preferring the very modest gain which they reap from this hard labor, to the uncertain and continually decreasing profits to be obtained by the cultivation of indigo.[45]

This is well illustrated in the 1797 inventory of the plantation of the late Jean Georges Haydel. The crops comprised only rice, peas, and corn. Among the facilities on the site were "deux vieilles paires de cuves en ruine" (two pairs of vats old and ruined).[46] In 1803, not more than 30,000 pounds of indigo were manufactured in Louisiana, and the planters were progressively turning to more lucrative staples, such as cotton and sugar cane.[47] Jean Jacques, the youngest child of Ambroise Haydel, and the last living member of the first Louisiana-born generation of the Haydels, witnessed two economic periods that were dramatically different. Indigo was booming at the time of his marriage, and by the time of his death, he had fully enjoyed the cultivation of sugar.

45 Collot 1826. *A journey in North America*, volume 2 (Paris: Arthus Bertrand), pp.166-167.
46 SCP-1797-1407/Inventaire au décès de feu Georges Haydel. 21 January 1797.
47 Holmes, "Indigo in Colonial Louisiana," (1967), p.340.

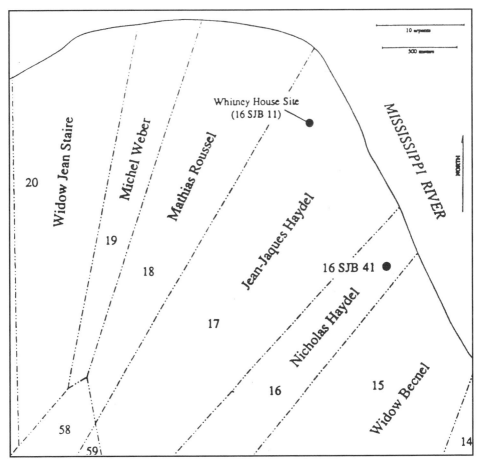

Fig. 4.7. The configuration of ownership based on the 1803 land claims. Lot 16 (Nicholas Haydel) and lot 18 (Mathias Roussel) were added to lot 17 (Jean-Jacques Haydel) respectively in 1822 and 1919. Lot 15 (Widow Becnel) is the site of the current Evergreen plantation.
Source: Hunter and als. 1991. Whitney Plantation: Archeology on the German Coast. Cultural Resources Investigations in St. John the Baptist Parish, Louisiana. Volumes 1, fig. 6.1, p.6-2.

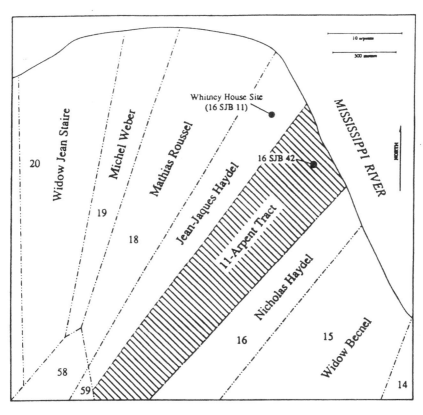

Fig. 4.8. The location of the 11-arpent tract which probably formed the habitation of Ambroise Haydel.
Source: Hunter and als. 1991. Whitney Plantation: Archeology on the German Coast. Cultural Resources Investigations in St. John the Baptist Parish, Louisiana. Volumes 1, fig. 6.2, p.6-6.

The Haydel Plantation under Jean Jacques Haydel Sr. (1770-1819)

According to Edward King, experiments on sugar were made in Louisiana since the 1750s by the Jesuits. In 1751, two ships transporting soldiers to Louisiana stopped at Hispaniola (Saint-Domingue), and the Jesuits on that island sent some sugar cane and some black slaves used in its cultivation to the brothers of their order in the new colony. The Jesuits at New Orleans undertook the culture of the crop but did not succeed, and it was only in 1795 that the seeds became thoroughly naturalized in Louisiana.[48] Sugar cane may have been first planted in Louisiana during the late 1600s by Iberville, the "Founder of Louisiana," but the year 1751 is the one usually accepted for the successful introduction of sugar cane into Louisiana. The Jesuits did not actually manufacture sugar, but they sold the sweet chewable stalks of the "Creole" cane. Joseph Dubreuil erected the first sugarmill in 1758, but the outcome was not satisfactory.[49]

According to Collot's observations, Etienne de Boré was the first planter to re-establish the cultivation of sugar cane and to succeed in its transformation into raw sugar of the finest quality. The produce of Mr. Boré's establishment during the 1795 grinding season amounted to twelve thousand piastres thus encouraging more Louisiana planters to undertake the cultivation of cane, but they had to deal with the lack of qualified workers. When Collot visited Boré's plantation in late October 1796, he found a mill "turned by five mules like those in St. Domingo," and the workforce was composed of forty slaves under the direction of "the only workman in the colony, and who is in Mr. Boré's service, (and who) refines for other planters when his master's work is finished."[50] This first sugar master in Louisiana was called Antoine Morin, an immigrant who arrived in the country in the early 1790s, probably through Cuba, like many others who fled the Haitian Revolution. In 1791, he was hired by Don Antonio Mendez, officer of the Spanish crown, to assist him in the establishment of a sugarhouse. The latter was apparently only producing molasses and rum after buying land, a crop of cane, and distilling outfit from Solis, a refugee from Saint Domingue. However, for different reasons the results were disappointing. Etienne de Boré purchased cane from Mendez and Solis and hired Morin. He began his experiments in 1794, and the next year he finally produced the first crop of sugar sufficiently large and profitable to serve as an incentive to others.[51] The new trend eventually caused a scarcity of rice, and the inhabitants of the riverbanks above and below New Orleans demanded renewed importation of slaves.[52]

Cotton was also cultivated with success in Louisiana, but it required a great amount of work and its value in the markets of Europe was inferior to the cotton of

48 Edward King, *The Great South; A Record of Journeys in Louisiana, Texas, the Indian Territory, Missouri, Arkansas, Mississippi, Alabama, Georgia, Florida, South Carolina, North Carolina, Kentucky, Tennessee, Virginia, West Virginia, and Maryland* (Hartford, Conn.: American Publishing Co, 1875), p.79.

49 200 years of progress in the Louisiana sugar industry: a brief history. Contributed by Dr. Charley Richard of the American Sugar Cane League for the American Society of Sugar Cane Technologists: www.assct.org/louisiana/progress.pdf (accessed 8 September 2011).

50 Collot 1826. *A journey in North America*, volume 2, p.169-174. This plantation was located in the area of present-day Audubon Park and Tulane University, in the city of New Orleans.

51 Rolph 1917, *Something about sugar. Its history, growth, manufacture, and distribution* (San Francisco: John J. Newbegin), p. 176.

52 Records and deliberations of the Cabildo (1769-1803), vol. 4, part 3, pp.165, 202; quoted in Blume, *The German Coast* (1990), p.101.

Surinam, Cayenne, the West Indian Islands, and the Indies.[53] When the Orleans territory became the state of Louisiana in 1812, sugar was definitely the main crop of the farmers of the Lower Mississippi River. The arrival of the first steamboat the same year soon turned New Orleans into the second most active port of the United States after New York. The core zone of sugar production ran along the Mississippi River, between New Orleans and Baton Rouge. In the 1830s and 1840s, other areas around Bayou Lafourche, Bayou Teche, Pointe Coupee, and Bayou Sara, and the northern parishes also emerged as sugar districts despite risks of frost damage. The farmers circumvented this ecological obstacle by windrowing their canes, which meant laying the harvested canes in furrows and covering them with leaves until the next grinding or planting season.[54] Windrowed canes were called "cannes en matelas" by the predominantly French-speaking population of the German Coast. In 1817, the introduction from Java (Indonesia) of ribbon cane, a frost-resistant variety, partially resolved the geographical limits to cane cultivation in Louisiana. The introduction of steam-powered mills in 1822 was most welcome since the tougher bark of ribbon cane was difficult to crush with animal-powered mills.[55] Sugar cane was planted in January and February and harvested from mid-October to December. The planting season was followed by miscellaneous tasks such as the cultivation of corn, the collection of wood, and the maintenance of levees and drainage canals. The grinding season (*roulaison* in French) started in early November, at the latest. According to Follett,

> Steam power profoundly shaped the sugar industry, but its economic success rested primarily on the mass importation of African American bondspeople to Louisiana. The seasonal nature of sugar production imposed a forbidding regime on the slaves (…), gravely affected slave women's capacity to bear children, and it left an appalling legacy of death in its wake.[56]

Sugar production was a dangerous process, involving the handling of boiling liquids. Sugar cane juice was heated in a series of open kettles and pans called the "Jamaica Train." The slaves poured juice from boiler to boiler with long-handled ladles. This old dangerous method of sugar production did not end until the 1840s when Norbert Rillieux (1806-1894), an African American born from a French farmer and his female servant, invented a sugar processing evaporator composed of multiple pans stacked inside a vacuum chamber. This machine called multiple-

---

53 Collot 1826. *A journey in North America*, volume 2, p.167.
54 Follett 2005. *The sugar masters: Planters and slaves in Louisiana's cane world, 1820-1860* (Baton Rouge: Louisiana State University Press), pp.21-22.
55 Ibid., pp.23-24; King, *The Great South* (1875), p.79.
56 Follett, *The sugar masters* (2005), pp.11-13, 24.

effect evaporation was patented in 1843. It improved the sugar refining process, saved time and money in the making of sugar, and protected lives.[57] The evaporated sugar juice crystallized in wooden vats, known as coolers. It was then packed in 1,000 to 1,200-pound wooden barrels called hogsheads or "boucauts" among the French-speaking communities of Louisiana and the French Caribbean islands.

Although a few refineries existed, including the Louisiana Sugar Refining Company in New Orleans, refining was not a significant part of the antebellum sugar industry. Louisiana's product was chiefly raw sugar, most of which was shipped to cities in the Upper Mississippi Valley either directly from the plantations or by way of New Orleans. The raw sugar that arrived in New Orleans by steamboat was sold daily at auction on the levee. Since sugar cane required greater capital investment than other crops, several planters' banks were created, including the State-chartered *Association Consolidée des Planteurs de Louisiane* (The Consolidated Association of Planters of Louisiana), established in 1828. Its members who bought shares in the bank could be reasonably certain of obtaining loans.[58]

Jean Jacques Haydel, Sr. was among the most successful planters of Louisiana. His main plantation was located in St. John the Baptist Parish, on the right bank of the river, between Mathias Roussel (above) and Jacques Haydel and Brothers (below). It was seventeen arpents wide, eighty arpents deep (*double profondeur*) and established in sugar (*habitation établie en sucre*). He also owned a second plantation established in sugar, nearly twelve arpents wide by the customary forty-arpent depth. It was also located in St. John the Baptist Parish, on the right bank of the river, and was bounded below by the habitation André Hymel and above by the farm of Alphonse Haydel, father of Marie Azélie Haydel. The main plantation was estimated to be worth 30,000 piastres. The main house standing on it was described as a "superbe maison de maître" (superb master's house), along with dependencies: *moulins à riz* (rice mills), *magasins à vivres* (granaries), and *cases à nègres* (slave cabins). There also was a sugar mill and enough windrowed cane to plant forty arpents. The second habitation also had its own sugar mill, enough windrowed cane to plant forty arpents of land, and newly planted cane was growing on eighty-five arpents. This was quite typical on large plantations where cane was always ready for harvesting. Since this inventory was held in December 1819 in the middle of the grinding season, Jean Jacques Haydel and the heirs of his late wife declared their inability to determine either the quantity of sugar to be produced or

---

57 The River Road African American Museum: online at http://www.
africanamericanmuseum.org/exhibits.html (accessed 17 September 2010). It was also another African American, Leonard Julien Sr. (1910-1995), who invented the sugar cane planting machine in 1964.

58 "Sugar at LSU- Cultivating a Sweeter Future", online exhibition based on the 1995 physical exhibition celebrating the 200th anniversary of commercial sugar production in Louisiana; curated by LSU librarians C. Riquelmy and D. Currie, and mounted by E. Robison: http://www.lib.lsu.edu/special/exhibits/sugar/ (accessed September 2004).

the expected income from it until the day of the auction. They were finally able to evaluate the production of the two sugar mills to 190 hogsheads of sugar and 110 hogsheads of syrup, which they intended to sell later because of low prices.[59] The latter were provoked by the economic crisis known as the Panic of 1819, which marked the end of the economic expansion that had followed the War of 1812. This crisis was partially due to the decrease of European demand for American foodstuffs because Europe was recovering from the Napoleonic Wars, which had decimated its agriculture. In this context of crisis and at a time when steam-powered sugar mills were not in operation yet in Louisiana, Haydel's production was quite impressive. Even after the invention of Rillieux's machine, the average output was 250 hogsheads in 1845 and 310 hogsheads in 1853.[60] The quantity of sugar produced on Jean Jacques Haydel's plantations was comparable to the output of many of the most successful plantations on the German Coast in 1860.[61]

Jean Jacques Haydel Sr. had married Marie Magdelaine Bozonnier Marmillon, a resident of New Orleans and member of a successful family of planters. The marriage was celebrated on February 7, 1774, but the marriage contract itself was signed three days earlier before Juan Baptista Garic, notary public of the city. Among the attendees were Antoine Bozonnier Marmillon and his wife Laurenza Guaitreto (Laurence Gachet in French), parents of the bride, and other individuals including Jean Georges Haydel, the brother of Jean Jacques Haydel.[62] He fathered eight children: Marguerite Aymée, Cesara, Charlotte Adélaide, Jean Jacques Jr., Erasie, Antoine Telesphore, and Jean François Marcellin. A child apparently born in 1777 and baptized privately died the same year and was interred on November 12, 1777.[63] Antoine Telesphore died a teenager on August 8, 1801.

---

59 SJB-1-1820; Vente des meubles et immeubles de la communauté d'entre le Sr. Jn Jacques Haydel père et la feue dame Marie Madelaine Bozonnier son épouse. January 13-14, 1820.
60 Follett, *The sugar masters* (2005), p.25.
61 See Menn, *The large slaves holders of Louisiana* (1964), pp.360-363.
62 Marriage Contract of Haidel, Jacques and Madalaine Bosonier", in *L'Heritage*, a journal of the St. Bernard Geneaological Society, 11, N°44 (October 1988), pp.297-299.
63 Sacramental Records, vol. 3, p. 55. Name is missing.

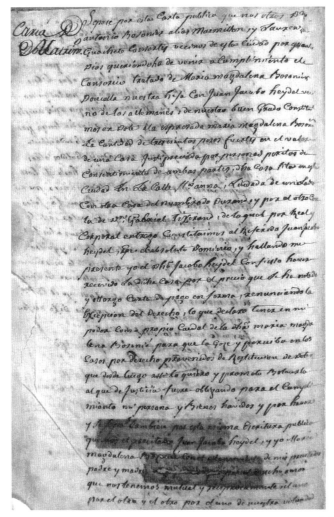

Fig. 4.9. Abstract of marriage contract between Jean Jacques Haydel and Madeleine Bosonier (Spanish records). Source: NONA, J.B. Garic, Vol. 5, Act 29, February 7, 1774.

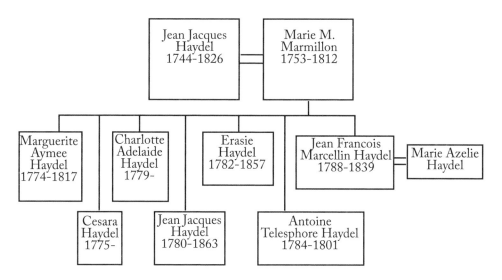

Fig. 4.10. Descendants of Jean Jacques Haydel

Marie Magdelaine Bozonnier Marmillon died on February 26, 1812. Following a death, a complete inventory of the deceased's assets was required to be filed in court under Louisiana law. For some reason, her community with Jean Jacques Haydel Sr. was not inventoried until seven years later. Among the sixty-one slaves listed in the inventory, nineteen were born in Africa. This group of Africans was 100 percent male and consisted of eleven individuals aged between twenty and thirty-five (58 percent) and eight others who were fifty up to sixty-six years old. Two slaves were from the sugar islands, precisely Jamaica and Saint-Domingue, and three were from the East coast of the United States. The rest of the slave force was composed of Creoles born in Louisiana. The oldest slave in the plantation was Marguerite, a sixty-six year old Creole woman, listed with her husband Sam, a slave of the Soso (Susu) nation, sixty years old and blind. They were estimated together to be worth zero piastres. One slave was affected with hernia, and another one had recovered from it. This sickness related to hard work was quite frequent among the labor force of the area. More than hard work, the loss of freedom and homesickness certainly affected most of them, especially those born in Africa like Bernard, a fifty-year old slave from the Kiamba (Tchamba) nation, who suffered with *moments de démence* (fits of madness).[64]

The value in the inventory of each slave was determined by many factors such as age, gender, health, personal behavior, and skills. The grown individuals, those aged between sixteen and thirty-five years and male, were generally more expensive than younger and older people. But within the same age range, women were generally lower priced. This tendency is shown in the comparison of the three most expensive

---

64. SJB-116-1819; Inventaire des communautés d'entre Sr. Jn Jques haydel père et ses enfants héritiers de la Dame Marie Madelaine Bosonnier. 7 December 1819.

males and the three most expensive females in the inventory.

TABLE 11. GENDER AND PRICES OF SLAVES

Name/Age	Qualification	Gender/Origin	Price (piastres)
Etienne, 19	cart driver, plough hand, herdsman	Male Creole	1,700
Azor, 19	cart driver, plough hand, herdsman	Male Creole	1,700
Joseph, 20	cart driver, plough hand, herdsman	Male Creole	1,700
Reguine, 18	house keeper	Female/East Coast	1,100
Sophie, 35	house keeper	Female Congo	600
Catherine, 16	house keeper	Female Creole	1,100

Illness or being a maroon (runaway slave) notably lessened the value of a slave. Isidore, a twenty-year-old slave of the Congo nation was affected by tinea, a fungous disease. He was estimated 500 piastres only, although he was a cart driver and a good house servant. Alexandre, of the Bambara nation, was a carpenter, a cooper, and a good domestic. He was only thirty years old but was estimated fifty piastres because he was sickly. Manuel, a twenty-three year old Creole slave, was described as *voleur et maronneur* (a thief and a maroon) and valued at 400 piastres. Skills made the difference between two individuals of the same age and gender and without any defaults. Most of the slaves on the plantation were field hands, some of them also referred to as *bons domestiques* (good servants) or *habiles à la garde des troupeaux* (good herdsmen). The two sugar makers (*sucriers*) were both born in West Africa, and they both belonged to the Bambara nation: Alexis, fifty years old, estimated 250 piastres, and Barnabe, thirty years old, estimated 1,000 piastres. The latter was also a *scieur de long* (sawyer), and a good house servant. François, a fifty-year-old "griffon" (Indian and African), was estimated 900 piastres despite his age. Besides being a good domestic and a carpenter, he was more importantly a *tonnelier* (cooper), a trade much needed in a refinery for the production of the sugar containers designated under the reminiscent name of hogsheads.

The inventory listed twenty-one female slaves (34 percent). Children under ten (14 percent) were listed with their mothers with whom they were priced and sold. Agathe, a forty-three year old Creole woman, was listed and priced 1,800 piastres, along with twins Jean and Jeanne, four years old, and Clemence, eighteen months old. There are no indications of death rates in the plantation inventories but further documentation from the Sacramental Records of the Archdiocese of New Orleans reveals earliness of motherhood among the enslaved women and high mortality among their children. Thirty-nine children died on this plantation from 1823 to 1863, only six reaching the age of five. Some of the children, either on this site or elsewhere, died in tragic circumstances such as drowning, epidemics, being burned, or hit by lightning. The cases of Françoise, a Creole slave and a domestic, born ca.1830 and Delphine, a

Creole slave born ca.1825, are quite symptomatic of the high infantile death rate on the site.[65] Each of them had lost more than half of her children by the time they were last inventoried on the Haydel plantation in 1860. Delphine lost three children between 24 July 1849 and 24 August 1849. On May 24 of the same year, Francoise also lost a baby. These deaths were probably related to the 1849 cholera epidemic, which was believed to have spread from Irish immigrant ships from England. It killed thousands in New York, a major destination for Irish immigrants, and spread throughout the Mississippi river system, killing over 4,500 in St. Louis and over 3,000 in New Orleans.[66] The Sacramental Records of the Archdiocese of New Orleans are quasi-silent on the causes of children's deaths. But, interestingly enough, the only entry mentioning the death of a child by cholera was recorded that year. The early 1850s were also known as the "cholera years," during which four babies (three of Françoise's and one of Delphine's) died on the plantation.

TABLE 12. INFANT MORTALITY ON HABITATION HAYDEL (1849-1860)

Name of child	Name of mother	Date of birth	Date of death	Age at death
Louis	Françoise	Oct. 1843	Aug. 20, 1855	11 years
Claire (from burns)	Françoise	1845	Jan. 21, 1852	6 years
Marie Delphine	Françoise	March 11, 1848	May 24, 1849	14 months
Fabien Sebastien	Françoise	April 12, 1851	Oct. 2, 1853	2 years
Florian	Françoise	1852	Oct. 14, 1853	1 year
Nancy	Françoise	1854		
Francois	Françoise	1857		
Lise	Françoise	1859		
Sam	Delphine	1841	July 29, 1849	8 years
Thomas	Delphine	Aug. 21, 1845	July 24, 1849	3 years
Marie Rose	Delphine	1847	Aug. 24, 1849	18 months
Valsin	Delphine	Nov. 6, 1848	Aug. 3, 1852	3 years
Mitilie	Delphine	1855		
Caroline	Delphine	1857		
Léontine	Delphine	1859		

65 Sacramental Records of the Archdiocese of New Orleans, 1823 through 1863. SJB-178-1860/Inventaire des biens de la succession de la dame Azélie Haydel décédée veuve   Marcelin Haydel. 10-12 November 1860. On the site of the Whitney Plantation Museum, a memorial called "Field of Angels" is dedicated to 2,200 slave children who died in St. John the Baptist Parish before reaching their third birthday and recorded by the Archdiocese of New Orleans.
66 Rosenberg, Charles E. (1962). The Cholera Years: The United States in 1832, 1849 and 1866. The University of Chicago Press.

The community of Jean Jacques Haydel and his late wife was estimated in the inventory at 112,383 piastres. On January 13, 1820, a first group of slaves was sold to Jean Jacques Haydel Sr., according to a decision of the assembly of his family.[67] The rest of the slaves and the plantations were auctioned the next day and mostly purchased by members of the family. The second habitation was sold to Pierre Becnel Sr. The main plantation was sold to Jean Jacques Jr. and Marcellin Haydel. Their father resided in the main house until his death. The slaves he owned during the last part of his life were auctioned on March 10, 1827. Raphael of the Kiamba nation, seventy-five years old, and Lubin of the Mandingo nation, sixty years old, were not sold because of age and illness. A family assembly decided that they were to be taken care of by the heirs, in accordance with the slave code. The rest of the slaves remained attached to the plantation except René, a twenty-three year old Creole slave, a cart man and ploughman, purchased by Becnel Frères & Brou.[68] Marie Joseph, sixty, and Claire, thirty-two, both Creoles born on the plantation, were sold to Jean Jacques Haydel Jr. He emancipated them on April 30, 1827.[69]

Jean Jacques Haydel Sr. was the most successful among his brothers. He built the main house standing today on Whitney Plantation, apparently in the early 1790s when the indigo business was still profitable. Improvements were done later with the boom of the sugar industry in the early 1800s. He passed away on December 1, 1826 at age eighty-two and was interred the next day in St. John the Baptist Cemetery adjoining the parish church in Edgard. The epitaph on his grave dates his birth back to August 11, 1744 and summarizes his life as a man of exceptional qualities: "Parrain de cette Église. Il fut époux tendre bon père ami sincère Homme de probité" (Godfather of this Church. He was a tender spouse good father sincere friend Man of probity).[70]

About seven years before his passing away, his reputation as a generous and welcoming person might have brought to his care an atypical stranger, who was taken back and forth between Europe and America by turbulences in the North-Atlantic world. This stranger's name was Yves Louis Jacques Hypolite Mialaret, a native of a hamlet, near Montauban, France. It is likely that he was somewhat of a royalist since he had to flee to Saint-Domingue with the breakout of the French Revolution. There he became a schoolmaster and eventually a friend and secretary

---

67 SJB-1-1820/ Sale of the community of Jean Jacques Haydel and Marie Madelaine Bosonnier. January 13-14, 1820; SJB-117-1819/Assemblée de famille et adjudication sur prix d'inventaire d'un certain nombre d'esclaves dépendants de la communauté d'entre le Sr. Jn Jques Haydel père et Marie Madelaine Bosonnier sa femme décédée au dit Sr. Jean Jacques Haydel.

68 SJB-29-1827/ sale of the estate of late Jean Jacques Haydel; 10 March 1827.

69 SJB-72-1827: Liberté par J. J. Haydel à la Négresse Marie Joseph ; SJB-71-1827: Liberté par J. J. Haydel à la Négresse Claire.

70 Sacramental Records, Volume 17, p. 193. Find A Grave Memorial# 10930993; contributed by Katy Morlas. May 08, 2005 (http://www.findagrave.com).

of the family of Toussaint Louverture, tutoring the latter and his son Issaac. He was able to escape the furies of the Haitian Revolution and returned to France, where he was forced to resign himself to the silent occupation of *employé* in the Government revenues at different places from the Pyrenees to Tuscany. In 1812, he was appointed to the Island of Elba (Italy), then under the control of France. There he met and supported Napoleon Bonaparte on his comeback to Paris, but after the downfall of the empire, he fled again from France and sought refuge this time in Louisiana. The eventful life of Hypolite Mialaret was recounted by his daughter Athenaïs, the spouse of the celebrated French historian Jules Michelet. The following lines depict the encounter of her father with Jean Jacques Haydel Sr., who welcomed him, hired him as a teacher, and eventually allowed him to marry his fourteen-year-old granddaughter, even though he was forty-one:

> My father, inconsolable, left the country, and sought a new home on the Mississippi. Following the course of the river, he approached, at evening, the door of a habitation far from town or any village […]. The family which he met was a representative type of the people and the races in Louisiana. It had a triple origin, Rhenish, English, and French. The Haydels from the Rhine, and the English Becknells, who came over in the time of Law, united themselves by marriage to the family of Francis Bozonier, a colonel from Provence, who had left this country on account of an unfortunate duel […]. After escaping his life from the fires of St. Domingo and the horrors of its massacres, and from the den of Toussaint; after having joined in the triumphal return of the Eagle […]; to live to recite these wonders, made (my father) a man of singular attractions […]. He made a conquest of the American family: not only of Mr. Haydel, its head; but of his children, his nieces—a charming circle of young girls. Mr. Haydel said, "You shall go no farther: all these shall be your pupils." The most beautiful, the most serious of the young ladies was Emma Becknell, still a child, but blooming and growing hour by hour in charms, like the flowers of that fertile land. Having lost her mother, she ruled her father's and her uncle's establishments; and, at twelve years of age, was mistress of a household […]. She was fourteen years old. One day, when he was reproving her with the authority of a master, without resisting him, she said, with her English gravity, "I would prefer to be scolded by my husband" […]. One month later, Miss Emma, robed and veiled in white, was led home from church by my father.[71]

---

71 Michelet, Madame J. 1868: *The Story of my Childhood*; translated from the French by M.F. Curtis. Boston (Little, Brown, and Company) and London (Sampson Law, Son, and Company), pp.180-183.

In fact, the matrimonial alliance of the Haydels and Becnels with the Bozonier family was done initially through Antoine Bozonier, a native of Dauphiné in southeastern France. François (Francis) Bozonier, the brother of Antoine, left no known descendants. The alias "Marmillion" was given to the Bozonier after they came to Louisiana. It is said to be a mispronunciation of "marmiton" and refers to the servant boy who carries the marmite (kitchen pot or chamber pot). As often happened in Louisiana, the name stuck and, for many generations, the family name was Bozonier-Marmillion. After the Civil War, part of the family living on the River took the Marmillion name and their New Orleans cousins retained the Bozonier name.[72]

The marriage contract between Hypolite Mialaret and Marguerite Becnel was signed on September 2, 1820 in St. John the Baptist Parish.[73] Marguerite Emma Becnel was the oldest daughter of Pierre Becnel Jr. and the granddaughter of Jean Jacques Haydel Sr. Her mother, Marguerite Aymée Haydel, died on April 12, 1817, about five years after the passing away of her grandmother, Marie Madeleine Bozonier Marmillon. Marguerite Emma Becnel and her brothers and sisters Pierre Aymé Becnel, Florestan Becnel, Ramire Becnel, Félix Becnel, and Amélie Becnel, were heirs of the community of J.J. Haydel Sr. and late Marie Madelaine Bosonnier for 1/5th, by representation of their deceased mother. They were present at the inventory, accompanied by Pierre Becnel, their father, curator, and tutor. Morel Guiramand (Jean Pierre), judge of peace in St. John the Baptist Parish, and Hypolite Mialaret were the witnesses. When Jean Jacques Haydel Sr. died in 1827, Marguerite Emma Becnel was living in France with her husband. Jean Pierre Morel Guiramand, her curator ad hoc, represented her at the inventory of the estate of her deceased grandfather.[74]

In 1823, Hypolite Mialaret and Emma Becnel moved to Montauban, in Southern France, where they engaged in farming. The house they built on their farm, "in the American style," was surrounded by a "covered gallery," "roomy and convenient," with magnificent vistas on the vast plains of Languedoc and the snowy peaks of the Pyrenees. It was somewhat a reproduction of the *maison basse* (one-story building) once standing on the Haydel plantation, where the couple may have lived before

---

72 Communicated by Norman Marmillion, initiator and curator of the Laura Plantation museum. The alias "Mermillon" was first mentioned on a marginal note near Antoine's name at the baptism of his daughter Marie Angélique held on December 15, 1764 in the St. Louis Cathedral of New Orleans (Sacramental Records, Volume 2, 1751-1771, p. 33).

73 SJB-94-1820. Mialaret I.J.L.H. Contrat de marriage avec Mlle A. Becnel. 2 September 1820.

74 SJB-116-1819: Inventaire des communautés d'entre Sr. Jn Jques haydel père et ses enfants héritiers de la Dame Marie Madelaine Bosonnier. 7 December 1819. SJB-4-1827: Inventory of the estate of late Jean Jacques Haydel. 30 January 1827. Marguerite Emma Becnel was the granddaughter of Magdelaine Haydel and the great granddaughter of Jean Christophe Haydel. Her paternal uncle, Drozin Becnel, and his wife died of smallpox in 1804 (Conrad 1972, p.296). Pierre Clidament Becnel, the son Drozin Becnel, took total control of the Evergreen plantation in 1830, after the death Magdelaine Haydel [SJB-CB-1830-H-248].

moving to France. Antonin Mialaret, the fourth of their six children, was born there in 1827. At age 61, declining fortune led Yves Mialaret back to Louisiana with the purpose of handling the estate he left behind when he moved to France. This last trip across the ocean explains his sudden return into official documents in St. John the Baptist Parish. He was mostly engaged in transactions with his brothers-in-law. To ensure that his son Antonin would get a good education in English, he took him to a school in Cincinnati, Ohio. When they arrived in this city, the school was temporarily removed into the country, to escape a typhoid fever epidemic. Yves Mialaret was unfortunately among the victims. His remains were transferred to Louisiana, in St. John the Baptist Parish, and buried near his father-in-law. In 1848, eight years after Mialaret's death, his widow was still settling affairs related to his estate in St. John the Baptist Parish. She died in France on October 14, 1865.[75] Antonin Mialaret settled in the same parish and married Amélie Becnel, the daughter of Ramire Becnel, his maternal uncle. Antonin was a brilliant physicist. He spent two years in St. Louis, Missouri as a photographer. He is credited with the discovery of the basic principles of photography on copper in 1866. The next year, he purchased the Roussel/Becnel plantation adjoining the Haydel plantation upriver. He was killed there in a tornado in 1884.[76]

When Yves Mialaret arrived at Habitation Haydel, the four surviving children of Jean Jacques Haydel Sr. were all married, the daughters away from home. Emma was very likely spending her time between the future Evergreen and Whitney plantations, caring for her widowed father and grandfather, and occasionally serving her maternal uncles Jean Jacques Haydel Jr. and Marcellin Haydel. The latter were then getting ready to carry on the management of the parental heritage.

The partnership of Jean Jacques Haydel Jr. and Marcellin Haydel (1820-1839)

From January 1820 to February 1839, the Haydel plantation was under the partnership of Jean Jacques Haydel Jr. and Jean François Marcellin Haydel. The partnership of the two brothers included a sugar plantation along with the buildings, tools, and animals, owned two-thirds by Jean Jacques Jr. and one-third by Marcellin. This joint partnership did not include the slaves present at the plantation. But "there is not enough room for two adult male crocodiles in the same pond," an African proverb says. After two decades, the management of the

75 Michelet, Madame J. *1868: The Story of my Childhood*, p.7 and pp.212-213. SJB-55-1832; SJB-76-1832; SJB-157-1832; SJB-135-1836; SJB-14-1846; SJB-114-1848. Biographical and Historical Memoires of Louisiana, volume 2, p. 252.

76 Simpson G.W. ed., The Photographic News. A weekly record of the progress of photography, volume X, N° 898, 20 April 1866. Printed and published in London by Thomas Piper, p.190. *Biographical and Historical Memoires of Louisiana*, volume 2, (Chicago, IL: Goodspeed Publishing Company, 1892), p. 252.

plantation became a matter of the Court when Jean François Marcellin Haydel filed a petition in the First Judicial District Court of the State of Louisiana in New Orleans, requesting the partition of the joint estate. Beside the fact that "his advice or observations were not taken into account," the petitioner also deplored "bad treatment inflicted by (…) Jean Jacques Haydel on (him) and his neglect to give proper accounts of his administration of (the) plantation and of the sale of the crops." Since J. J. Haydel had refused an amicable partition of the tract of land in kind without resorting to a sale, the petitioner "further prayed for a partition of the land and improvements and for the citation of his brother before the Court."[77]

The inventory described the plantation as established in sugar, located in St. John the Baptist Parish on the right bank of the Mississippi River, twenty-three arpents wide by the customary depth (forty arpents). There was also a second concession, which meant forty additional arpents, to the rear of the plantation. It was bounded above by habitation Charlotte Haydel, the widow of Mathias Roussel, and below by the plantation of Pierre Clidamant Becnel and Mrs. Félicité Becnel. On this habitation were a *maison à étage* (two-story building) and dependencies consisting of a kitchen, an oven (*four*), a hospital, a cabin for domestics, *magasin à vivres* (granary), *écurie* (stable), *moulin à pierre* (grindstone), *moulin à riz* (rice mill), two *pigeonniers* (pigeon houses), four *poulaillers* (hen houses), and a barn. On the premises were also a *maison basse* (one-story building) and dependencies consisting of a kitchen, a hospital, a granary, and a cabin for domestics.[78] The other buildings included a small house for the accountant, a ruined barn, and twenty slave cabins. The landed property included 150 arpents of standing cane, 200 arpents of sprouting cane, and about enough windrowed cane to plant 60 arpents. The sugar mill was operated by two crews, each one equipped with four *chaudières* (boilers) and all the accessories, a cane crusher equipped with a *machine à vapeur d'Angleterre* (British steam engine), a *purgerie* (sugar juice extractor), enough coolers to contain 250 hogsheads of sugar, a barn, and a blacksmith shop. The inventory also mentioned 241 hogsheads of sugar in the coolers and a certain quantity of molasses.[79] The slave population was not inventoried since it was not included in the partnership. But one can easily imagine its size since, in this particular time, a crew usually consisted of 76 slaves.[80] It is clear that by June 1834, Jean Jacques Haydel owned 78 slaves attached to Habitation Haydel according to documents presented at his meeting with his creditors in the office of Felix Grima, notary

---

77 SJB-27-1839: Marcellin Haydel vs. Jean Jacques Haydel/Marcellin Haydel petitioner to the Hon. T. Le Blanc Parish Judge of the Parish of St. John the Baptist. 5 January 1839.
78 The "maison basse" was probably the house built by Nicolas Haydel.
79 SJB-27-1839/Procés verbal d'inventaire des biens situés dans cette paroisse possédés indivisément entre les sieurs Francois Marcellin Haydel & Jean Jacques Haydel. 21 February 1839.
80 Follett 2005. *The sugar masters*, p.24.

public in New Orleans.[81]

Judgment was rendered on June 15, 1839 by Judge Buchanan of the First Judicial District Court of the State of Louisiana in New Orleans. He ordered that a sale be made by Terence Le Blanc, Judge of St. John the Baptist Parish, that a stay of execution be granted until the last Monday in November 1839, and that defendant pays all costs of the suit.[82] The sale of this business was finally held on February 27, 1840, but Jean Francois Marcellin Haydel was never to witness it. He died at his house on Saturday, November 16, 1839 and was interred the next afternoon. Martian Belfort Haydel, the oldest child of Jean Jacques Haydel Jr., was in the crowd that took Marcellin to his grave, but his father's name was not mentioned anywhere on the burial certificate, which listed the names of some of the attendants and those who signed it. Marcellin's grave is still in good condition at St. John the Baptist cemetery in Edgard, between the Catholic Church and the courthouse.

Besides their partnership, each of the two brothers owned other plantations. In March 1835, Marcellin Haydel bought the farm of his deceased mother-in-law, Marie Troxlair.[83] Three years later, he bought 103 acres from the General Land Office of the U.S. government.[84] It has been stated that Marcellin took over all operations of the Haydel Plantation in 1830 and proceeded to enclose the side galleries of the main house. The same source also gives him credit for having commissioned Dominique Canova to paint murals on the interior of the main house between the 1830s and 1840s.[85] Another study evokes a legend, which attributed the murals to Dominique Canova and dates them back to the 1850s:

> The legend is that an artist (possibly Dominique Canova) was taking River Road when suddenly he became ill (probably the yellow fever epidemic of 1853). Marcellin Haydel came across this sick stranger and brought him home. Marcellin and his wife nursed the stranger back to health. The stranger was so grateful to them for saving his life that he offered the only riches he had, his skill as a painter. He proceeded to stay on another six months and paint these murals which can be seen today.[86]

---

81 NONA, Felix Grima, Vol. 2, Act 201: Meeting of the creditors of Jean Jacques Haydel. 30 June 1834.
82 SJB-42-1840: Marcellin vs. Jean Jacques / Decision of Justice No. 17.045. 15 June 1839.
83 SJB-116-1835/Vente d'une habitation par les héritiers de la feue dame Marie Troxler veuve Alphonse Haydel au Sieur Marcellin Haydel. 30 March 1835.
84 SJB-CB-1851-Z32. Marcelin Haydel: Registration of a patent to him delivered by the US.
85 Dillard and als. "Whitney and Evergreen Plantation". In *River Road Preservation and Promotion*. Tulane University, School of Architecture: Preservation Studies, Spring 2005, p.28.
86 Alva B. See III, *Whitney Plantation*, Architectural Thesis, Tulane School of Architecture, November 1982, pp.24-25.

In fact, Marcellin never really took control of the plantation before his death. It is even doubtful he ever lived in the main house after his marriage. The *maison basse* (one-story building) and dependencies were more likely his private premises. Jean Jacques Haydel Jr. was wealthier than his brother, but he was heavily indebted in the 1830s. At that time he owned other plantations, including a small farm attended by three slaves in St. James Parish and an eleven-arpent plantation he bought from Emile Doumeing and Martian Belfort Haydel in St. John the Baptist Parish. Jean Jacques Haydel Jr. also owned two-thirds of another plantation in St. John Parish and the remaining one-third belonged to his son Martian Belfort Haydel. The plantations mentioned above, including Habitation Haydel, and the slaves attached to them were mortgaged either to the Union Bank of Louisiana or the Bank of the Consolidated Association of the Planters of Louisiana. Jean Jacques could not honor all his engagements with his creditors and had to file a petition asking for a respite of one to three years from them. Emile Doumeing, his son-in-law, was one of his attorneys and his middleman for all acts related to those banks. A meeting with his creditors was scheduled for June 30, 1834 in the office of notary public Felix grima. Meanwhile all his assets were inventoried and were evaluated at $208,360. His debts were evaluated at $197,559, including 23,411 dollars for the Consolidated Association of the Planters of Louisiana, 14,950 dollars for the Union Bank and $2,880 for the Bank of Louisiana. The rest of the debt was contracted with individuals living in Louisiana or in France. Substantial amounts had to be paid to close relatives such as Marcelin Haydel ($12,757), his sister Érasie Haydel Lebourgeois of St. James Parish ($22,815), and Mialaret ($8,935) who had relocated in France, leaving his estate in the hands of Jean Jacques Haydel, Jr. himself. The preparatory documents of the meeting also mentioned circumstances unfavorable to the petitioner such as the destruction of several crops by natural elements, mostly frost damage, the loss of slaves, and other losses evaluated at a total of $100,000. He had to borrow large sums of money at a high interest rate but he still could not assume the payment of several promissory notes endorsed by him.[87]

The return of Mialaret to Louisiana was partially related to the bankruptcy of the maternal uncle of his wife. Érasie Haydel appointed her son-in-law Vinaux Lebourgeois as her prosecutor general and to represent her in any matters related to debts owed her by Jean Jacques Haydel, including filing suits against her brother or his syndics.[88] Like his father, Martian Belfort Haydel was also affected by the loss of crops related to the same factors, the great pressure in the money market, and his subsequent failure to meet his engagements. A meeting was held the same

87 NONA, Felix Grima, Vol. 2, Act 201. Meeting of the creditors of Jean Jacques Haydel. 30 June 1834.

88 SJ-B18-P56-1839. Érasie Haydel appoints Vinaux le Bourgeois as her prosecutor general. 16 February 1839.

day with his creditors, also allowing him to get respite from them.[89] The father and his son were finally able to keep their heads above the water but the cost was high, especially for the former. Their partnership was broken on March 27, 1840 by a judgment of the First Judicial District Court of the State of Louisiana in New Orleans. The plantation and 114 slaves attached to it were auctioned and the father's share was distributed to his creditors.[90] The plantation was thirteen arpents wide and was bounded above by Pierre Clidamant Becnel, the future Evergreen Plantation. Martian Belfort Haydel kept control of the property until his untimely death in 1863. Martian was also a partner of Emile Doumeing but the latter was apparently having the same problems as Jean Jacques. In October 1840, the syndics of his creditors sold to Belfort two valuable lots in Faubourg Washington, in the area known today as the Bywater District in New Orleans.[91]

Under Louisiana law, slaves were real property and their sales had to be officially recorded by notaries in the city and parish judges who also served as notaries assisted by sworn recorders. In St. John the Baptist Parish, Adolphe Sorapuru, a member of a family of Creoles of color, served as the sworn recorder of sales and mortgages during the decade preceding the Civil War. Terence Le Blanc (1774-1857), his father in law, was Judge and ex-officio notary public of the same parish during many decades in the first half of the 19th century. The sale of a slave could be subjected to conditions such as the manumission of the slave by the buyer. Marie Joseph and Claire were sold to Jean Jacques Haydel, Jr. for this purpose following the family meeting which settled the estate of his deceased father. Another condition would be the transfer of the slave far away from the seller for security reasons. On January 26, 1840 Érasie Haydel Lebourgeois sold a young male slave named Africain to Hosie Edwards, a Medical Doctor. The condition was that the slave could not be either kept or resold in St. James Parish because he had threatened revenge against the overseer of the vendor.[92] Auctions were a common way of liquidating estates and settling debts, and auctioneers made a living selling slaves. In New Orleans, the auctions were held every Saturday, and they drew large crowds of onlookers beneath the rotundas of the city's luxury hotels.[93] On March 24, 1840, a group of seventy slaves, owned by Jean Jacques Haydel and most of them from Habitation Haydel, were displayed on the auction block at the Bath Saloon of the St. Louis Hotel in New Orleans and sold to the highest bidders. These sales were officially

89 NONA, Felix Grima, Vol. 2, Act 200. Meeting of the creditors of Marcian Belfort Haydel. 30 June 1834.
90 SJB-161-1840 / Procès verbal de l'inventaire des biens dont deux tiers indivis ont été abandonnés par le Sieur Jean Jacques Haydel à ses créanciers et dont l'autre tiers indivis appartient au Sieur Martian Belfort Haydel. 8 May 1840. SJB-CB-1841-S14/ "The syndics of the creditors of Jean Jacques Haydel: Act of partition of the result of the sale". 9 March 1841.
91 CHREO/Vendees/B27-28/Fo. 499. October 16, 1840.
92 SJ-B18-P377-1840. Erasie Haydel: sale of rebellious slave. 26 January 1840.
93 Johnson 1999, p.54.

recorded before Felix Grima on June 27, 1840. A week before the auction, Terence Le Blanc had issued a certificate ascertaining that all of them were mortgage free. The Haydel slaves exposed and cried by auctioneer Joseph Le Carpentier comprised a majority of young males and females, with eight infants. There were also elderly people, twelve of them born in Africa, and some affected by ailments such as asthma, hernia, and the piles. Jacob, an African affected by an hernia and the oldest person in the group (seventy years), was sold to Lucien Wells for $175. Little Guim, a fifty-year-old African, and Marianne, a fifty-six-year-old Congo slave, were probably delivered from the horrors of slavery when they were bought by Etienne Villeré, a free man of color and a possible relative. Mental illness did not prevent the sale of Sery, a twenty-five-year-old female described as an "idiot" and sold for $105, the lowest price recorded that day. One of the most striking views on the auction block was that of twenty-eight-year-old Queto with his rags revealing a maimed arm which gave him the distinctive name Queto Manchot (one-armed man in French). He live at Habitation Haydel where he served as a carter and ploughman. Despite his infirmity, this Creole slave was sold for $350 to Widow Choppin, a resident of St. James parish. The most active buyer was Felix Garcia of St. John the Baptist parish, a higher-ranking official who was at that time the President of the Louisiana Senate. The twenty-three slaves he purchased were also acquired in the name of Achille Lorio, his partner and co-owner of a plantation located in St. Charles parish.[94] Although most of them were not displaced too far, this was a trying time for these enslaved people who were forced to reconstruct new lives away from their loved ones.

Lady, thirty years old, was part of the group sold to Garcia & Lorio with her five children. Thirteen years later, a female slave named Lady, aged about 44 years, was sold with her daughter to Séraphine Haydel, a free woman of color who lived since 1847 in a house located on Ursulines Street in Faubourg Tremé. The vendor was another free woman of color identified as Widow Louis Boisdoré. In this same sale was another female slave named Marie, about 48 years old, and her three children, the youngest one named Lady and aged seven years.[95] The age of the mature Lady in 1853 indicates some probability that the documents were referring to the same person. It is also plausible that this group was related to Séraphine Haydel who

---

94 NONA, Felix Grima, Vol. 30, Acts 456 through 482. Sales of slaves by the syndics of the creditors of Jean Jaques Haydel. 27 June1840. Felix Garcia owned plantations in both St. Charles and Jefferson parishes. Felix Garcia was the President of the Louisiana Senate from 1839 to 1845. His brother, Manuel Garcia, also a slave owner, was the sheriff of Jefferson parish for nine years before his election at the Louisiana Senate in 1845. Their father was an officer in the Spanish Navy [Biography of Manuel Garcia: http://files.usgwarchives.net/la/orleans/bios/g-000043.txt (Accessed April 2, 2014)].

95 CHREO/Vendees/B45/Fo. 36. Land slae; Joseph Dumas to Miss Séraphine Haydel. 14 July 1847. CHREO/Vendees/B60/Fo. 501. 5 March 1853. Sale of slaves; Veuve Louis Boisdoré to Miss Séraphine Haydel.

may have bought them for the purpose of freeing them. Although the name of the father of Séraphine is yet to be uncovered, it is quite clear that she knew Lady when this person was enslaved on the Haydel Plantation. This is an interesting path for further research on the black Haydels. It appeared that their history did not start with the relationship of Antoine Haydel, the brother in law of Marcelin Haydel, and Anna, one of the slaves who saw Lady leave the plantation with the coffle bound for the auction block in New Orleans. Marguerite Adèle Haydel, the wife of Martian Belfort Haydel, owned a house near the domicile of Séraphine within the block delimitated by Ursulines, St. Claude, St. Phillip, and Rampart.[96] Across this street, in the French Quarter, Jean Jacques Haydel also owned a house located at the corner of Rampart and St. Peter, within the block delimited by St. Peter, Rampart, Orleans, and Burgundy.[97] He was in this city during the summer of 1855 when a yellow fever epidemic broke out and took the life of Marie Laure Haydel, his second wife, along with thirty-two slaves. *Le Meschachébé*, the official newspaper of St. John the Baptist Parish, covered the event with an article stating hastily that the man was himself "sur le point de mourir" (about to die).[98] Later that year, his community with his deceased wife was inventoried. It included eighty-nine slaves and the only plantation he did not lose to the benefit of his creditors in St. John the Baptist Parish.[99] Jean Jacques Haydel Jr. apparently sold that place and the next year he moved permanently to New Orleans where he spent the rest of his life.[100] At that time, his property included a plantation in Orleans Parish, below New Orleans on the right bank of the Mississippi River and the house on Rampart and St. Peter. He also owned another house located in Faubourg Marigny, 102 Rue St. Antoine (St. Anthony Street), where he passed away on February 1, 1863. He was eighty-three years old. The service was held on February 2nd at the St. Augustine church in Tremé where a growing population of people of color lived, some of them linked to the Haydels by blood. Jean Jacques was interred the same day in his family vault at Saint-Louis Cemetery Number 1.[101] This was the end of the life of a man who was baptized privately (*ondoyé* in french) because he was in danger

---

96 CHREO/Vendees/B79-82/Fo.? Etienne Villavaso to Marguerite Adèle Haydel (land sale). New Orleans May 6, 1859. For sixteen years, Marguerite Adèle Haydel was also the owner of the square bounded by New Levee (now South Peters), Gravier, Tchoupitoulas, and Common streets, where the Bottle Tree Hotel is standing today [CHREO/Vendees/B79-82/Fo. 88/ New Orleans May 21, 1859].

97 CHREO/Vendees/B60/Fo. 423. Land sle; Justin Durel to Jean Jacques Haydel. 5 February 1853.

98 *Le Meschachébé*, 12 August 1855.

99 SJB-271-1855/Inventaire des biens de la communauté qui a existé entre Jean Jacques Haydel et Marie Laure Haydel son épouse décédée. 31 October 1855.

100 SJB-144-1856. Déclaration de domicile par Jean Jacques Haydel. 6 May 1856.

101 CHREO /Vendees/B80/Fo. 117. Jean Baptiste Fleitas to Jean Jacques Haydel: Retrocession of land and slaves. 8 June 1859. Obituary posted in *L'Abeille de la Nouvelle Orleans* (The New Orleans Bee). 2 February 1863, p.1, col. 5.

of imminent death in his early infancy.[102] Despite fateful events, the most painful being the loss of two beloved wives, he lived a comfortable life that was sustained by the sweat and tears of hundreds of enslaved people.

The Haydel Plantation under Marie Azélie Haydel (1840-1860)

The auction of the property of Jean Jacques Haydel Jr. and Marcellin started in February 1840. Marie Azélie, the widow of Marcellin, was there buying land, tools, and animals. Despite competition from other bidders, the habitation and dependencies were sold to her for 41,100 piastres. We will probably never know the number and the names of all the slaves owned by Marcellin Haydel since they were not part of the auction. Azélie inherited them according to Marcellin's will. Some of them appear in the inventory of Azélie Haydel's estate following her death in 1860. So was the case of Gabriel, of the Congo nation, and Reguine, a female slave from the East Coast, sold to Marcellin Haydel at the auction of the community of his parents in January 1820. The Congo slave was then seventy years old and respectfully called Vieux (Old) Gabriel. He spent more than fifty years of his life on the plantation under four different masters. Two other slaves listed in the 1827 inventory of the estate of late Jean Jacques Haydel Sr. and sold to Marcellin were also still living at the place: Hilaire, a sixty-five-year old Creole, and Julien alias Doudou, an overseer married to Lilite, fifty-five, born on the East Coast.[103]

Marie Azélie Haydel was born on October 17, 1790. She was the oldest among the thirteen children of Alphonse Haydel and Marie Troxlair. Alphonse died on January 29, 1814, leaving behind Marie Azélie, her mother, and twelve brothers and sisters, most of them minors. This probably gave her a strong sense of responsibility, which later allowed her to become a successful entrepreneur. On her father's side, Marie Azélie Haydel was the granddaughter of Mathias Haydel and the great granddaughter of Ambroise Haydel. Marcellin Haydel, whom she married on June 12, 1810, was a first cousin of her father. They grew up together on adjoining plantations. Their marriage lasted nearly three decades without being rewarded with any offspring. The couple adopted Alphonse Becnel, the son of Joséphine Haydel (Azélie's sister) and Florestan Becnel. Joséphine died in 1844, followed by her husband ten years later. This was probably the year Marthe Becnel joined her brother Alphonse as a member of Azélie's household. The 1840 census listed Widow Marcellin Haydel as head of household, along with two white males, four

---

102 Sacramental Records, Vol. 3 (1772-1783): "Baptismal ceremonies supplied on 6 June 1783." His first wife Clarisse Becnel died on October 12, 1811.
103 SJB-178-1860/Inventaire des biens de la succession de la dame Azélie Haydel décédée veuve Marcelin Haydel. 10-12 November 1860.

white females, and forty-eight slaves. In the 1850 census, Azélie's sister Carmelite
Haydel and Ursin Weber, the plantation overseer, were also listed on the plantation
along with their children.[104]

In her first will, recorded in New Orleans on March 25, 1839, Azélie Haydel
appointed her husband as her testamentary executor, allowing him total disposal
of her wealth until his death.[105] Marcellin Haydel's last will was recorded the
same day in the same office of Louis T. Caire, public notary in New Orleans. It
was a mystic or a secret will, secured in a sealed box. He designated his wife as
his universal heir and the sole executor of his estate. The sickness of Marcellin
probably dictated changes to his first mystic will recorded in St. John the Baptist
Parish on August 27, 1836.[106] Azélie continued successfully the operation of the
plantation after Marcellin's death. She was most likely the actual commissioner
of the paintings, which are still adorning the interior and the exterior of the main
house on Whitney Plantation. These were not just mere decorations since she used
them to pay homage to her deceased husband by having his initials monogrammed
in cartouches and disposed at the four corners of the paintings drawn on the ceiling
of the upstairs living room. This was very likely done in the 1840s when increased
tariff protection generated higher profit and the subsequent rise in the number of
sugar plantations. Dominique, Domenico, or Dominici Canova, the alleged artist,
was born in 1800 in Italy where he began his artistic training. Canova arrived in
Louisiana about 1837 to teach art at Jefferson College. Later, he moved to New
Orleans where he died in 1868. Many decorative paintings in New Orleans and
its countryside are attributed to Domenico Canova, including an altar piece and
a fresco for the St. Louis Cathedral and the decorative paintings of San Francisco
Plantation. The Marmillions, the owners of San Francisco, were closely related to
the Haydels. Given this kinship and the proximity of the two plantations, it is not
improbable that Canova painted the two houses standing on them.[107]

---

104 Roberts, Erika Sabine. *Digging through discarded identity: archaeological investigations
around the kitchen and the overseer's house at Whitney plantation, Louisiana.* Thesis submitted
to the Graduate Faculty of the Louisiana State University and Agricultural and Mechanical
College in partial fulfillment of the requirements for the degree of Master of Arts in the
Department of Geography and Anthropology, May 2005, p.22.
105 St. John the Baptist, Will Book 1, 11 December 1846 through 6 December 1967.
106 SJB-254-1839. Marcellin Haydel's last mystic will. New Orleans 25 March 1839. SJB-
305-1836/Testament du Sieur Jean Francois Marcellin Haydel.
107 Kilpatrick 1992, *A Conservation Study Of The Decorative Paintings At Whitney Plantation,
St. John The Baptist Parish, Louisiana.* A Thesis in the Graduate Program in Historic
Preservation. Presented to the Faculties of the University of Pennsylvania in Partial Fulfillment
of the Requirements for the Degree of Master of Science, University of Pennsylvania (Section
2.3.1: Biography of Domenico Canova). Edwards 1991. *The Preservation and Restoration of the
Whitney Plantation, St. John the Baptist Parish, Louisiana. Volume I: Historic Structures Report.*
Department of Geography and Anthropology, Louisiana State University, Baton Rouge, 15
November 1991, pp.36-37.

In the 1840s, official records often mention Marie Azélie buying or selling slaves and landed property, or otherwise making donations of slaves and money. The slaves were mostly bought from New Orleans, where she was represented by Georges and Théodore Lanaux, two residents of the Crescent City. On April 30, 1842, she sold one arpent of land to her brother-in-law Félix Becnel for 1,300 piastres.[108] The same day she leased three arpents of land to her brother Antoine Haydel for eight years.[109] The latter died in 1857, and three years later, buildings belonging to his heirs were still standing on the main plantation.[110] He was survived by many children, including a mulatto boy born from his relationship with Anna, his sister's slave. The boy's name was Victor, and he is the ancestor of all the black Haydels, including those who later rose to fame in New Orleans.

Marie Azélie Haydel became one of the major planters of Louisiana. In 1844, her sugar mills produced 356,000 pounds of sugar. In March 1845, she signed an agreement with Pierre Lezin Becnel allowing her to dig a canal on her neighbor's property, which drained floodwaters into the swamp through Bayou Becnel. Lezin would also use the same canal to drain his own land.[111] The 1845-46 grinding season yielded 275,000 pounds of sugar. The production of the plantation peaked in 1854-55 with 407,000 pounds of sugar, but frost-damage soon brought the worst years in the history of the sugar industry in Louisiana. Champomier ended his 1856 report with a sad prediction: "Taking all things into consideration I shall not be at all surprised if I have again a short crop to report upon in 1856-57." That year, Azélie's production dropped dramatically to 60,000 pounds and only 3,603,000 pounds were harvested in St. John the Baptist Parish. Severe cold and a devastating flood ruined the 1858-59 crop. According to Champomier, on the 19th and 20th of November 1858, a severe frost suddenly fell upon the state at the very moment when it was yielding the most cane. It found the farmers unprepared and left some of them without seed cane. In the spring of 1859, several breaches in the levees, on the right bank of the river, combined their work of destruction of cane, corn, and other crops in the country situated between Bayou Lafourche and the Mississippi River and down in St. Charles, St. John the Baptist, and to some extent St. James and Assumption parishes.[112] These breaches profoundly affected the next year's crop, and only 20,000 pounds of sugar were produced on the Haydel plantation.

---

108 SJB-110-1842/Vente d'un lot de terre par la dame veuve François Marcellin Haydel au Sieur Felix Becnel. 30 April 1842.

109 SJB-111-1842/Bail d'habitation par Mme veuve François Marcellin Haydel au Sieur Antoine Haydel Junior. 30 April 1842.

110 Succession Azélie Haydel, 10-12 November 1860.

111 SJB-CB-1845-X6. Acte sous seing privé par lequel Pierre Lezin Becnel accorde à Mme Veuve Marcellin Haydel le droit de fouiller un canal sur sa propriété. 22 March 1845.

112 P.A. Champomier, *Statement of the Sugar Crop Made in Louisiana* (New Orleans: Cook, Young, & Co., 1844, 1845-46, and 1849-50 to 1858-59).

In 1860, a few months before her death, Azélie was listed among the largest slaveholders in the state. Her landed property encompassed 2,200 acres of land of which 1,200 were improved. That same year, Azélie Haydel's crops were partially destroyed by the natural disasters mentioned above, but her work force secured 5,500 bushels of Indian corn, 75 bushels of peas and beans, 75,000 pounds of sugar, and 14,000 gallons of molasses.[113]

From the time of Ambroise Heidel to that of Marie Azélie Haydel, a small farm entirely dedicated to foods crops was turned into a huge agro-industrial unit. A modest farmer in 1724 with a single pig for all livestock, Ambroise became a wealthy landowner engaged in the business of indigo. His legacy was mostly carried on by Jean Jacques Haydel Sr., his youngest child, who transitioned the plantation from indigo to sugar before passing it to the next generation. The inventory of Azélie Haydel's estate was completed in two days by Adolphe Sorapuru, the recorder of the parish. The total succession was estimated to nearly 187,000 piastres. The landed property was composed of several farms operated by a work force of one hundred and one slaves. For Kilpatrick, the high-quality and complex decorative paintings, both interior and exterior applications, place the main house on the plantation in a category by itself in Louisiana and the South, since no other application of exterior decorative painting is known to survive or even have existed in Louisiana. This author is also right to suspect that the elaborate ornamentation conveyed to all visitors at Whitney the high level of economic success and cultural sophistication the Haydels had attained.[114] However, it should never be forgotten that the process of perpetual economic growth, which led to luxury, was made possible by the hard work of hundreds of African slaves and their descendants. The last chapter of this monograph examines some aspects of their fate and legacies.

---

113 Menn, *The large slaveholders of Louisiana* (1964), pp.359-361.
114 Kilpatrick 1992, A Conservation Study of the Decorative Paintings at Whitney Plantation, p.3.

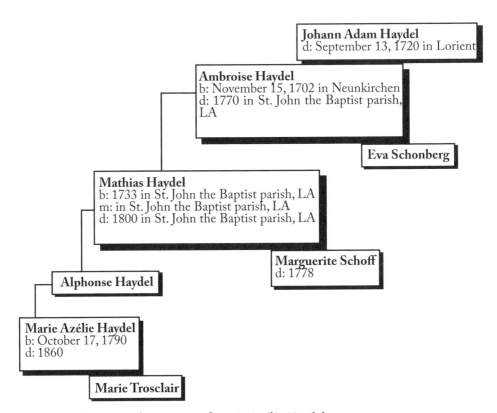

Fig. 4.11. The paternal ancestors of Marie Azélie Haydel.

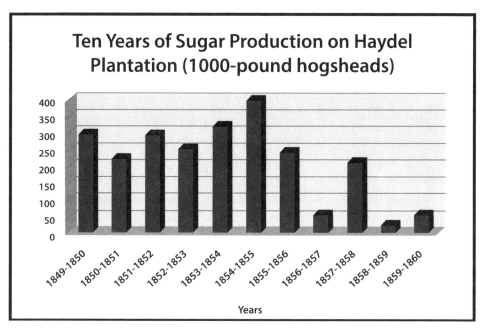

Fig. 4.12. Sugar production on Haydel plantation (1849-1860)
Sources: P.A. Champomier, Statement of the Sugar Crop Made in Louisiana, (from 1849-50 to 1858-59); and Menn, The large slaveholders of Louisiana, for the 1859-1860 crop.

TABLE 13. SUGAR PRODUCTION IN ST. JOHN THE BAPTIST PARISH (1849-1859)

Grinding seasons	Number of sugar houses	Number of steam-powered mills	Parish production 1,000-pound hogsheads
1849-1850	69	42	12,077
1850-1851	67	50	8,584
1851-1852	-	-	10,920
1852-1853	-	-	11,944
1853-1854	67	51	17,601
1854-1855	61	51	13,339
1855-1856	60	51	8,356
1856-1857	60	51	3,603
1857-1858	60	51	11,303
1858-1859	63	51	11,271

Source: P.A. Champomier, Statement of the Sugar Crop Made in Louisiana, (New Orleans: Cook, Young, & Co., 1849-50 to 1858-59).

TABLE 14. SUGAR PRODUCTION IN LOUISIANA, 1834-1873

Year	Production, Hogsheads	Year	Production, Hogsheads
1834	100,000	1853	449,000
1835	30,000	1854	346,000
1836	70,000	1855	231,000
1837	65,000	1856	74,000
1838	70,000	1857	279,000
1839	115,000	1858	362,000
1840	87,000	1859	221,000
1841	90,000	1860	228,000
1842	140,000	1861	459,000
1843	100,000	1864	7,000
1844	200,000	1865	15,000
1845	186,000	1866	39,000
1846	140,000	1867	37,600
1847	240,000	1868	84,000
1848	220,000	1869	87,000
1849	247,000	1870	144,800
1850	211,000	1871	128,461
1851	236,000	1872	105,000
1852	321,000	1873	90,000

Source: King, The Great South (1875), p.79.

Fig. 4.13. Haydel Family vault in St. Louis Cemetery Number 1.
Photo by Ann Davis (http://www.findagrave.com).

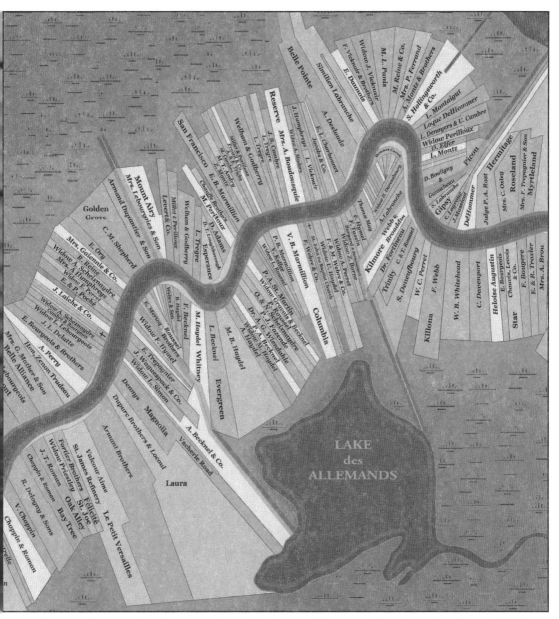

Fig. 4.14. Section of the Norman's chart of the Lower Mississippi River by Adrien Persac (1858). Reprint by the Zoe Company (2013), Laura Plantation, Vacherie, Louisiana. Courtesy of Norman Marmillon. The Haydel/Whitney plantation is located between Félix Becnel (F. Becnel) and L. Becnel (Evergreen).

Chapter Five

LAPIN MANGÉ LI
Resistance, Freedom, and Legacies

"Quand la mémoire va chercher du bois mort, elle ramène le fagot qui lui plaît." ["When Memory goes a-gathering firewood, she brings back the sticks that strike her fancy."]
—African proverb.[1]

Marronage as prelude to revolt

The institution of slavery was based on violence inflicted to the bodies of the enslaved people. Whipping, branding, ear cropping, and other mutilations, along with various instruments of torture were so many means used to generate the pain inflicted to the flesh of the people who were put to work against their own will. This violence was institutionalized through the so-called black codes and the expected result was total obedience from the slaves. The life of a slave was marked by permanent fear of punishment and tireless quest for freedom. Manumission was relatively easier for the slaves with special skills, especially those who lived in New Orleans and who were hired out by their masters. Either in this city or elsewhere in the country, manumission was obviously easier for the slave women engaged in concubinage with their masters and for their offspring of mixed race. For the vast majority of the enslaved people emancipation came only with death and they had to find paths of accommodation to the "peculiar institution" through passive resistance which included various and often unsuspected tools built around cultural matters such as music, storytelling, and even foodways. Active resistance involved

---

1 In Birago Diop, *Les contes d'Amadou Koumba*, Paris, Présence Africaine, 1947, p. 28. Translation by Dorothy S. Blair. *African Literature in French.* Cambridge University Press, 1976, p. 44.

mostly men and consisted of radical reaction to violence which culminated with revolts. But marronage was a common way of escaping violence and enjoying temporary or definitive freedom. The increased intensity of this phenomenon was a potential factor of revolt or, at least, an indicator of its imminence.

Marronage is a French word indicating the status of the maroons or runaway slaves who escaped for different reasons. According to Le Page du Pratz, many of the Africans brought to Louisiana in the early years of the French regime either committed suicide or ran away: "*Some of them have killed or drowned themselves and many have fled (…). In this case they attempt to return to their homes and think it possible to live in the woods with fruits which they expect to be everywhere similar to those at home; they even think that they will get home by roaming around the sea (…).*"[2]

Technically, any slave who left the plantation without a permit from their master was a maroon. Some slaves may have used *petit marronage* to avoid punishment, escaping for brief periods of time, allowing an enraged master to calm down and become less vengeful. Others may have left the plantations to pay nighttime visits to lovers, visit friends and relatives on other properties, or simply for a short break from hard work.

The *grand marronnage* was defined by its duration, the considerable distances involved and, above all, the chronic rebelliousness of the actors. For Gabriel Debien the *grand marronnage* always involved people who did not have any intention of returning to their masters. Some lived for a long time in isolation, others organized themselves around a leader or joined already existing gangs. They lived on resources found in nature or taken from granaries and smokehouses on the plantations. This generated much anxiety for the masters although it was not a real threat to their lives. Expeditions operated by the regular troops and the local militia resulted in the capture of fugitive slaves, but the phenomenon did not end until the abolition of slavery.[3] The environment was very important to the existence and survival of maroon communities. Rafael Lucas distinguishes three "grand ecosystems of marronage": the mountainous lands (Martinique, Guadeloupe, Haiti, the Dominican Republic, Jamaica, Cuba), the forested countries (Surinam, Guyana), and the milieus colonized by swampy thickets (Mato Grosso in Brésil).[4] Louisiana belonged to this type of ecosystem where maroons found refuge from the beginnings to the end of slavery. Besides the pillaging of resources on the plantations, marronage was a permanent loss of labor for the masters who resorted to ferocious repression through legislation provided by the slave codes established by the different regimes.

---

2 Le Page du Pratz : *Histoire de la Louisiane*, tome 1er, De Bure, Paris, 1758, p. 334.

3 Gabriel Debien. *Marronage in the French Caribbean*; in Richard Price, *Maroon Societies, Rebel Slave Communities in the Americas*, Baltimore et London, Johns Hopkins University Press, 1996, pp. 107-134.

4 Rafael Lucas, « Marronnage et marronnages », *Cahiers d'histoire. Revue d'histoire critique*, 89, 2002 [Online], p. 8. Accessed 5 September 2013. URL : http://chrhc.revues.org/1527.

Punishment was particularly severe for runaway slaves. Article 32 of the Code Noir promulgated in Louisiana in 1724 stipulated gradual sentences, which included whipping, marking with the *fleur-de-lys*, mutilation, and death:

> The runaway slave, who shall continue to be so for one month from the day of his being denounced to the officers of justice, shall have his ears cut off, and shall be branded with the fleur-de-lys on the shoulder; and on a second offense of the same nature, persisted in during one month from the day of his being denounced, he will be hamstrung, and be marked with the fleur-de-lys on the other shoulder. On the third offense, he shall suffer death.

Article 34 of the same code was designed to prevent the harboring and concealing of runaway slaves by the free population, with fines three times heavier for the free people of color, who were more likely to provide such support to fugitive slaves:

> Freed or free-born negroes, who shall have afforded refuge in their houses to fugitive slaves, shall be sentenced to pay to the masters of said slaves, the sum of thirty livres a day for every day during which they shall have concealed said fugitives; and all other free persons, guilty of the same offence, shall pay a fine of ten livres a day as aforesaid; and should the freed or free-born negroes not be able to pay the fine herein specified, they shall be reduced to the condition of slaves, and be sold as such. Should the price of the sale exceed the sum mentioned in the judgment, the surplus shall be delivered to the hospital.[5]

Despite the threat of severe punishment, marronnage was always a serious problem for planters throughout the history of antebellum Louisiana. The French were unsuccessful in eliminating it, and slave control became an even higher priority in Spanish Louisiana with the arrival of large numbers of African slaves. By the time of the American Revolution, the maroons of Louisiana had control over Bas du Fleuve, the area between the mouth of the Mississippi River and New Orleans. The Spanish authorities were concerned that the maroons had formed several bands of considerable numbers in various places such as Ville Gaillarde and

---

5 B. F. French 1851, *Historical Collections of Louisiana: Embracing Translations of Many Rare and Valuable Documents Relating to the Natural, Civil, and Political History of that State* (New York: D. Appleton). The flawed translation of fleur-de-lys (flower de luce) has been discarded for the initial French term. The fleur-de-lys, a stylized lilly, was the emblem on the flag of the French ancient regime. It has become a symbol of unity as the logo of the New Orleans Saints, the winning NFL team of Super Bowl XLIV. Every touchdown scored by this wonderful team should be dedicated to the people who suffered from what used to be one of the most feared instruments of punishment.

Chef Menteur in Gaillardeland, a vast and uncharted territory in what is now St. Bernard Parish. The leader of this community was St. Maló, a former slave of Karl d'Arensbourg, the commander of the militia and leader of the German Coast.[6]

Maroon communities sometimes involved entire families fleeing together. The maroons developed their own economy cultivating corn, squash, and rice or gathering herbs, roots, and wild fruits. They made baskets, sifters, and other articles woven from willow and reeds. They carved indigo vats and troughs from cypress wood. They trapped birds, hunted and fished, and acted as independent contractors for their labor in the cypress industry. Some even went to New Orleans to trade and gamble.[7] The maroons were usually armed with stolen rifles. Many stayed in the neighboring *cyprières* (cypress swamps) and returned nightly to their masters' premises where they procured supplies from smokehouses or from the cabins with the complicity of female slaves. The testimony of Albert Patterson, once a slave of the Lasco Plantation in Plaquemines Parish, indicates some of the strategies used by the fugitives in order to escape the bloodhounds:

> If a nigger hide in de woods, he'd come in at night to get [a] meal. They bore a little hole in the floor, and they break into de meat house too. De dogs couldn't catch dem nohow 'cause they put bay leaves on de bottom of their feet and shoes. Then they go and walk in fresh manure, and a dog can't track them. That way a man could come and see his family.[8]

The tighter control on the slave community that developed after the Louisiana Purchase did not prevent slaves from running away. The black code of 1808 was a synthesis of the slave laws passed under French and Spanish rules. Those caught harboring a fugitive slave were still subjected to the penalty of heavy fines. In June 1808, Charles Paquet, a free black man living in St. Charles Parish, was fined for hiding two maroons at his home: Honoré, a slave of Judge Alexandre Labranche, and Lindor, a slave of Sieur Pierre Reine. They were all taken to court, and it is from this case among others that it is possible to confirm the day-to-day life of maroon slaves described above. Honoré confessed having settled with Lindor and another maroon named Gabriel in the *cyprière* of Sieur Pizéros, captain of the local militia and chief of patrol. From there, they settled on the land of Sieur Delhomme where they built a cabin. Gabriel made frequent trips into the quarters where Rosette, a female slave, provided food for them to eat. They stayed at this place for a month. Sometimes they ran errands out of the swamps, in the prairie, or on Lake Pontchartrain at the junction of Bayou St. John. From there Gabriel went all the way to New Orleans to sell items and buy groceries. Gabriel and Lindor often

---

6 Hall, *Africans in Colonial Louisiana* (1992), p.232.
7 Hall, *Africans in Colonial Louisiana* (1992), p.202.
8 Clayton, *Mother Wit*, p.178.

slept at Charles Paquet's house.

Lindor confessed to having stayed for one week in the cypress swamp. Then he joined Honoré and Gabriel on the highlands of Mr. Pizéros, where he found them with a calf they had killed, and they stayed there for one week before moving to the *lataniers* (dwarf palmetto grove) of Mr. Cabaret. Louis and Célestin, two slaves owned by Pizéros, joined them there and stayed with them for one week. They went back to their master's house with a ticket of grace, a note of forgiveness written by Sieur Zénon Trude (Trudel) in order to avoid being punished. A few days later, Louis went back to the *lataniers*, probably as a spy for his master. From there, the party moved to the rear of Pierre Reine's habitation where they killed a cow. Fifteen days later, they settled on the limits of the plantations of Sieurs Adelard Fortier and Pizéros. The group moved on to the *cyprière* of Mr. Destréhan where they stayed for two months, killing and eating domestic animals. Then Lindor and Gabriel settled in the house of Charles Paquet where they killed yet another cow and occupied themselves cutting wood with Léveillé, a slave of their host. Lindor and Honoré also slept for one week in the cabin of one of Fortier's female slaves named Ciba. The Chief of the Militia arrested Honoré in this place, then he caught Lindor in Charles Paquet's house where he found him hidden in the flue of the chimney.[9]

On the same plantation, four months later, a slave named Lindor, who may or may not have been the same Lindor, became the overseer of the plantation of Sieur Pierre Reine. There he found himself in the role of a maroon hunter. During the night of October 5th and 6th, 1808, around four o'clock, he was awakened by the dogs barking after Charles, a slave of the merchant Alexandre Chopin. The intruder opened fire on Lindor with a rifle that he had hidden in a barn but missed his target. The runaway slave was shot by Ursin Chalaire, the manager of the Reine plantation, who later caught him in the canes of the neighboring plantation of Sieur Alexandre Labranche.

This Charles was a rebel par excellence. A witness named François Levasseur described him as a "*marroneur de profession*" (maroon by trade) and affirmed knowing him well since his birth in Natchitoches Parish. The witness also revealed what he considered the defendant's "pronounced tendency to the rape of white women." According to Sieur Baptiste Prudhomme, Charles' former master, he sold him in New Orleans where he served several masters. Then he was bought by Sieur Paillet and brought back to the Natchitoches. The return of the rebel generated much anger. Sieur Prudhomme and other inhabitants managed to have him expelled from the parish. From there, he was probably sold in St. Charles Parish to Sieur Alexandre Chopin. At his trial, Charles confessed that he had been a maroon

---

9 SC-37-1808, "Interrogatoire du nommé Charles Paquet, nègre libre, et jugement rendu contre lui pour avoir recelé deux nègres marrons, l'un appartenant à Mr Reine et l'autre à Mr Alexandre Labranche." Procès verbal N° 37, 4 June 1808.

for one month and that he followed the woods toward Bayou St. John into the plantation of Sieur Canterille where his mother lived. In a boat out on the bayou, he found a bag of gunpowder and a rifle with which he attempted to shoot Lindor. The tribunal headed by Judge Alexandre Labranche condemned him "to be hung and strangled until death follows," a sentence regarded as "necessary for the public peace."[10] Three years later the biggest slave rebellion ever known in North America broke out on the plantations of those who had chosen to hang the slave Charles.

Marronnage remained a permanent issue on the German Coast, from its beginnings through the Civil War. During the decade preceding this conflict, the local press regularly published advertisements of runaway slaves. As discussed above, the maroons killed domestic animals, mostly cows, which improved their diet. Pigs were certainly targeted, but their noisy agony would have discouraged many nocturnal visitors. The frequency of the butcheries operated by the maroons is part of the evidence of a then on-going underground market where they sold meat to their fellows or to poor whites in exchange for commodities such as whiskey. Chronicles posted in the local newspaper often lamented the problem as shown in the following lines:

> The number of maroon Negroes is considerable on all the (German) Coast. These gentlemen are so sure not to be threatened they build cabins in the woods, very close to the habitations where they live in quietude. Three Negroes have been arrested in the rear of the habitation of Mr. Rousselle. Milk cows and theirs calves left out at night become prey to the butcheries of the Negroes…[11]

In February 1855, the inhabitants organized another hunting party against the runaway slaves in this same area. Jim, "the captain of the band" and a slave of Adelard Fortier, was among the captured maroons after he was wounded in the thigh. He declared that there were many camps further away. Groceries stolen at night were taken to his camp by Toby, a slave of Theodule Rousselle, and three other slaves. Among many other things, whiskey was found there. Another conclusion was that "all the animals that disappear […] serve to maintain the butcher shop of these Congo gentlemen." Before being restored to his master in St. Charles Parish, "Captain Jim assured [the maroon hunters] that he found our hams excellent and that our barrels of cod fish were exquisite."[12]

Planters generally resented the relations between slaves and economically disadvantaged whites. In October 1854, the Court of the Third Judicial District,

---

10 SC-52-1808, "Procès du Nègre Charles appartenant à Alexandre Chopin. Jugement, exécution et estimation dudit nègre". Procès verbal N°52, 6 October 1808.
11 *Le Meschacébé*, 3 December 1854.
12 *Le Meschacébé*, 25 February 1855.

seated at St. Charles Parish, condemned one Charles d'Arensburg for buying merchandise from a slave and selling him whiskey. The defendant chose to pay a $250 fine instead of the sentence of three months in jail.[13] During the summer of 1858, *Le Meschacébé* reported that a Committee of Vigilance was formed in St. James Parish, "in the goal of purging the coast of all whites, accused and convicted of partaking in the infamous traffic with the negroes." It further reported that the members of the Committee have transported themselves to the homes of two white men, Louis Rome and Adolphe Guillaume, in order to expel them from the parish. The former was found sleeping in his bed, and the latter was found cutting down trees in the woods. The two men were completely undressed by the Committee and subjected to outrageous torture. Then the Committee made them embark in a skiff, warning them if they ever set foot in the parish again they would be hanged.[14]

There were many Roussel plantations in the area and most of them very close to the Haydel and Becnel (Evergreen) plantations. They adjoined each other by their rear swampy lowlands toward Lake des Allemands. When Marie Azélie Haydel died in November 1860, two maroon slaves were listed in the inventory of her estate. Alphonse Becnel found one of them seven months after the beginning of the Civil War, in a cabin on the Becnel Plantation. After the runaway slave was summoned in vain to surrender himself, Alphonse Becnel shot at him twice with a rifle and four times from a revolver but was unable to stop him. One Mr. Allen, son-in-law of Dr. Wiendahl, a nearby planter, found himself in the way of the fugitive. He tried to seize him, but, as he was not armed with more than a stick, the maroon threw himself on him, hit him on the arm with a cane knife, and took flight back into the woods.[15]

Uprising: the 1811 slave revolt

By the time of the Louisiana Purchase, the booming sugar industry encouraged marronnage and required renewed imports of slaves. Governor Claiborne was deeply concerned by the potential factor of slave revolts, and he expressed his feelings in a letter to President James Madison: "At present I am well assured, there is nothing to fear either from the Mulatto or Negro population: but at some future period, this quarter of the Union must (I fear) experience in some degree the Misfortunes of St. Domingo [Haiti], and that period will be hastened if the people

---

13 *Le Meschacébé*, 13 October 1854.
14 *Le Meschacébé*, 4 August 1858.
15 *Le Meschacébé*, 23 November 1861.

should be indulged by Congress with a continuance of the African trade."[16] This prediction was confirmed seven years later with the outbreak of the biggest slave revolt in the southern United States.

On January 8, 1811, slaves from St. Charles and St. John the Baptist parishes rose up and walked downriver toward New Orleans. Armed with rifles, sabers, fire-hardened oak sticks, or simply with their tools, they killed two white men and caused considerable damage to the plantations they crossed. They were stopped only the next day after a rough battle against the local militia. The insurrection started on the property of Manuel Andry, then the head of the local militia of St. Charles Parish. His own son was killed, and he was wounded. After the turmoil, seven of his slaves were missing: Gilbert, Janvier, Valentin, Moreau, Alsindor, Jacques Bambara, and Jupiter. The latter, a Congo slave, was finally captured with a rifle and a pack of clothes in his hands, which he claimed to have found on a slave who died in the action. One of the questions directed to him at his trial was about the intention of the insurgents when they left the Andry plantation. His answer was quite clear: "ils allaient en ville pour détruire tous les Blancs" (they were going to the city [New Orleans] to destroy the lives of all the white people).[17]

The 1811 revolt had several leaders from various ethnic origins. At least six slaves played a major role in the insurrection:

- Charles Deslondes, a Creole slave owned by Widow Deslondes.
- Dagobert, a thirty-five year old Creole slave owned by Sieur Delhomme. He was described as a Negro of choice, overseer, *indigotier* (indigo maker), cart man, and ploughman.
- Amar, forty-five years old, a slave of Widow Charbonnet, was a "hoe and ax Negro" (nègre de pioche et de hâche), who was also qualified for work in a sugar mill. His name indicates a Wolof or Moor origin.
- Komlan, also called Komina or misspelled Qualmley in the official documents, was a slave owned by James Brown. He was qualified for work in a sugar mill. Komina and Komlan are variants of Kwabena, an Akan name for a male born on Tuesday.
- Cook, a twenty-year old African slave also owned by James Brown, was also qualified for the work in a sugar mill. His name, sometimes transcribed as Coock, also indicates Ewe or Akan origin: Kwoku/kweku/kwaku is a name for a child born on Wednesday.
- Lindor, twenty-eight years old, a slave of Kenner and Henderson, was a field hand, a cart man, and qualified to work in a sugar mill.

16 Governor William C.C. Claiborne to James Madison, New Orleans 12 July 1804; in Elizabeth Donnan, ed. *Documents Illustrative of the History of the Slave Trade to America*, vol. IV, *The Border Colonies and The Southern Colonies*, p.663.
17 SC-17-1811, "Interrogatoire et jugement rendu contre le nègre Jupiter appartenant à Manuel Andry." Procès verbal N°17, 20 February 1811.

Two other slaves named Lindor (Gros Lindor and Petit Lindor), who belonged to Sieur Destréhan, were also judged and executed. This prominent planter also lost one slave in the battle, and another one was held in jail in New Orleans.[18] Joseph l'Espagnol, probably a slave from Cuba, was also among the twenty insurgents held in jail in New Orleans. Cupidon, a slave of the Labranche brothers, denounced the mulatto Charles Deslondes during his trial as being the main leader ("premier chef des brigands") of the insurrection. He also denounced Dagobert and Cook as "chefs de brigands." Cook was also accused of giving a stroke of an ax to François Trépagnier who had already died, an act he strongly denied during his hearing. James Brown, his master, denounced Cook before the court as being a "mauvais nègre" (bad Negro). Brown also denounced Komina with the same phrase. Komina eventually participated in a meeting at Manual Andry's plantation, the day before the insurrection, along with Charles Deslondes. Amar was also a "chef de brigands" according to all the insurgents present at the trial. He could not defend himself because an injury to the throat had deprived him of his voice. According to Dagobert, Amar was a leader and encouraged the others. Lindor of Kenner and Henderson served as a drummer to the insurgents, and Joseph l'Espagnol was believed to have assembled his friends on the levee, in front of the habitation of Charles Paquet, and served them tafia liquor.[19]

The trial of the "brigands" took place on the plantation of Jean Noël Destrehan, January 13-15. The jury was composed of five landowners and presided over by Judge Pierre Bauchet St. Martin. This bench was shaped in accordance with the 1806 Black Code, which mandated that the tribunal in charge of capital punishments had to be composed of the parish judge or two justices of peace, assisted by three to five landowners. The judgments were rendered without appeal. Several death sentences were pronounced. The procès verbal of the judgment specified that the convicts would immediately be delivered to be shot to death, each before the habitation to which he belonged; that the death penalty would be applied to them without torture, but the heads of the executed would be cut and planted on poles at the place where each convict would have undergone the right punishment due to his crimes, in order to frighten all malefactors who would attempt any such rebellion in the future.[20]

The statistics of the insurrection reveal a real bloodshed: twenty-five slaves were killed in the action, twenty were reported missing, forty-five were condemned to death and were executed, and twenty-two slaves, including twenty in New Orleans,

---

18 *Louisiana Slave Database*, Doc. # 49211 [http://www.ibiblio.org/laslave/revolt/individ. php?sid=49211 (accessed 28 September 2010)].
19 SC-2-1811, "condamnation des Brigands pris dans la dernière insurrection." Procès verbal N°2, 15 January 1811.
20 Ibid.

were still awaiting their judgment.[21]   On January 16, 1811, a temporary end of arrests was ordered at the request of the planters. A procés verbal of St. Charles Parish courthouse evoked "the opinion of all respectable inhabitants" and specified that the decision was dictated by "difficult and imperious circumstances."[22] Indeed the local economy had already lost many highly qualified young workers. The state of losses presented two months later reveals that most of the slaves who had been killed were aged between twenty and thirty years, many among them described as skilled sucriers.[23] In St. John the Baptist Parish, a separate tribunal led by Judge Achille Trouard sentenced seven slaves to death, including Charles Deslondes, and a slave named Jacques owned by Pierre Becnel, the immediate neighbor of Jean Jacques Haydel Sr.[24] This may indicate the possible involvement of some of the slaves on Habitation Haydel since the two plantations were owned by people with very close family ties and their slaves interacted widely and provided support to their maroons.

The history of the 1811 revolt is yet to be fully uncovered. The most challenging fact is the scarcity of original documents and their availability. The parish of St. Charles has conserved most of the original documents related to the event. This is not the case for St. John and Orleans parishes. The few authors who wrote significant pages on the uprising make a link with external factors, the most important being the slave uprising in Saint-Domingue and the birth of free Haiti.[25] For Albert Thrasher, Charles Deslondes was a slave from St. Domingue. But it is clear that the leader of the uprising was a Creole slave born in Louisiana. For Fernin F. Eaton, if one considers the international environment, notably the risk of British subversion, Spanish retaliation for having lost West Florida, and the ongoing intrigues of French sympathizers, the histories of the events of January 1811 would have us believe that Charles Deslondes decided that this was the opportune time to lead a spontaneous uprising of slaves with the goal of capturing enough of New Orleans to secure ships with which to navigate to a free country. [26]According to Gwendolyn Hall, Joseph l'Espagnol was probably a Spanish or Cuban agent trying to protect Spain's interest in lower Louisiana and West Florida after the 1810

21 SC-(?)-1811, "Etat des Ateliers de MM. les habitants constatant le nombre des esclaves tués, arrêtés et absents depuis l'insurrection." Habitation Destréhan, 18 January 1811.
22 SC-(?)-1811. Procès verbal N°(?), 16 January 1811.
23 SC-21-1811, "Déclaration des pertes faites en nègres et maisons par divers habitants dans l'insurrection du 9 janvier et estimation des dites pertes." Procès verbal N°21, 7 March 1811.
24 Albert Thrasher, *On to New Orleans, Louisiana's Heroic 1811 Slave Revolt*, 2nd edition (Author's publication, 1996), p.65.
25 Thrasher, Albert. *On to New Orleans: Louisiana's Heroic 1811 Slave Revolt*. 2d ed.
Rasmussen 2011. *American uprising. The untold story of America's largest slave revolt*. New York: HarperCollins Publishers, p.40-49.
26 Fernin F. Eaton. The 1811 German Coast Slave Uprising-Fact, Fiction and Folklore. Online article [https://www.academia.edu/1245448/The_1811_German_Coast_Slave_Uprising--Fact_Fiction_and_Folklore (accessed April 30, 2014)].

revolt gave the Louisiana Florida parishes over to the United States.[27] Although external factors can't be disregarded, the main factor of the 1811 uprising cannot be separated from the harsh conditions imposed on the slaves with the new sugar industry as described by Richard Follett. Instead of monitoring the entrance of the Mississippi River, Governor Claiborne would have done a better job by paying attention to the worsening working conditions in the cane fields and the sugar mills. Although the biggest slave revolt in the United States, the 1811 uprising was very limited in its scope. The prompt and merciless massacre which followed it has a link with what Rafael Lucas and other historians call the *Haitian syndrome* or the *Haitian peril*, both concepts designating the psychosis generated by the successful slave uprising which knocked down the Colonial system in Saint-Domingue after a long phase of marronage.[28] Beyond the rewriting of the history of the 1811 slave revolt, historians must interrogate the collective amnesia which shadowed such an important event. On the other hand, since one of the most celebrated persons in Louisiana today is Jean Lafitte, a sort of white maroon, we also need to understand why a once-popular figure like St. Malo totally vanished from the collective memory.

The persistence of violence

The antebellum Louisiana plantation society, including the German Coast, was a brutal one. Life was cheap, and violence affected both white and black people, men and women. From 1802 to the 1860s, the Clerk of Court Records of St. John the Baptist Parish contain an amazing number of cases of battery and assault, many with intent to kill, some resulting in murder. Violence was also echoed by the local newspapers. Even children were not spared. On May 20, 1854, a young slave, only 15 years old, was playing with a white child when a quarrel came up between them. To bring it to an end, the white boy took a gun and shot his playmate to death.[29]

The levees were places of socializing for residents of the riversides. They were nicknamed "chemins d'amour" since much courting was conducted there.[30] These "love walkways" also proved to be deadly because of the many duels and murders that occurred there. In his 1858 annual report to the Legislature, Attorney General M.E. Warren Moise emphasized the prodigious development of crime in the state with 44 homicides and 25 suicides committed the previous year. Since this was a time of crisis with the approaching Civil War, an scapegoat had to be found. In

---

27 Personal communication, Summer 2007.

28 Lucas, Rafael, 2002, "Marronnage et marronnages," in *Cahiers d'histoire. Revue d'histoire critique*, 89: Les enjeux de la mémoire. Accessed 5 September 2013. URL: http://chrhc.revues.org/1527.

29 *Le Meschacébé*, 21 May 1854.

30 Edwards and du Bellay de Verton, *A Creole Lexicon, Architecture, Landscape, People* (Baton Rouge: Louisiana State University Press, 2004), p.124.

order to stop crime, one of the recommendations of this official to the Legislature was the prohibition of the establishment of free blacks in the state.[31]

Some of the many criminal cases brought before the Court in St. John the Baptist Parish were related to violence inflicted on slaves by their masters or overseers. In the 1850s, the marking of slaves, so that they might be easily described and detected when they escaped, was still performed by some slave owners. On August 16, 1851, the Fourth Judicial District Court of St. John the Baptist Parish sentenced Etienne Daunoy to pay a fine consisting of three hundred and one dollars and the costs of prosecution for cruelly beating and mutilating his female slave named Aspasie. The defendant admitted the crime and pleaded guilty of "cropping" the ears of his slave and branding her on the back with his initials: *E. D.*[32] Etienne Daunoy lived in St. John the Baptist Parish where he owned a plantation priced at $50,000 in the 1850 Census files. He was listed with his wife, Rosa Nora Daunoy, and seven children, including Frederick Daunoy and Emile Daunoy. At the time of his father's trial, Frederick was facing charges for "willfully, maliciously and feloniously shooting at one Henry Lèche with a pistol, with intent to kill and murder him."[33] Emile was seventeen at the time of the trial.[34] Six years later, Emile was an overseer on the Marmillion's plantation when he was allegedly killed by a slave.

Nelson, a slave of Jacques Clement, apparently often left his master's plantation to court a female slave named Louisa, owned by Charles Parent, the overseer of the nearby plantation of Pierre Landreaux. One day, "the husband of Louisa" (as Nelson was called by one of Landreaux's slaves before the Court) was severely whipped by Charles Parent, who did not want Nelson around his slave. This caused Ben, one of Landreaux's slaves, to kill Charles Parent with a gun. When asked why he killed the overseer, the answer was: "he caused the slaves to work too hard and whipped them too much." According to a female slave brought before the Court as a witness, the night following the whipping, Nelson went into Ben's cabin and awakened him. There started this dialogue:

> Nelson: "I have been whipped for nothing and if you will join me I will procure a gun and you will shoot Mr. Charles Parent."
> Ben: "Bring me the gun and I will kill him."

Soon thereafter, Nelson went back to Landreaux's plantation, handed Ben a

---

31 *Le Meschacébé*, 13 February 1858.

32 The State of Louisiana vs. Etienne Daunoy [SJB-CCR, Loc. 17106, Box # 2 (1815-1852)].

33 The State of Louisiana vs. Frederick Daunoy [SJB-CCR, Loc. 17106, Box # 2 (1815-1852)].

34 The 1850 United States Federal Census, the Seventh Census of the United States, St. John the Baptist Parish, Louisiana, Page 278, Household 495, 16 August 1850. This property is on the 1858 Persac's map, on the Bonnet Carré bend, on the right bank of the River under the name E. Daunois.

single-barreled gun and told him: "mind you don't miss him." "I will not miss him," Ben responded. The following night, a little after dusk, the firing of a gun was heard from the barn where Charles Parent was feeding a mare. The day following the murder, the same witness was on her way to the river to get a bucket of water, when she saw the two fellows engaged in a discussion near the gate:

> Ben: "Old fellow is dead neat, don't care to look for him again, I got his life."
> Nelson: "Mr. Charles Parent whipped me for nothing, but now he is gone to hell and he will whip me no more."[35]

The sentence of this trial held in May 1841 is missing from the file, but it is very likely the two slaves were condemned to death respectively for murder and complicity of murder. There were many other similar cases of slaves perpetrating violence against their drivers and masters. In 1856, Peter Smith, a slave of Valsin Marmillion, intended to kill his master and the two drivers of the plantation. He finally killed one of the overseers, wounded two other slaves, and was condemned to be hanged outside the Courthouse.[36] That same year, Eugene, another slave attached to the same plantation was the suspect in the "mysterious assassination" of Emile Daunoy. Since the case was examined by many juries who could not reach an agreement, the Legislature authorized its transfer to the Court of the First District of New Orleans. Finally, with the death of the principal witness, it was decided that the affair would be abandoned, and Eugene was restored to his master after being held in prison for two years.[37] During the following winter, six Mulatto slaves, all female but one, were also arrested in a mysterious affair of poisoning. They belonged to Martian Belfort Haydel, and the arrest was done at the request of a member of this planter's family. Four of the women were arrested in New Orleans and brought to the St. John the Baptist Parish prison. According to the source of this information, the man included in the accusation "is one of those vulgarly called medicine men."[38]

Towards the end of the Civil War, *The Harper's Weekly*, sometimes known for its moderate editorial position on the issue of slavery, published a document describing a group of emancipated slaves from New Orleans, who had been set free by General Butler. The name of one slave's master was misspelled, but there is no doubt it referred to Valsin B. Marmillion, the owner of the plantation known later as the San Francisco Plantation:

> Wilson Chinn is about 60 years old; he was "raised" by Isaac Howard of

---

35 SJB-CCR, Loc. 17106, Box # 2 (1815-1852), F 16.

36 *Le Meschacébé*, 13 January 1856.

37 *Le Meschacébé*, 20 March and 7 May 1858.

38 *Le Meschacébé*, 8 January 1859.

Woodford County, Kentucky. When 21 years old he was taken down the river and sold to Volsey B. Marmillion, a sugar planter about 45 miles above New Orleans. This man was accustomed to brand his Negroes, and Wilson has on his forehead the letters "V. B. M." Of the 210 slaves on this plantation 105 left at one time and came into the Union camp. Thirty of them had been branded like cattle with a hot iron, four of them on the forehead, and the others on the breast or arm.[39]

Valsin Marmillion did not own 210 slaves at this particular time. In 1860, he was the second largest slaveholder in St. John the Baptist Parish, but his slave force consisted only of 142 slaves.[40] The 1856 inventory of the Marmillion plantation, the last predating the Civil War, listed only 87 slaves, men, women, and children. Two slaves were described as "borgnes" (one-eyed), one named Mingo (30 years old), and the other one Smith (55 years old). Unlike Smith, Mingo had not yet lost his eye by the time of the 1843 inventory of the plantation.[41] This may be interpreted as proof of violence exerted on the slaves or, to the least, as the result of accidents related to hazardous working conditions. However, the branding of slaves on this plantation was not mere fiction although some of the stories about extreme cruelties need careful consideration. According to the testimony of one Mrs. Webb, a former slave, Valsin Marmillion was the cruelest master in St. John the Baptist Parish during slavery time. One of his cruelties was to have a disobedient slave stand in a box, in which nails were placed in such a manner that he was unable to move. He was powerless even to chase the flies or sometimes, ants crawling on some parts of his body. Mrs. Webb also spoke of a young slave who had been raised with the children of his master and thus had been accustomed to all the good things on the plantation. At the death of his master, the slave boy was put on the auction block where Mr. Marmillion bought him, and the next day, the new master gave the order to put the young man to the plow. But the boy refused to do such hard work. Mr. Marmillion, hearing of this, went to the slave and told him, "I give you until tomorrow. If by then you still refuse, you will dig your grave." The next day the boy had not yielded. He was made to dig an immense hole in which they made him stand, and, bandaging his eyes, he was shot, falling into the

---

39 From *Harper's Weekly*, Saturday 30 January 1864.

40 The 1860 United States Federal Census, the Eighth Census of the United States, St. John the Baptist Parish, Louisiana, p.79B. This census is the last to list slaves. The largest slaveholders were in the upper parishes. The first of them was John Burnside of St. James Parish (940 slaves). See Joseph K. Menn, *The large slave holders of Louisiana-1860*.

41 Inventaire communauté E.B. Marmillion & Jeanne Antoinette Bozonier Marmillion, 1 May 1843 [SJB-97-1843]. Succession Edmond B. Marmillon, 14 May 1856 [SJB-165-1856]. San Francisco Plantation Museum: [http://www.sanfranciscoplantation.org/history.asp]. Accessed 3 October 2011.

hole he had dug. [42]

If Marmillion did commit all the cruelties attributed to him, his behavior may be explained by the devastating events that plagued his life. Antoine Valsin Bozonier Marmillion, to call him by his full name, was born in 1828 in St. John the Baptist Parish. He never envisioned his future as a Louisiana sugar planter. But, when his father passed away in 1856, he returned from Europe and was forced to take over the plantation. He had been educated at prominent Catholic universities on the East Coast and had worked as an accountant in New Orleans and Paris for many years. He had only been 15 when his mother, Jeanne Antoinette Bozonier Marmillion, died from tuberculosis, a disease which eventually claimed the lives of some of his siblings as well. The loss of his loved ones and his own developing illness continuously made him want to leave his home. As early as 1859, Valsin and his younger brother Charles attempted to sell the estate but were halted by a legal conflict with Victorine Zoé Luminais, the widow of their deceased brother Pierre Edmond Bozonier Marmillion (1826-1852). When the argument was settled in 1861, it was too late. War and reconstruction prevented any possibility of a sale for the following fifteen years. Valsin was married to Louise von Seybold of Munich, and his dream of moving to Southern Germany remained unfulfilled. He died of tuberculosis in 1871.[43] His father, Michel Edmond Bozonier Marmillon (1803-1856), was the son of Pierre Bozonier Marmillon and Françoise Haydel. On his mother's side, he was the grandson of Jean Christophe Haydel and the great grandson of Ambroise Haydel.

African Foodways and Resistance

In plantation societies throughout the Western Hemisphere, slaves responded to bad treatment by running away and sometimes by returning violence against their masters and overseers. But retaliation and marronnage were not the only means by which the enslaved opposed the violent system of slavery. Passive resistance, meaning any kind of resistance that does not involve violence, was also conducted through songs (secular and sacred), dance, and storytelling. Slaves sang while performing collective duties and individual tasks, and the very field of their labor was the bedrock of blues, jazz, and rock & roll. They also used their foodways to lessen the burden of slavery and to reconnect themselves with their lost homes.

Pierre Landreaux was a businessman of French origin, and one of the most

---

42 Interview by Harriette Michinard on 17 August 1940; in Clayton, *Mother Wit. The Ex-Slave Narratives of the Louisiana Writers' Project*, p.208.

43 Marmillion (minors Pierre Edmond Bozonier, Antoine Valsin Bozonier & Michel Charles Bozonier). Assemblée de famille…; 18 May 1843 [SJB-121-1843]. The San Francisco Plantation Museum: [http://www.sanfranciscoplantation.org/history.asp]. Accessed 3 October 2011. The Family Tree Maker Online [http://familytreemaker.genealogy.com]. Accessed 8 October 2011.

successful planters in Louisiana before the Civil War. He owned the Trinity Plantation in St. Charles Parish, and his approach to the management of slaves was unique, according to the testimony of Elizabeth Ross Hite. When the interviewers of the Louisiana Writers' Project approached this lady in the early 1940s, she remembered that entertaining their master and his guests was part of their duties. "Dey would make music wid pans, beat on pots wid sticks, and sing." Whenever there was a contest, a man named Jolly, "a tall fellow, skinny, wid long legs and a peanut-lookin' head," would win all of them. The old master, who would holler when Jolly started "twirling his legs and stickin' out his back," took him around the other plantations to dance against the slaves of his friends. But, in one instance, success came along with trouble when Jolly was caught in the bed of his defeated competitor's wife. On the Landreaux plantation, the real "good time" occurred in the quarters or in the sugarhouse, where "dey played guitar, and danced 'fore de light went out" to the rhythm of a drum made of a "skin over a barrel," doing "de buck dance and de shimmy." Often slaves would sneak out of the cabins and go dance, way out in the fields, where the master could not hear them, and come back to the quarters just before daylight.[44]

It was also out in the fields that the Black Church was born. Elizabeth Ross Hite further recalled their master bringing a priest from France, but they preferred the preaching of Old Man Mingo in the fields without regard to the risks involved:

> My master brought a colored man, John Adams, from France to teach us how to pray, read, and write […]. But we had our own church in de brickyard way out on de field. We hid behind de bricks and had church every night. We was only supposed to have church on Sunday, but we wanted to pray all of de time. Old Man Mingo preached and dere was Bible lessons […]. Nothing could stop us from prayin' to Gawd. We didn't use light, we prayed in de dark, children and all. Sometimes we would put grease in a can and burn it. De preacher had to sit over de can to read his Bible. One time de preacher caught on fire. Dere was some screaming. One of the drivers caught us, and de master whipped all dem dat was late for work de next day.[45]

In this study, I have chosen to focus on foodways and storytelling, two passive resistance tools attached to the nightly activities of the slaves. Dinner was usually cooked after work at night within each individual compound, lunch being a collective meal in the fields, except on Sundays. For practical and mystical reasons, as demonstrated further in this chapter, storytelling was performed after dinner. For French historian Michel Faucheux, "il y a toujours une dimension symbolique

---

44 Clayton, *Mother Wit. The Ex-Slave Narratives of the Louisiana Writers' Project*, p.105-106.
45 Ibid., p.102.

du repas contenu dans le lien fait entre ce qu'on mange et l'imaginaire auquel il renvoie" (there is always a symbolic dimension to food nested in the link made between what one eats and the imaginary it reflects).[46] A rather famous French saying is "dis-moi ce que tu manges, je te dirai qui tu es" (tell me what you eat, I will tell you who you are). Thus, food is an important part of the identity of a community. For people living in exile, what is better than the smell of familiar food to bring about fond memories of home? For Carney and Rosomoff, "food is vested with symbolic ties to homelands left or lost. The emphasis on meaningful foods and familiar forms of preparation enriches the memory dishes with which migrants connect past and present."[47] In other words, "food gives material expression to the way exiles commemorate the past and shape new identities amid alien cultures, diets, and languages."[48]

The recreation of Africa was partly done through the raising of specific food crops and the continuation and transformation of recipes such as okra gumbo, jambalaya, and couscous. In his *Histoire de la Louisiane*, Le Page du Pratz strongly encouraged masters to provide their slaves with land toward the swamp on which they would work on Sundays:

> It is your interest to give them (the slaves) a plot of new land at the end of yours, & to engage them to cultivate it in order to give them good spirit with the product that you buy from them fairly; it is better to give them such an occupation on Sunday if they are not Christians...[49]

Since the French had a very long experience of master/slave relationships in Northern Senegambia, the practice was probably inspired by this region of West Africa where slaves owned land on which they worked on Thursdays and the produce of which belonged entirely to them.[50] This policy was not inscribed in the 1724 Louisiana slave code, but it remained unchanged through the Spanish period and into the Civil War. The 1825 Civil Code eventually allowed slaves to own property with the consent of their owners. This created at the periphery of the masters' premises a domain of liberty where African material culture survived,

---

46 Interview by Ludovic Viévard for the Center of Prospectives Ressources of Greater Lyon (September 2004): http://www.millenaire3.com/michel-faucheux----dis-moi-ce-que-tu-manges--je-te.122+M596fa33280c.0.html (accessed 14 September 2010).

47 Carney J.A. and Rosomoff R.N. 2009. *In the shadow of slavery. Africa's botanical legacy in the Atlantic world*. Berkeley, Los Angeles, and London: University of California Press, p.185.

48 Howard P.L. 2003, "Women and the plant world: An exploration," in Patricia L. Howard, ed., *Women and Plants: Gender Relations in Biodiversity Management and Conservation* (London: Zed, 2003), p.11; quoted in Carney J.A. and Rosomoff R.N. 2009, p.185.

49 Le Page du Pratz, *Histoire de la Louisiane* (Paris: De Bure, 1758), pp.351-352.

50 Diop, Abdoulaye Bara. 1981. La Société Wolof, Tradition et Changement: Les systèmes d'inégalité et de domination. Paris: Karthala.

especially culinary art. Maroon slaves extended this space to the swamps where they cultivated food crops. The produce of the small plots supplemented the diet of the slaves, and surplus was sold to the master or taken to the local market with the permission of the master. They planted primarily corn and rice, the latter requiring particular skills in its processing from the paddies to the pot. Elizabeth Ross Hite remembered well her kin eating self-grown crops and her mother's patch where corn was king:

> My mother planted corn, but de master bought it from her. He paid fifty cents per barrel for corn […]. Sure, we ate good food […]. Everything was made on de plantation by plantation people […]. We had a garden right in front of our quarter. We planted everything in it. Had watermelon, mushmelon, and a flower garden.[51]

Louisiana historian Charles Gayarré (1805-1895) spent his childhood on the sugar plantation of his grandfather, Etienne de Boré, who is credited for being the first producer of granulated sugar at the industrial level in Louisiana. In a rather famous article, he evoked with deep nostalgia the skills of the African cooks (apron-girt Sambos), especially the way they handled rice and seasonings:

> Who knows how to roast? Who knows how to season just à point? (...) How many delicious dishes have vanished forever of which the best cooks of France have never dreamed! To invent them it had required the constantly improving genius of several generations of apron-girt sambos (…). Who but Sambo knew how to bake rice in an iron pot? I say iron, because it must be nothing else, and the rice must come out solid, retaining the exact shape of the pot, with a golden crust round its top and sides. You think this easy, presumptuous mortal. Well, try it, and let us see if your farinaceous production will have its required shape and color, and its precise proportions of salt and lard.[52]

In Louisiana, slaves also produced vegetables, which followed them from Africa. Among these were black-eyed peas (*Vigna unguiculata*), called *ñébé* by the Wolof and Fulbe of Senegal. The French called them *fèves des marais* (marsh beans), and many inventories of farms in colonial Louisiana mention *fèves* among the food crops. For their high level of protein and for being easy to cook, black-eyed peas were the most convenient and maybe the richest food used to feed slaves during the crossing of the

---

51 Elizabeth Ross Hite, in Ronnie W. Clayton, *Mother Wit: The Ex-Slave Narratives of the Louisiana Writers' Project* (New York: Peter Lang Publishing, Inc., 1990), p.100.
52 Charles Gayarré. "A Louisiana Sugar Plantation of the Old Regime," *Harper's Magazine*, 74, 442 (1887), pp.620-621.

Atlantic Ocean. There is also a deep cultural significance attached to this food crop in Senegambia, where it often serves as an icebreaker, due in part to its implications as a "fart food." Cousins or people of different origins exchange jokes about *ñébé*, accusing each other of liking this flatulence-inducing food too much.

Watermelons (*Citrullus vulgaris*) are also extensively cultivated from West Africa to Egypt since the second millennium B.C. This plant was introduced into Louisiana at the earliest time of French colonization. But okra (*Abelmoschus esculentus*) is the African plant that became a real symbol in Louisiana and in all the southern United States. At first, okra was a food used exclusively by African slaves, but white masters discovered that they loved it, too. After a second trip to Louisiana at the end of the eighteenth century, Baudry des Lozières wrote about "gombeau" (okra), emphasizing its value as a nutraceutical plant:

> There is no emollient substances used in the affections of the chest in the colonies that are more multiple than those of okra... All parts of okra enter in stews of the indigenous of the colonies, and Europeans as well as Creoles find in the fruit of this small bush, an excellent food.[53]

For Catherine Kolb, the success of okra is bound to its multiple properties. The oleaginous seeds are rich in proteins. The pod is a source for vitamins A and C. The stalk can be used to manufacture ropes. The viscous texture of the plant provides good gastric protection. The grilled seeds were used as a surrogate for coffee when blockades denied the Confederates access to coffee beans.[54] The word "okra" is of West African origin: "okuru" in the Igbo language of Nigeria, "ṇkrūmā" or "ṇkrakra" in some Akan languages spoken along the Gulf of Guinea, from the Ivory Coast to the Volta River. Among the Fon of the Bight of Benin, okra is called *févi*.[55] In various Bantu languages of Central Africa, okra is called *kingombo* or simply *ngombo*, and this is the word that made its way into the French language (*gombeau* or *gombo*). In Louisiana, *ngombo* became *gumbo*, a style of cooking more than a dish, whose components are traceable to specific regions of Africa. Elizabeth Brandon identified three kinds of gumbo in the description of the Acadians of Vermilion Parish in the 1950s: *gumbo févi*, *filé gumbo*, and *gumbo z'hèbes*.[56]

Gumbo févi or okra gumbo is most common. It shows a direct linguistic connection with the Bight of Benin and is quite reminiscent of cooking styles one can still find

---

53 Baudry des Lozières, *Second Voyage à la Louisiane, 1794 à 1798* (Paris: Chez Charles, 1934), p.308.
54 Carolyn Kolb, "Beyond Gumbo: The Secret Life of Okra," *Reckon: The Magazine of Southern Culture 1*, Première Issue (N° 1-2) (1995), p.150.
55 "Fon is Fun," a website dedicated to *Fon* or *Fongbe*, the predominant language of Southern Benin. Produced and edited by Chris Starace, a former Peace Corps volunteer: online at www.fon-is-fun.org.
56 Elizabeth Brandon, "Les mœurs de la paroisse Vermilion en Louisiane," in *Le Bayou*, N° 64 (1955).

in the westernmost countries of West Africa such as Mali, Senegal, the Gambia, Sierra Leone, Guinea, and Guinea Bissau. But this recipe is more linked to Mande foodways. Among the Bambara and the Mandingo, true eating means eating *kanja* (okra) smothered with *tiga dege* (peanut butter), and served over rice or *tò* (paste made with millet or corn meal). A famous Wolof joke about the Bambara is about them eating too much okra and peanut butter sauce (*maafé*) and being so prompt to fart (*bëgg maafé gaawa doxot*). Interestingly enough, there is no other word for okra in Senegambian languages except the word from the Mande that literally means "easy on the throat" [*kan* (throat); *ja* (good)]. Other okra-related dishes are *soupe kanja* (okra and palm oil) and *thiou kanja* (okra and tomato sauce) but are mostly limited to the coastal line running from Saint-Louis, Senegal to Casamance and Guinea Bissau.[57]

Filé gumbo is made with *filé*, a powder made from the leaves of the sassafras tree and used for its flavor and as a thickener. Although Native Americans pounded sassafras leaves into a powder and added them to soups and stews, the people of Mali, more precisely the Songhai of the Niger River, use a similar product in their stews called "fako hoy."[58]

Gumbo z'hèbes, a French Creole word which stands for *gombo aux herbes* or "greens gumbo," is made with varieties of greens such as mustard greens, collard greens, turnip greens, red cabbage, and eventually sliced okra. A signature ingredient of the foodways of Africa and the diaspora is greens. In West Africa alone, more than one hundred and fifty indigenous species of edible leaves, including more than thirty different cultivated species, were identified by the mid-1950s.[59] In West and Central Africa, the leaves from an even greater variety of plants are used to make various kinds of stews such as *boroxe* (manioc leaves), *saka-saka* (sweet potato leaves), *ndole* (the bitter leaf / *Vernonia amygdalina*), *haako ñebbe* (black-eyed-pea leaves), the leaves of the "never-die tree" (*Moringa oleifera*), and many others. Today these dishes are designated in Francophone West and Central Africa under the generic name of *sauce feuilles* (greens sauce).

In Louisiana, the preparation of gumbo always begins with the making of *roux*, a mixture of oil and flour that provides color and acts as a thickener. The oil and flour are mixed together in a heavy pot and cooked over a low flame with constant stirring until the color of the mixture turns dark brown. In Senegambia, peanut

---

57 *Soupe kanja* is very similar to *Awara soup*, a signature dish for Easter among the Black communities of French Guiana. A popular belief is whoever eats *Awara soup* while there will always travel back to this country.

58 Personnal communication with Hassimi Oumarou Maiga, professor of History, and Paramount Chief of the Songhai community. Gao (Mali), January 2000, over the festivities of the coronation of his predecessor.

59 F.R. Irvine, "The edible cultivated and semi-cultivated leaves of West Africa," *Qualitas Plantarum et Materiae Vegetabiles*, N°2 (1956): 35-42; quoted in Carney J.A. and Rosomoff R.N. 2009, p.177.

butter, tomato, and palm oil are used as thickeners or for food coloring. In both countries, the dishes are served with rice instead of *fufu* (pounded tubers), which is more common along the Gulf of Guinea beyond Sierra Leone.[60] In Louisiana, gumbo has evolved into a soup-like dish in which white rice is drowned instead of being a bed for the sauce. Smothered okra, a recipe very typical of southwest Louisiana and very similar to the Haitian *calalou*, is closer to what one stills finds in West Africa. Jambalaya is another rice-based dish prepared in a very similar way to the Wolof cooking style, which developed on the coast of Senegal and is known as Jollof rice but includes a variety of dishes such as *cheebu jën* (fried rice and fish), *cheebu yapp* (fried rice and meat), *cheebu ñébé* (fried rice and black-eyed peas), and *daxin* (rice cooked in peanut butter sauce). Just like in jambalaya, each of these dishes may be improved with seafood and spices.

It is also noteworthy that grits were deeply rooted in the eating habits of the people of North Senegambia. While South Senegambia is "Riceland," North Senegambia should be called "Gritsland," as is suggested by the map drawn by Chastanet and entitled "Les principaux lieux du 'sanglé' (XVIIe-XIXe siècle)".[61] Men raised the crops, mostly millet (*Pennisetum typhoides*) and different varieties of sorghum (Guinea corn), but women made the grits through an ingenious and rather tiresome process, using mortars, pestles, and sifters. They turned the flour into *couscous* through slight wetting and steam-cooking. Before the introduction of maize and manioc from America and until the early eighteenth century, millet was also the basic food crop in the hinterland of the Bight of Benin. It was supplemented with sorghum, rice, and yams. Now it has been relegated to the status of "sacred food" or "memory dish," exclusively processed with the traditional grindstones, and partly used to feed the *vodun* (deities) and to commemorate the ancestors.[62] Today, sub-Saharan Africans have massively turned to rice mostly imported from Asia. African food crops favored for the making of grits were deeply affected by the colonial system, which imposed the cultivation of commercial crops like peanuts. In Senegal, the French trading companies found an additional source of profit through massive importations of rice from their Indochina colony, which they sold to the farmers who were forced to grow commercial crops destined for the industries of Marseille and Bordeaux. Thus, an entire section of African culture is still under threat since the readiness of

---

60 Carney J.A. and Rosomoff R.N. 2009, p.180.

61 Chastanet M. "Le « sanglé », histoire d'un plat sahélien (Sénégal, Mali, Mauritanie)." In M. Chastanet, F.X. Fauvelle-Aymar & D. Juhe-Beaulaton, 2002, *Cuisine et société en Afrique, histoire, saveurs, savoir-faire*. Paris: Karthala, pp.173-90.

62 Juhe-Beaulaton (Dominique). "Alimentation des hommes, des *vodoun* et des ancêtres, Une histoire de céréales dans le golfe de Guinée." In M. Chastanet, F.X. Fauvelle-Aymar & D. Juhe-Beaulaton, 2002, *Cuisine et société en Afrique, histoire, saveurs, savoir-faire*. Paris: Karthala, pp.53-66. The concept of "memory dish" is from Price (Richard) 1983. *First Time: The Historical Vision of an Afro-American People*. Baltimore: Johns Hopkins University Press, p. 129; quoted in Carney J.A. and Rosomoff R.N. 2009, p.93.

imported rice, moreso than the introduction of gasoline-powered mills, is silencing the mortars and pestles, which, some time ago, awakened villagers like church bells and provided inspirational rhythm to male drummers, including those who laid the roots of the heavy Rub-A-Dub style so characteristic of Jamaican reggae. In Senegal, many elders cloistered in remote villages would not eat any grains other than those processed the traditional way.

In the French colonial literature related to this country, grits are called *sanglé*, *sanglet*, or *senglet*. This word is the corruption of *cenle* or *sanqal*, local terms used by the Fulbe and the Wolof, respectively, for the raw product they cook in countless and variegated manners, like other peoples disseminated on the Sahel and savanna lands, from Saint-Louis to Timbuktu, between the Atlantic and the great bend of the Niger River.[63] Among the Fulbe, *ñiiri bunaa* (grits and ground salt fish) is improved with spices and served with *nebam sirme* (cooked butter) put to melt in the middle of the hot dish. Using their fingers, diners make balls of *ñiiri*, which they swallow after dipping them in the butter. *Ñiiri kosam* (grits and sweetened sour milk), called *lax sow* by the Wolof, is cooked without spices. Grits may also be cooked with salt fish, ground peanuts, the fruit of the tamarind tree, and the acid sorrel leaves (*Hibiscus sabdariffa*) and served to the sick, especially those affected by malaria.[64] Called *gar* by the Wolof, this food may be cooked with a great amount of red pepper and served to people intoxicated by alcohol as was usual around the trading posts where African and European traders met. As reported to French explorer Raffenel, it was believed to be a radical cure for the most severe hangover.[65] It has also become a popular food in Senegalese bars whose owners increase their profits by selling it to their customers thus causing them to absorb more of the "nectar of Bacchus." The most popular names for this recipe are *laro* or *laru* among the Mandingo and the Fulbe, *gar* or *laax bisaap* by the Wolof, and *ngurbaan* among the Sereer of Senegal. For the Sereer, a real treat destined for the family and guests would be *ngurbaan fo ceek* (chicken grits). A particularly interesting description of the making of *sanglé* was done in the mid-19th century by a Franco-Senegalese priest, who lived in Saint-Louis among the Wolof:

> The grain from the pounded millet [...] is cooked in a pot with flat water to the consistency of a mush; then it is served in a calabash along with sour milk, cooked butter, or the cutch of the fruit of the tamarind or baobab tree. Sometime it is sweetened with honey. This meal does not take long

---

63 For an exhaustive list of the French authors, see Chastanet (2002), figure 2 (tableau chronologique des sources), p.175. This article offers a very interesting and well-informed study of this food.

64 The Jamaica sorrel plant (Hibiscus sabdariffa) originated from West Africa where its most popular names are *bisaap* (Wolof) and *Kucha* (Mandinka). The flours are used to making a refreshing cranberry-like drink.

65 Raffenel A. 1856. *Nouveau voyage dans le pays des Nègres*. Paris: Imprimerie et Librairie Centrales des Chemins de Fer, p. 54.

Fig. 5.1. Senegal: women with mortars and pestles.
Source: Senegal National Archives, collection Fortier, No. 244.

Fig. 5.2. Senegalese girls grinding grain for couscous, sifter in hands of little girl.
Source: Senegal National Archives, Anonymous author.

Fig. 5.3. Acadian woman hulling rice with mortar and pestle (pile et pilon). Sifter
on the side of mortar.
Source: Crowley Signal, 30 January 1904.

to cook [...]. This sanglé is the ordinary early breakfast.[66]

The omnipresence of grits in southern breakfasts and the so-called "southern cornbread dressing" can be related to the legacies of the African slaves. In Louisiana, they also made the even more complicated couscous, which they passed on to the Acadians (*couche-couche*) along with their spicy foodways. This kind of food was unknown to the French, and they usually resorted to eating it only when supplies from France did not reach the shores of Senegal on time. It was only later, with the development of the "marriage à la mode du pays," which brought together African women and Europeans, that it became a habit, in this mixed society, to eat both African and European food. According to Boilat, "les habitants de Saint-Louis et Gorée qui déjeunent à la française, dînent [...] le soir au kouskou."[67] On his return to France, Le Page du Pratz explained in his memoirs how African slaves made couscous out of rice or cornmeal and how good it tasted when put into broth (bouillon). He also urged the planters to provide herbs from their gardens and some salt to make their "couscous" more palatable:

> Pour nourrir vos Nègres plus doucement, il leur faut donner toutes les semaines une petite quantité de sel & des herbes de votre jardin pour rendre leur couscous plus mangeable... Le couscous est une graine qu'ils font avec de la farine de Riz ou de Mahis, qui est bonne et trempe bien dans le bouillon. (To feed your slaves smoothly, give them every week a small quantity of salt and herbs from your garden to make their couscous more eatable... Couscous is a grain they make with rice or cornmeal, which tastes good and soaks well in bouillon).[68]

Also writing from eyewitness, Pruneau de Pommegorge, a former administrator of the French Company of Senegal, noticed that couscous was the signature food to the point that "ces peuples croiroient n'avoir point dîné, quelque bonne chose qu'on leur servit à la place" (whatever else you serve them, these peoples would think they have not eaten at all).[69] In these lines, Pruneau was also referring to the Pulaar (Fulbe) of Fuuta Tooro, cattle raisers and agriculturalists and the neighbors of the Wolof to the east on the Senegal River. The association of *gawri* (the generic cereal for couscous) and *kosam* (milk) is a core part of the identity of the Fulbe. The two elements have a sacred nature and people swear on "barke gawri e kosam" (the sacred value of millet

---

66 Boilat 1984. *Esquisses sénégalaises*. Paris: Karthala (1st edition 1853), p.299.
67 Boilat 1984, p.299. The "marriage à la mode du pays" was the Senegalese parallel of Louisiana *plaçage*, which brought together white males and their colored mistresses. In both cases, children were recognized and often times given the opportunity to pursue their education in France. The early political elite of modern Senegal came from this "custom".
68 Le Page du Pratz 1758, *Histoire de la Louisiane*, tome 1, p.351.
69 Pruneau de Pommegorge, *Description de la Nigritie*, p.37.

and milk).[70] Like the Bambara, they are also targeted by Wolof jokes, this time for their alleged dreams of a postmortem world with rivers of "kosam" (milk) and dunes of "lacciri" (couscous).

African-related cuisine is still enjoyed in Louisiana, and this legacy has been passed on to many restaurants around the United States, mainly through spicy recipes labeled "Cajun." However, these dishes should rather be considered as part of the global Indian, Mediterranean, and Atlantic worlds since so many material cultures have been intermingled through many centuries. Behind the name jambalaya one can think of the Wolof verb *jamb* (to mix), which may have been used to express the use of so many ingredients cooked with rice in one pot. Jambalaya is the Louisiana version of Jolof rice, a recipe born among the Creoles of African and European descent along the coast of Senegambia. Since eating habits travel faster that agricultural practices (Pélissier 1966), Jolof rice has also become the most popular rice recipe along the Gulf of Guinea reaching as far as Nigeria. The use of tomato and peanut butter for cooking is relatively new in West Africa since the basic plants came from America. As suggested by Carney and Rosomoff (2009), the history of food crops and foodways cannot be fully explained and understood out of the context of a world that has been going global since the ancient times. African food crops and foodways have followed the bondspeople wherever they were taken, from the ancient settlements of the Garamantes in the desert of Libya to the medieval plantations of the Middle East, and from the sugar islands of Madeira and the Canary Islands to the New World. Everywhere familiar foodways were revitalized, thus contributing to the shaping of the identities of diasporic Africans.[71]

After a lecture in the fall of 2001 in St. Martinville in southwest Louisiana, a Cajun elder approached this writer and acknowledged the legacy of Africans in Louisiana. As far as food is concerned, he was able to provide anecdotic proof. He was part of a delegation from Acadiana that was invited north for a pilgrimage to their former settlements in Canada. Everything went right except for the fact they could not eat well because the food was tasteless for lack of spices. They would have had the same impression in Poitou-Charentes, their ancestral origins on the west coast of France. The history of Louisiana foodways is yet to be written.

Entertainment and resistance through storytelling

Beyond the reconstruction of their foodways, storytelling also played a very important role in African slaves' survival in the absurd world in which they were forced to live. Storytelling eased the pain in their limbs and minds and allowed

---

70 Sall (Ibrahima Abou). "Les céréales et le lait au Fuuta Tooro (Mauritanie, Sénégal): un métissage culinaire." In M. Chastanet, F.X. Fauvelle-Aymar & D. Juhe-Beaulaton, 2002, *Cuisine et société en Afrique, histoire, saveurs, savoir-faire*. Paris: Karthala, pp.191-204.
71 Carney J.A. and Rosomoff R.N. 2009, chapter 2 (African plants on the move).

many to deal with their fate instead of crying or drowning in homesickness. Storytelling was also a means for the oppressed to create fictional situations where the weak could overcome the domination of the powerful. This function is well rendered by Moroccan humorist Ahmed Sanoussi Bziz: "le rire est une forme de résistance, une revanche de l'opprimé, un pied-de-nez à la bêtise, une manière de rendre la parole confisquée aux petits" (humor is a form of resistance, a revenge of the oppressed, a 'thumb-to-the-nose' against stupidity, a manner of giving the confiscated speech back to the powerless).[72] This form of resistance is partly conveyed through the stories of Ole Massa and his slave John or Jack.[73] In the next lines, we will only consider the animal tales since the bestiary in them is a convenient way of identifying their links to sub-Saharan Africa.

On the continent of Africa, the hare is the main character of a series of trickster stories called the "cycle du lièvre" (cycle of the hare) by Marcelle Diarassouba. This cycle is found primarily in the savanna regions of Mauritania, Guinea, Senegal, Côte d'Ivoire, Upper Volta (now Burkina Faso), Mali, northern Nigeria, Niger, and Chad. But since the stories move easily by word of mouth and given the similarity of the spirit and themes of the African tales, it is not surprising to find the stories of the hare throughout sub-Saharan Africa. The cycle of the hare exists alongside many other cycles, like those of the tortoise, the leopard, the antelope, the praying mantis, the tree frog, and many others. The hare also makes incursions into the forest countries, and thus we can encounter these stories in the southern Côte d'Ivoire and in Togo.[74]

The hare carries different names depending on the country, but his characteristics are constant. In Senegal, the Wolof call him *Lëk*, a weak animal but reputed for being very cunning, just like *Njombor* (rabbit). *Lëk/Njombor* is associated with *Bouki*, the "stupid and greedy hyena," eternal victim of the tricks of his little companion. In Mali, the hare is called *Samba*, the name given to the second son of the family, considered the most intelligent. Other names confer female characteristics to the hare, because of its craftiness and cunning, which are characteristics generally assigned to women. The hare is called *bojel kumba* (little hare kumba), Kumba being the Fulbe name of the second daughter of the family.

Like the hare or the rabbit in the savanna lands, the spider is the main character of another important cycle of animal tales, the "cycle de l'araignée" (cycle of the spider). If the domain of the hare is the vast grasslands of the savanna, the forest is the domain of the spider. In fact, it is in the forest regions of West Africa

---

72 In *Afrique Magazine*, a publication of Groupe Jeune Afrique, N°125, July-August 1995, p.23.

73 Levine, Lawrence W. 1977. *Black Culture and Black Consciousness: Afro-American Folk Thought From Slavery to Freedom*. Oxford: Oxford University Press. Zora Neale Hurston. 1990. *Mules and Men*. New York: Harper & Row.

74 Marcelle Diarassouba, Le lièvre et l'araignée, deux animaux des contes de l'Ouest africain. Thèse de 3e cycle, Universités de Lille et d'Abidjan, 1970, pp.5-6).

where the stories of the spider abound: northern Guinea, Sierra Leone, Liberia, southern Côte d'Ivoire, Ghana, Togo, and so forth. The spider may also be found in the savanna, most notably among the Hausa of Niger and Northern Nigeria, and in Burkina Faso. The spider is known by many diverse names depending on the ethnicity: *Akédéba* or *Kakou Ananzé* among the Agni of Côte d'Ivoire and *Anansi* among the Asante of Ghana. Kakou, Kouakou, or Kweku is the name the Akan give to male infants born on Wednesday.[75] Among the Ewe of Togo, *Hevi Golete* (spider) is also the main character of the animal tales. In their culture, they joke about spider urine as being the source of the flavor attached to leftover food from the previous day.[76]

Central Africa, more precisely the Congo basin, is the domain of various tales unquestionably dominated by the tortoise. In this region, animals such as *Tsétsé* the gazelle, *Moloko* the antelope, *Kafulu* the tortoise, and *Kalulu* the hare use their intelligence and trickery against *Ngo* the leopard who is ambitious but is always caught in a trap.[77] In the collection of stories published under the direction of Gaston Canu (1975), the tortoise plays tricks on all the other animals: the antelope, the eagle, the leopard, the hippopotamus, the elephant, and so forth. The tortoise is also found along the Bight of Benin where some call him *Awon*. The tortoise is also the trickster hero of tales throughout the Bight of Biafra, from the Niger Delta to Cameroon and Gabon.

The tales of the hare, spider, and tortoise were transported to the Western Hemisphere by the slave trade. They were popularized in North America beginning in 1880 with the publication by Joel Chandler Harris of a collection of thirty-four stories entitled *Uncle Remus: His Songs and Sayings*. In 1883, Harris published another collection titled *Nights with Uncle Remus, Myths and Legends of the Old Plantation*.[78] Harris was a journalist in central Georgia where he worked for one of the first southern rural newspapers, *The Country Man*. Then later he worked more than twenty years for the newspaper *Atlanta Constitution*, of which he was a member of the board of directors.[79] Other folklorists subsequently added their findings to those of Harris.

---

75 Bernard B. Dadié, *Le Pagne Noir* (Paris: Présence Africaine, 1955); see also Diarassouba, "Le lièvre et l'araignée" (1970), pp.154-156). Agni and Asante are components of the larger Akan group, which also includes the Baule of Côte d'Ivoire.

76 Communicated by Kofi Kondo Awute (Togo), then a graduate student at the University of Mississippi in Oxford, Spring 1996.

77 Gaston Canu, ed., *Contes du Zaïre, Contes des montagnes, de la savane et de la forêt au pays de fleuve Zaïre* (Paris: EDICEF, 1975), Introduction.

78 Joel Chandler Harris, *Uncle Remus: His Songs and Sayings* (New York: D. Appleton and Company, 1880), and Harris, *Nights with Uncle Remus, Myths and Legends of the Old Plantation* (New York: McKinley, Stone & Mackenzie, 1883).

79 Richard M. Dorson, *American Negro Folktales* (Greenwich, CT: Fawcett Premier Book, 1967), p.13.

In the southern United States, the repertoire of animal tales is dominated by the stories of the hare/rabbit. The tortoise is also present in the United States but in a less common way even though, as A. B. Ellis suggested, the tortoise was the prototype for Terrapin in the Uncle Remus stories.[80] In North America, Anansi lives a marginal existence, notably in the Carolinas and in Georgia in a few stories titled "Aunt Nancy Stories." In the Uncle Remus stories, the spider also appears under the name Miss Nancy. In the Anglophone Antilles, the spider is the primary character within the bestiary of animal folklore. His name was anglicized, and some refer to its stories as "Nancy Stories." Anansi is present under the name B'Anansi (Brother Anansi) in the Bahamas where he is no longer a spider but a monkey or a malicious child. The spider is also present among the blacks of Suriname where all their trickster stories, regardless of the characters, are designated under the generic term "Anansitori." It is the same way among the blacks of Curaçao who refer to their tales as "Cuentas de Nansi."[81] The British Antilles were heavily populated by slaves taken from the Gold Coast. The existing folklore on these islands is a direct stem of the African cycle of the spider. Martha Warren Beckwith, a renowned folklorist, collected an entire volume of Anansi tales in Jamaica, but her search was in vain in the southern United States where the spider gave way to Brer Rabbit.[82]

The U.S. South is the archetypal domain of the cycle of the rabbit. The bestiary is overwhelmingly dominated by Brer Rabbit or Buh Rabbit, who is associated with Fox, rather than with the hyena. In Louisiana, it is more correct to speak of the cycle of "Bouki and Lapin." The rabbit took the place of the hare, but it is not difficult to recognize the minor variation between the two. The Wolof name of the small trickster (Lëk/Njombor) was not kept by the folk collective memory. Louisianans had for some time forgotten the meaning of Bouki and thought of him as a he-goat or sometimes as a raccoon, but the characteristics and role of the character remain the same. Bouki is also present in folktales collected in Florida, the Bahamas, Haiti, and French Guyana. In Haiti, Bouqui is partnered with his nephew Ti-Malice, who never misses an occasion to play dirty tricks on his uncle.[83] In this country, the two characters have returned to their human features, which is understandable since animals are used all over the world by human beings to

---

80 Colonel A. B. Ellis, "Evolution in Folklore. Some West African prototypes of the Uncle Remus Stories," *Appleton's Popular Science Monthly* (Nov. 1895 - April 1896), p.93.
81   Lawrence W. Levine, *Black Culture and Black Consciousness: Afro-American Folk Thought from Slavery to Freedom* (Oxford: Oxford University Press, 1977), p.103; see also Melville J. Herskovits and Frances S. Herskovits, *Suriname Folk-Lore* (New York: Columbia University Press, 1936).
82 Martha Warren Beckwith, *Jamaica Anansi Stories* (New York: American Lolk-Lore Society, 1924); Dorson, *American Negro Folktales* (1967), p.17.
83 *Contes et Légendes d'Haïti*, Centre de Recherches Littéraires et Sociales, (Port-au-Prince, Haiti : Editions Christophe, 1993). See also Harold Courlander, *The Drum and the Hoe: Life and Lore of the Haitian People* (Berkeley: University of California Press, 1960), pp.175-178.

portray their own defaults and qualities. In Senegal, Bouki is also the uncle of Lëk/Njombor, his little partner. This can be explained by the matrilineal frame of many African societies in which heritage goes from maternal uncles to nephews, who are bound by very special relationships that involve love, caring, and the exchange of jokes.

Alcée Fortier (1856-1914) was the leading folklorist to have systematically collected the French-speaking oral tradition of Louisiana. In his childhood, the tales of Bouki and Lapin were likely all over the place, but he was probably also inspired by the series of tales published in *Le Meschacébé* after the Civil War. He was born on a plantation in St. James Parish to a father who inherited a large sugar plantation. His mother, Edwige Aime, was the daughter of Valcour Aime (1798-1867), owner of the first sugar refinery built in Louisiana before the Civil War.[84] In 1880, he was elected Professor of Romance Languages at the University of Louisiana and was re-elected when that institution became Tulane University. His academic career allowed him to conduct a remarkable work with the collection and publication of stories, songs, and proverbs in Creole, at a time when the former slaves who remembered the stories were still alive, and their stories carried much more weight than those compiled by the interviewers working for the Federal Writers Project in the 1930s.

Fortier first published the results of his fieldwork in 1887, in the form of an article ("Bits of Louisiana Folklore") presented at the December 1887 meeting of the Modern Language Association. His second major folklore publication, *Louisiana Folktales*, published in 1895, remains today a work of reference for the study of Louisiana folklore.[85] The first part of his work was devoted to fifteen animal tales, of which ten are tales of "Bouki and Compé Lapin" in their original Creole version, followed by translations in English. Fourteen tales, in English versions, were published in an appendix, of which eight have Bouki and Compé Lapin as principal protagonists. A single story is related to the tortoise, and the spider is never brought into play. A century later, the *Cajun and Creole Folktakes* of Barry Jean Ancelet, published in 1994, represents the second largest systematic collection of popular Louisiana folktales. Of the seventeen animal stories collected by Ancelet, mostly from Wilson "Ben Guiné" Mitchell, ten are stories of Bouki and Compé Lapin, and the other seven bring other animals into play: the elephant and the serpent, the owl and the birds, the fox, the little toads, Fourmi (the ant) and Grasshopper, and stories such as "Neige casse la patte de la fourmi" ("Snow breaks the paw of the ant") and "Bicoin et les choux" ("Bicoin/Goat and the cabbages").

---

84 *Biographical and Historical Memoirs of Louisiana, I* (Chicago, IL: Goodspeed Publishing Company, 1892), pp.420-421; see also Alcée Fortier, *Louisiana Folk-Tales, In French Dialect and English Translation* (Boston, MA: Houghton, Mifflin and Co., 1895), preface.

85 Fortier 1895. *Louisiana Folktales*. Boston, MA: American Folklore Society.

No story discusses the tortoise or the spider.[86]

At the time of Fortier's fieldwork, Creole was still the first language of the majority of the population of Louisiana. For Fortier, it was not a simple corruption of French. It was a veritable idiom with its own morphology and grammar. He was also surprised to note the way in which the "ignorant African slave" transformed the language of his master into a concise and simple speech that was also "sweet and musical."[87] Fortier had also found the fact strange that the old people didn't like to relate the stories with which they had enchanted their little masters before the American Civil War. In his book, he confessed that it was with much difficulty that he succeeded in obtaining the stories. The reticence of the storytellers can be explained by the fact that Fortier had presented himself multiple times during daylight hours, unaware that one does not ask an African to tell a story before dusk. This can be related to practical reasons since daytime is meant for work. And taboo is always protected by myth as far as Africa is concerned. In Burkina Faso, for example, if this taboo is violated, the storyteller must say the following expiatory expression, "Soleil prends toute ta cécité et laisse-moi sain" (Sun, take away the blindness in your rays and leave me clean).[88] In Senegal, one says that a daytime storyteller risks losing his mother. This belief is also found in Haiti, where one says, "Si ou tiré kont lajounen wa va pédi Manman'w" (If you tell a tale in the day, you're going to lose your mother).[89]

The reticence from Fortier's interviewees can also be explained by the fact that they were dealing with a stranger who belonged to a different milieu and, by consequence, was incapable of appreciating the true value of their humor. A show of tales among Africans is a type of communion where each participant brings his own "grain de sel" (bit of wit) or even participates in the inevitable songs that punctuate the tale. Fortier was not an adequate listener for the storytellers. This is verified in the comments preceding his repertoire: "while reading these tales, one must bear in mind that most of them were related to children by childlike people; this accounts for their naïveté." Then he wrote: "while singing, he (a storyteller) writhes in a horrible manner and gesticulates wildly, rubbing his shoulders against all the persons present, who sing with him the refrain and dance to the tune of a most primitive music."[90]

In Fortier's repertoire, strong historical links between Louisiana and Senegambia are suggested even beyond the names of the main characters. In "Compair Bouki

86 Barry Jean Ancelet, *Cajun and Creole Folktales, the French Oral Tradition of South Louisiana* (Jackson: University Press of Mississippi, 1994).
87 Fortier, *Louisiana Folk-Tales* (1895), p.8.
88 Ansomwin Ignace Hien, *Le Conte de la Volta Noire-Contes Dagara*, Corpus II (Ouagadougou, Burkina Faso: Editions G.T.I., 1995), p.12.
89 Communicated by Marie Monique Moléon, a Haitian student at the University of Mississippi, Spring 1996.
90 Fortier 1895. *Louisiana Folktales*, pp.9-10.

and Compair Lapin No.1," a story published in the appendix of Fortier's *Louisiana Folk-tales*, Bouki and Lapin decide to sell their mothers in order to buy food. Bouki ties his mother with a very solid cord, and Lapin uses a leash made of the burr from an ear of corn. Of course, Lapin's mother escapes, and the mother of his partner is sold in exchange for a pot of gruel and a pot of gumbo. Bouki puts the two pots on his cart and heads back down the road home. Twice Bouki sees a "dead" rabbit on the road but does not stop. Seeing a rabbit for the third time, he steps down from his cart and goes back to search for the other two rabbits. His search is in vain because this is all another ruse of Lapin's. Lapin takes possession of the cart, cuts the horse's tail off, and plants it in the ground. On his return, Bouki thinks his harness has sunken into the lithosphere. He pulls with all his strength and endsup with a tail in his hands.[91] In *La Belle Histoire de Leuk-le-Lièvre* (1953), under the same circumstances Bouki's aunt is sold in return for a steer and a donkey loaded with millet. Bouki's little companion uses the same ruse in order to appropriate the donkey and its load. Alerted by Leuk, Bouki pulls the donkey, supposedly buried under the earth, and retrieves nothing but a tail. Then the two companions decide to roast the steer. To pass the time while cooking, they sit on a tree and braid each other's hair. Each time Leuk makes a braid in Bouki's hair, he ties it to a branch. When the time comes to eat, they both jump down from the tree, but Bouki remains suspended above the ground. Leuk eats the roasted steer and violently throws each cleaned bone at Bouki's mouth.[92] In "Bouqui et Malice vendent leur mère" ("Bouqui and Malice sell their mothers"), a tale from Haiti, Malice tricks his partner into selling his mother in order to get money for food.[93]

Another story involves the rabbit/hare, the elephant, and the whale. The version published by Fortier is identical to that of Senghor and Sadji. In Senegal and Louisiana, the same animal (the rabbit or the hare) is found begging for the help of the elephant to pull an imaginary treasure from the bottom of the ocean. Then he approaches the whale and asks the giant of the oceans to help him pull a treasure or a cow, also imaginary, from the mud of the continent. When the two giants discover the hoax, they decide to forbid the small animal to graze upon the grass of the continent or to drink from the water of the ocean. In Louisiana, Compé Lapin gets past the problem by pretending he has acquired a diabolic power. He covers himself with the skin of a roebuck eaten by vermin and goes to see the two giants in order to pass for a victim of Lapin. In Senegal, Lëk covers himself with the skin of a deer in order to escape the vigilance of the two giants.[94] A similar tale

---

91 Fortier, *Louisiana Folk-Tales* (1895), pp.109-110.

92 Léopold Sédar Senghor and Abdoulaye Sadji, *La Belle Histoire de Leuk-le-Lièvre* (Paris: Hachette, 1953).

93 Suzanne Comhaire-Sylvain 1940, *Le roman de Bouqui*. Port-au-Prince, Haiti: Imprimerie du Collège Vertières.

94 Fortier, *Louisiana Folk-Tales* (1895), pp. 2-7. Senghor and Sadji, *La Belle Histoire* (1953), pp. 30-33.

was collected on the Red Sea island of Mauritius where the hare challenges the elephant and the whale, but instead of pulling himself, he ties each end of the cord to one of the giants, thus provoking a duel of titans.[95]

There is a remarkable representation of Africa in the series of tales published in *Le Meschacébé* during the 1870s. But still the main characters are of Senegambian origin. In *Compair Lapin et Ti Négresse Congo*, one of the many versions of the tar baby tale, several African regions are represented. The name of the storyteller (Coffee) originates from the Gold Coast and the Bight of Benin, and the names Bouki and Lapin originate from Senegambia. Ti Négresse Congo is the tar baby made by Bouki to catch Lapin, who has been stealing water from his well. After making a *catin* (doll in Creole) out of a piece of wood of the bay tree, "li godroné li, godroné li si tan jika li té noi com négresse guinain" (he applied tar on it, again and again, until it looked like a Negress from Guinea).[96] The tale "Compair Bouki avé Compair Dahomey" ("Compair Bouki and Compair Dahomey"), also collected in 1878 in St. John the Baptist Parish from one Pa Lindor, shows a stronger link between Louisiana and Senegambia although the second character suggests another link with the Bight of Benin. Congo is represented through the *caçambo* (pipe) Compair Dahomey smokes when Madame Rahoutan visits him. The old lady is the victim of Bouki, who steals her livestock until he is caught and punished by Compair Dahomey. Compair Dahomey finds the whole family clinging to the girders supporting the roof of their house and nearly exterminates them. Bouki manages to have his older son escape in order to perpetuate his race.[97] In the story "Bouki et la vieille fermière" (Senghor & Sadji 1953), an old lady is also the victim of the cupidity of Bouki who literally wipes out her livestock. Bouki and his family are punished under the same circumstances, but justice is carried out by Uncle-Gaïndé-the-Lion. In "La mort de la famille Bouqui," another tale from Haiti, there is no old lady as a victim but a strange character called "Tête-sans-corps" (Head-without-body) who punishes Bouki and his family in the same manner.[98] By all evidence, these stories traveled from Senegal to Haiti and later to Louisiana. Whereas over 2,300 Senegambia slaves were already in Saint-Domingue in 1681[99],

95 Gerber 1893, "Uncle Remus traced to the Old World", p.250. The majority of the slaves transported to this former French island between 1730 and 1735 came from Senegal [Hall 1992, *Africans in Colonial Louisiana*, p.191].

96 This tale originally published in *Le Meschacébé* of June 10, 1876 was retrieved from Bibliothèque Tintamarre, a website built by the students of the Centenary College in Louisiana and dedicated to make the literature of French Louisina available to the grand public: http://www.centenary.edu/french/creole/ccl1.htm (accessed September 26, 2010).

97 Originally in *Le Meschacébé*, 27 April 1878. Retrieved from Bibliotheque Tintamarre: www.centenary.edu/french/creole/ccl5.htm (accessed September 26, 2011).

98 Comhaire-Sylvain, *Le roman de Bouqui* (1940).

99 Pierre Pluchon, *Vaudou-Sorciers-Empoisonneurs, de Saint-Domingue à Haïti* (Paris: Karthala, 1987), p.305. The first shipment of slaves to arrive in Louisiana was sent from Saint Domingue in 1812.

the first direct shipments of slaves from Africa did not arrive in Louisiana until 1719.

Louisiana and the rest of the southern United States inherited the cycle of the hare/rabbit stories through the slave trade. The fundamental impetus incontestably stemmed from Senegambia and more precisely from the Wolof countries. The Trans-Atlantic Slave Trade Database shows that in the years 1751-1775, 58.2 percent of all the slaves imported into South Carolina and Georgia (35,774) came from this region.[100] Bouki's name has journeyed across centuries to appear even today in the tales of southwest Louisiana. In this area, like in Africa, the opening and closing of a tale were always accompanied by a ritual. The storyteller spoke an inaugural phrase: "Bonne foi! Bonne foi!" and the audience responded, "Lapin! Lapin!"[101] The closing phrase depended on the inspiration of the storyteller. Among the Wolof, the end of a tale always includes the formula "fa la lèèb jogee tabbi gèèj" ("from there the story ended its journey in the ocean"). This may translate as the memory of the deportation of many of the Wolof to the other side of the Atlantic. Since women are the primary transmitters of culture to their children, the massive presence of Wolof women in Louisiana explains in part the fact that Bouki is kept by the folk memory. It is also necessary to take into account the massive presence of the Bambara in Louisiana and what the hyena (Souroukouba) represents among their people from an esoteric point of view. Bouki is the symbol of African wisdom and his character traits sum up, in an eloquent way, the dramatic experience of Africans in their contact with the Western world. For the Komo secret society of the Bambara:

> The hyena is a gifted animal with intuition and an infallible prescience. It possesses the "black knowledge": "darkness (which is to say the mystery) has no secret from the hyena." A nocturnal animal living in holes, its name is constantly associated with the night which shelters mating, with the secrecy of pregnancies; to all the works and cults of the earth (rites of fertility and abundance). The hyena is the guardian of life of the Earth. If the hyena is often presented as naïve, maladroit, saying "bah" to contingencies, these character traits – accused in the popular stories where it is the butt of the joke, notably to the ruses and treason of the hare – are, in reality, typical of "people of knowledge" who are always

---

100 Jane G. Landers, Atlantic Creoles in the Age of Revolutions (Cambridge, Massachussetts and London, England: Harvard University Press, 2010), p.19.
101 This call-and-response begins the iconic Tar Baby story; Fortier, *Louisiana Folk-Tales* (1895), p.98. See also Marcus Christian unpublished Manuscript, "Folklore of French and English-Speaking Negroes of Louisiana," Earl Long Library, Special Collections, University of New Orleans, pp.6-7.

disinterested and carefree.[102]

Alcée Fortier's Louisiana Folktales were collected in New Orleans and Vacherie in St. James Parish. The Laura Plantation, formerly known as the Duparc and Locoul Plantation, was located in this area. It is now a museum where visitors can buy Fortier's work as well as *La Belle Histoire de Leuk-le-lièvre*, a collection by Senghor and Sadji from Senegal. Fortier died nearly forty years before the publication of *La Belle Histoire*, but he knew the Wolof folktales collected by Baron Jacques-François Roger, the French governor of Senegal in the 1820s.[103] If Fortier and partners Senghor and Sadji could produce two nearly identical works from two sides of the Atlantic Ocean but never met, it is because they drew from the same heritage, the same patrimony, at different places and different times. The work of Barry Jean Ancelet further indicates the resiliency of these tales still found in Louisiana especially in the southwestern part of the state along Bayou Teche. This is also the region where one can still find many people with the family name "Senegal," the name under which the Wolof people were listed on the plantations of Louisiana. This is also Acadiana, the land of the Cajuns, where both black and white people grew up with these enchanting tales.

The wording "Bouki fait gombo, lapin mangé li" (literally, Bouki makes gumbo, Rabbit eats it) is a genuine African proverb transcribed into Louisiana Creole language. A Wolof proverb, similar in meaning, says, "Golo di bay, Baabun di dundee" (Monkey makes the crops, Gorilla eats everything). The proverb depicts the master-slave relationship or any situation where one performs services without getting any reward or even credit for it. Fortier did his fieldwork with the help of his nieces Désirée and Marguerite Roman. One of his "most valued" assistants was Widow V. Choppin, a plantation owner and the one who bought Queto Manchot from the group of the Haydel slaves auctioned in New Orleans in the spring of 1840. If the latter was still alive after the Civil War, he was probably among the informants of Fortier. The Duparc and Locoul plantation (Laura) was just downriver from the Choppin, Roman, Fortier, and Aime plantations, in St. James Parish. Whether Fortier conducted his search in this particular place or anywhere else along the river does not matter. But it is unfortunate that his informants were not always recognized with a clear identity. One of them was just an "old negro from La Vacherie" and another one an "old negress, 77 Esplanade Avenue." Fortier did appreciate the contribution of his assistants but did not bother to do so for the storytellers who gave him much of their time and definitely helped inscribe his

---

102 Germaine Dieterlen and Youssouf Tata Cissé, *Les Fondements de la Société d'Initiation du Komo* (Paris-La Haye: Mouton & Co., 1972), p.26. Translated by Sarita Henry.

103 Baron Jacques-François Roger 1828, Fables sénégalaises recueillies de l'ouolof et mises en vers français : avec des notes destinées à faire connaître la Sénégambie, son climat, ses principales productions, la civilisation et les mœurs de ses habitants. Paris: Nepveu, Firmin Didot, Ponthieu.

name into posterity. He was probably right not to use additional lines of gratitude since he knew that none of these "rude, ignorant and childlike people," as he called them, would ever read his book. However, Fortier was the product of the plantation society and his prejudiced view on the former slaves must be understood in this context. The folktales he collected are a perfect illustration of the resistance to slavery. Besides the survival of their memory dishes the slaves were able to keep the memory of Africa alive through their folktales. In other words, the masters had control on their bodies but never had any control on their souls. This is why America enjoys today soul food and soul music. Bouki is still around in Louisiana and the gumbo he makes is eaten worldwide since he has gone global under the disguise of a wild coyote along with Bugs Bunny, the Warner Bros. cartoon rendition of *Compère Lapin* alias *Brer Rabbit*.

The hard way to freedom

The manumission of slaves was quite early a reality in the history of colonial Louisiana. As early as the 1720s slaves were emancipated by their masters and the Superior Council of Louisiana confirmed many cases brought before it. Many of the freed people were of mixed race since concubinage between white men and slave women was extensive and openly accepted. Moreover, there was a strong consensus shared by white women that the concubines and children of white men should be free.[104] After the US takeover of Louisiana, the race relationships remained unchanged and concubinage between white men and slave women carried on through the Civil War. The Black Code provided relatively simple procedures for the manumission of slaves, but great distinction existed between law and practice. For example, the early age restrictions on manumissions were apparently intended to keep the most fertile women enslaved and to reduce the freed population. The Civil Code of Louisiana, promulgated June 20, 1825, stipulated two conditions to qualify for freedom: the slave had to be at least thirty years of age and have "honest conduct." This was defined as not having run away or committed a criminal act for four years before the emancipation. These stipulations could be waived if the slave to be freed had saved the life of his or her owner or a member of the owner's family. In 1827, the Louisiana legislature softened the age requirement. A slave under thirty years of age could be freed if she/he was a native of the state, but permission had to be given by the judge and the police jury of the parish where the owner lived. An act of 1830 required all newly freed slaves to leave the state within thirty days of their emancipation and required that the former owner post a $1,000 security-bond to ensure the ex-slave's departure. This requirement was softened by an act of the Legislature passed on

---

104 Gwendolyn Midlo Hall, Africans in Colonial Louisiana, the Development of Afro-Creole Culture in Eighteenth Century Louisiana (Baton Rouge: Louisiana State University Press, 1992), pp.129-130 and 238-240.

March 16, 1831. Parish juries could, by a three-fourths vote, allow emancipated slaves to remain in the state.[105]

The emancipation of Marie Joseph and Claire, both slaves of Jean Jacques Haydel Jr., proved to be very easy. The two cases were brought before the parish judge on March 10, 1827. Freedom was granted to them soon after the forty-day legal period during which the notices of emancipation were posted at public places by the sheriff of the parish.[106] The manumission of Arthémise for her "good conduct and services" took much longer to come to a conclusion. Jean Jacques Haydel Jr. filed a petition to emancipate his thirty-year old Mulatto slave on March 16, 1831. The case was transmitted on June 11, 1831 to the Parish Police Jury. On its meetings of June 13 and June 27, this institution decided unanimously that freedom should be granted to Arthémise and ordered the secretary to deliver a certificate of manumission. For some reason, Haydel did not file a second petition before the parish judge until April 3, 1833. The slave was finally manumitted on May 30, 1833.[107] Arthémise moved to New Orleans. In August 1844, she was back in the courthouse of St. John Parish, this time for the purpose of freeing Phélonise, a six-year old quadroon who was the daughter of her niece Paméla. Paméla was a Mulatto attached to the estate of Martian Belfort Haydel, who would receive 120 piastres for the transaction.[108]

During the 1850s, as the controversy rose between the North and the South about the "peculiar institution" of slavery, emancipation became more difficult though not impossible. Finally, in 1857, the Louisiana legislature totally closed the doors to freedom. In 1859, although the free people of color were not responsible for the atmosphere of violence described earlier in the book, the Legislature confirmed the law prohibiting the manumission of slaves, and those who were already emancipated had to each choose a master and return into bondage for the rest of their lives.[109]

The Haydel family was also deeply affected by these changing laws. Paméla was the daughter of Céleste, the younger sister of Arthémise. In 1840 she was listed with her mother and two siblings on one of the plantations owned by Martian

---

105 Judith K. Schafer, *Slavery, the Civil law, and the Supreme Court of Louisiana* (Baton Rouge: Louisiana State University Press, 1994), p. 181-182.

106 SJB-72-1827: Liberté par J. J. Haydel à la Négresse Marie Joseph ; SJB-71-1827: Liberté par J. J. Haydel à la Négresse Claire.

107 SJB-242-1833/Acte de liberté de la mulâtresse Arthemise par Jean Jacques Haydel. 30 May 1833.

108 SJB-252-1844/Acte par lequel le Sieur Martian Belfort Haydel s'oblige d'affranchir une petite quarteronne nommée Phélonise fille de sa mulâtresse Paméla. 17 August 1844.

109 Schafer, *Slavery, the Civil law, and the Supreme Court* (1994), pp.182-183. Marcus B. Christian, "The Free Colored Class of Louisiana," p. 41. In Manuscript for a Black History of Louisiana (unpublished), The University of New Orleans, Earl K. Long Library, Special Collections.

Belfort Haydel.[110] In the 1850s Belfort was separated from bed and board of his legitimate wife Marguerite Adèle Haydel and Paméla was called "*sa mulatresse*" (his Mulatto). Seven quadroon children were born from this relationship. Phélonise and Germaine, the two oldest daughters of Paméla, were emancipated on April 20, 1857 after many years of judicial procedures.[111] They moved to New Orleans where they met and married free men of color. But later in the 1850s, when Paméla had her last three surviving children, the law had changed. Belfort declared them free at their baptisms and had the priest record their status as such—with Belfort's wife watching and signing her name as a witness. But the document was not considered legal by the state, so Paméla's children remained slaves of their father, Belfort Haydel. Finally, in 1859, Belfort's white legitimate son (Georges Ambroise Haydel) purchased his illegitimate half-brothers and sisters and his father's slave mistress. In a legal act, he expressed "*his wish and determination to emancipate (them) from the bonds of slavery but that the laws of this State forbidding the emancipation of slaves (…), he has resolved to send (them) into a foreign country where slavery does not exist.*" The destination mentioned on the file was Tampico in Mexico, a country where many Creoles of color found refuge. After the Civil War all of Paméla's children, except Emma, returned to New Orleans and lived in a community of Creoles of color. [112]

For most of the slaves who remained on the former masters' plantations, freedom brought new hardship for which they were not prepared. In 1940, Julia Woodrich still remembered the hard days following Emancipation: "After us was set free we stayed in a shack in de pasture. Our missis told us she could not take care of us any longer. We lived off of berries and fish, crawfish and everything like that for a long time after us was free." The experience of Silas Spotfore was not different; although "missis" said they could stay, "my pa didn't want to. We hung around for a few days, den pa went to work for something to eat. You see, we didn't have a thing; left empty-handed with nothing."[113]

Marie Azélie Haydel, the last owner of the Haydel Plantation before the Civil War, passed away in November 1860. Since she was a widow and had no children, many relatives were present or represented as lawful heirs in the inventory of her

---

110 NONA, Felix Grima, Vol. 2, Act 200. Meeting of the creditors of Marcian Belfort Haydel. 30 June 1834.

111 SJB-90-1857/Belfort Haydel. Affranchissement de Phélonise et Germaine. 20 April 1857. Also in the Katy Morlas' files at the office of the Whitney Heritage Plantation Corporation in New Orleans, 416 Gravier Street.

112 SJB-7-1859/Belfort Haydel: Vente d'esclaves à Georges Haydel, 19 January1859. SJB-31-1859/Belfort Haydel: Vente d'esclaves à Georges Haydel, 23 February 1859. SJB-102-1860/ Georges Haydel: Consentement au départ de 7 esclaves, 25 May 1860. Also in the Katy Morlas' files at the office of the Whitney Heritage Plantation Corporation in New Orleans, 416 Gravier Street.

113 Clayton, *Mother Wit* (1990), pp.195 and 217.

property.[114] The estate was not auctioned until November 15, 1867 partly because of judicial procedures filed by relatives willing to defend their interests in her succession. The Civil War imposed a longer delay and the loss of the one hundred and one slaves attached to her estate. Many of the slaves who lived on the Haydel plantation by the time of the Civil War, exactly forty-three of them, became either Alphonse Becnel's sharecroppers or his day laborers.[115] Many of their descendants may still be living around the Whitney Plantation area, notably in Wallace, where the racial makeup is overwhelmingly African American (93.8 percent) with 45.5 percent of the population living below the poverty line.[116]

Marie Céleste Becnel was born on the Haydel plantation the natural daughter of Florestan Becnel, a cousin and brother-in-law of Marie Azélie Haydel. Francoise, the mother of Céleste, was a slave of Marcellin Haydel. She was granted freedom and became the cook of Widow Marcellin. She died on December 29, 1841.[117] When the legitimate wife of Florestan (Joséphine Haydel) died in 1844, Céleste was one of the slaves listed in the inventory of their community. She was described as a quadroon and an orphan, seven years old, and estimated 300 piastres. When Florestan passed away ten years later, his estate was estimated at 6,117 piastres. The inventory was held on January 4, 1854 at the house of his brother Félix Becnel, next door to Azélie on the future Mialaret plantation. It did not mention any land property. Céleste was one of the five slaves he owned. She was described this time as *mulâtresse créole* (Creole Mulatto), aged around 17 years old. She was priced 600 piastres and sold to Léo Becnel, her half-brother. The latter granted her freedom along with Henriette, who was for many years the cook of Florestan Becnel. This is why the 1860 US Census listed Céleste, 20 years old, and Henriette, 80 years old, within the household of Léo Becnel, a 30-year-old engineer apparently established at that time in the city of Edgard. They were both described as black women.[118] Beyond the inconsistencies respecting the complexion of Céleste, her age was obviously underestimated whereas that of Henriette was overestimated. The

114 Inventaire des biens de la succession de la dame Azélie Haydel décédée veuve Marcelin Haydel; 10-12 November 1860 [SJB-178-1860].

115 National Archives, Washington DC: M1905, Records of the Field Offices for the State of Louisiana, Bureau of Refugees, Freedmen, and Abandoned Lands 1863-1872, Record Group 105. Subordinate Office Plantation Department, Rolls 27-28-29; Register of Black Persons, undated.

116 Dillard and als. "Whitney and Evergreen Plantation". In *River Road Preservation and Promotion*. Tulane University, School of Architecture: Preservation Studies, Spring 2005, p.29.

117 The Morlas Files: Interment record of Françoise, free woman of color [died 29 December 1841].

118 SJB-223-1845/Inventaire Communauté Florestan Becnel et dame Joséphine Haydel décédée, 1 July 1845. SJB-4-1854/Succession Florestan Becnel, 4 January 1854. SJB-209-1854/Vente d'esclave par l'administrateur de la succession de feu Florestan Becnel à Léo Becnel, 15 May 1854. St John the Baptist Parish, LA, 1860 US Census, 12 June-21 July 1860, Page 7 of 9. Accessed 31 December 2013 at http://freepages.genealogy.rootsweb.ancestry.com/~montz/census/sjb1860g.htm.

inventories which listed them before freedom indicate that they were respectively born around 1837 and 1785. There is strong evidence that Henriette raised Céleste after the death of her mother.[119]

Céleste Becnel married Victor Théophile Haydel, also born on the Haydel plantation, the son of Antoine Haydel, a brother of Marie Azélie Haydel.[120] Anna, the mother of Victor, was also attached to the estate of Azélie. Because of their close ties with the Haydel family, Anna, fifty-years old, and Victor, twenty-five years old, were the last two names listed in the inventory of the estate of late Marie Azélie Haydel. Anna was described as *mulâtresse américaine*, which meant she was a Mulatto from the East Coast, probably Virginia. She had very poor health (*maladive*) and was priced 100 piastres. Victor was described as *mulâtre créole* (Creole Mulatto) and priced 800 piastres.[121] The enslavement of Anna in Louisiana is still kept alive in the memories of her descendants. The following story was transmitted to Curtis M. Graves born in 1952 the son of Mabel Haydel Graves (1908-1999), the grandson of Elphège Haydel (1879-1959), and the great-grandson of Victor Haydel (1835-1924). According to the story,

Anna was bought from the slave market in New Orleans by Marcellin Haydel and brought to the plantation and given to Azélie as a gift. Azélie had no children and always wanted a girl. My grandfather also said that she was not real black. So they thought she might have been mixed with Indian [I have done my DNA and I have no Indian. So I think her father was white]. Her brother or brothers were sold off to another plantation and she was standing crying. She remembered her mother falling asleep on the ship and being dropped off the side of the boat. She did not understand death at the time. I was told that Azélie raised her in the big house. She had a child in her teen years with Azélie's brother Antoine, and never liked him. So I think it was a rape (since a slave girl could not say no!). She did not marry anyone and also had no other children. She never saw or found her brothers or brother after she was

119 According to the Morlas Files, Marie Céleste Becnel was officially born 15 January 1833 on the Haydel plantation. So she was 52 when she passed away in 1885. Henriette was described in the two successions as "négresse créole," which means she was not of mixed race.
120 Marriage record of Theophile Haydel, son of Antoine Haydel and Anna, and Celeste Becnel, daughter of Florestan Becnel and Françoise [2 September 1871]; in the Katy Morlas' files. Baptism record of Victor, born August 1st 1835 of Antoine Haydel and Anna [13 December 1835]; in Belmont F. Haydel. *The Victor Haydel Creole Family: Whitney (Haydel) Plantation — Plantation Beginnings And Early Descendants*, 3rd ed. 2009. Warminster, PA: Cooke Publishing Company, p. 85.
121 Succession Azélie Haydel [SJB-178-1860].

sold in New Orleans.[122]

Anna passed away in the 1860s, probably during the Civil War. Victor Haydel and Céleste Becnel were listed as domestic servants in the 1870 Federal Census, within Ward 3 of St. John the Baptist Parish, apparently near the parish line in Wallace. Their children were Victor Jr., Théophile, Emma, and Clay. In the same household was Celina Becnel, born in 1854, probably Victor's stepdaughter. They were all described as Mulattoes. The 1880 census was held after the downfall of Reconstruction and the gradual entrance of Louisiana in the era of Jim Crow with the Constitution of 1879. This time all the members of the household were described as "Black." Victor had become a farmer and a landowner, and Céleste stayed at home as a housewife. Celina was no longer there and the couple was listed in Ward 2 with nine children. Clay Haydel was then ten years old.[123]   He later married Nellie Ory Haydel, the sister of the celebrated jazz musician Kid Ory. Their oldest son, Clarence Clement Haydel, was the father of Sybil Haydel, an educator, activist and community leader, who became an executive at Xavier University and a member of the Blue Cross and Blue Shield of Louisiana Board of Directors from 1993 to 2008. Sybil Haydel also bore the honorific title of First Lady of New Orleans when her husband, Ernest N. Morial, was elected the first African-American mayor of the Crescent City. Their son, Marc Morial, also rose to fame and was elected President of the U.S. Conference of Mayors, while serving two full terms as the Mayor of New Orleans like his father. He is currently the president and CEO of the American Urban League. For Sybil, there is no doubt her ancestors came from St. John the Baptist Parish, where some of them were

---

122 Discussion with Curtis M. Graves at the 9th annual conference of the Louisiana Creole Research Association (LA CREOLE), Xavier University in New Orleans, 19 October 2013. Confirmation done through email on 31 October 2013. Curtis presently serves as the regional representative of Quality Plan Administrators of Washington, D.C., a dental care provider. He retired from the National Aeronautics and Space Administration in August of 2003. In 1966, Curtis M. Graves was the first Black elected to the Texas House of Representatives since 1891.
123 The 1870 and 1880 Federal Censuses, St. John the Baptist, Louisiana; Microfilms in the Louisiana Division of the New Orleans Public library.

enslaved.[124] For another great-grandchild of Victor Haydel Sr. (alias Pépère), the German ancestry does not count in the measurement of the achievements of his/her family:

> True, the German, Antoine, contributed his seed, but then he vanished (…). Our heritage is one of exceptional accomplishments. As minorities, we, as a family, have overcome much of the depravation and discrimination of the times in which each generation excelled. That is what our family should be noted for, our capacity to overcome, not that one German stepped in for a nano-second.[125]

Slavery is a brutal institution imposed mostly on innocent and helpless people. There is no shame in being the descendant of people who were denied their freedom, exposed to all kinds of abuse, and put to work for the comfort of theirs exploiters. Nevertheless there are some conflicting memories about the origins and the social status of Anna and her only child. According to one source,

> When Elphège (Anna's grandson) signed Pépère's death certificate in 1924, he identified the origin of his grandmother with the letters "Ind," which could be interpreted either that Anna came from the state of Indiana or she was an Indian. I am inclined to believe that Elphège meant that his father's mother, Anna, was an Indian, since Elphège and his siblings were closer to reality than anyone else to oral history that claims Anna had come from Virginia; (…). As a child, I had always heard that Anna was from Virginia. Also, one only needs to look at Anna's grandchildren and some offspring thereafter, to safely determine about their Indian ancestry (…). Victor was dearly cared for by his aunt, Antoine's sister, Marie Azélie Haydel, who also raised one of her sister's children, Alphonse Becnel. Both Victor and Alphonse were born in the

124 Interview with Sybil Haydel Morial, Baton Rouge, Spring 2013. There are many other success stories among the descendants of Victor Haydel. The late Haydel White, Sr.– son of Victor, Jr., was among the famous 992 Tuskegee Institute Airmen, the first African Americans to integrate U.S. Air Force pilots. He was awarded the US Congressional Medal of Honor in 2007. The late Adam Haydel – son of Victorin- was a leading New Orleans entrepreneur and a well-know philanthropist, notably to private African American institutions and religious groups. He was the founder of Majestic Funeral Home & Industrial Insurance Co, Le Rendezvous Restaurant, Rest Haven Memorial Park Cemetery, and the Haydel Subdivision Construction. Dr. Belmont Haydel (Ph.D. in organization theory, economics, and strategic management) is an international economist, a retired US diplomat (twice appointed by Presidents Kennedy and Johnson), and a university administrator and professor. He is the author of *A Rendezvous with My Professional Destiny: Making a Difference* (2004). Like Curtis M. Graves, he is a grandson of Elphège.

125 Anonymous remark; in Belmont F. Haydel. *The Victor Haydel Creole Family*, p. 36.

same year, 1835. The two boys most likely were playmates (from reliable oral history). Likewise, Victor and Cèleste Becnel, who lived on the Haydel Plantation for several years after their cohabitation, were not treated as slaves, although they lived during the end of slavery time. Baby Victor was baptized "Victor Haydel" in the Catholic Church, on Dec 13, 1835, an occasion that was probably orchestrated by Azélie. At that time, slaves were not usually baptized. This act might also show that Azélie cared much for baby Victor, perhaps equally with her nephew Alphonse. We know, too, that Azélie considered Anna a "companion" servant, not a slave, perhaps due, in part, because Azélie was barren.[126]

Collective memory is mostly selective memory resulting from a universal human propensity to discard the so-called inglorious facts and to keep those considered more gleaming for the group. Memory is not history. The role of the historian is to find a path through conflicting versions of historical facts, not for the sake of finding the absolute truth, but in order to make the facts understandable. In confronting some family memories with recorded historical evidence, the intention of this writer was only to help shed light on the history of a particular group of people who accomplished exceptional achievements despite the fact that the odds were against them since their ancestors were bogged down in the horrors of slavery and racial discrimination. The baptism of Victor in the Catholic Church cannot be interpreted as a proof of freedom because a law that later became a custom established since the 1724 Code Noir of Louisiana encouraged the baptism of slaves. It is also noteworthy that the historical data does not sustain the Indian origins of Anna. The mention "Ind" on Victor Haydel's death record can also be interpreted as "indéterminé" (undetermined in French). Whether an Indian or not, Anna was undeniably enslaved on the Haydel plantation and was never granted freedom by Azélie Haydel. If she was still alive after the Civil War, Anna did not receive a single piastre from the auction of the huge fortune of her former mistress held in 1867. Neither Victor nor Celeste inherited a single acre of land from their respective fathers. Antoine Haydel and Florestan Becnel were not wealthy men and, even had they been prosperous, their natural children would not have been legally allowed to inherit from them. Without any doubt, Victor Haydel and Alphonse Becnel grew together as playmates on the Haydel plantation. But when Alphonse Becnel inherited 1/50th of Azélie's succession, like Léo Becnel and other siblings, Victor received nothing, and it took him several years of hard work to finally become

---

126 This point of view is presented by Belmont F. Haydel as the official position of the descendants of Victor Haydel. For the sake of equity, large excerpts from a digest stating what Dr. Haydel considers as the point of view of his family are reproduced at the end of this book in appendix 5.

a landowner.[127] It is possible that if freedom had not come at the conclusion of the Civil War a serious offense could have caused him to be sold away by his former playmate and administrator of the last will of his deceased mistress. The best way to honor the memories of Anna, Victor, and Celeste is to let the world know the hardship they went through and the injustice of being considered chattel for many years with a price imposed on each of them. In doing so, much respect would also be paid to those who sacrificed their lives in the defense of freedom and civil rights in this country and beyond.

TABLE 15. VICTOR HAYDEL'S HOUSEHOLD IN THE 1880 FEDERAL CENSUS

Name	Age	Relation to head of household	Complexion	Occupation
Victor Haydel	45		Black	Farmer
Celeste	40	Wife	Black	Housewife
Victor	22	Son	Black	Laborer
Théophile	21	Son	Black	Laborer
Emma	18	Daughter	Black	at home
Clay	10	Son	Black	at home
Andreas	8	Son	Black	at home
Dizième	7	Son	Black	at home
Victorin	6	Son	Black	at home
Marcel	3	Son	Black	at home
Elphège	1	Son	Black	at home

127 SJB-107-1867/Partage (sharing) de la succession de feu Dame Azélie Haydel Veuve Marcelin Haydel. 15 July 1867.

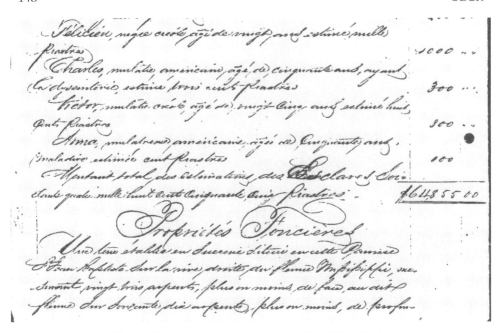

Fig. 5.4. Anna and Victor Haydel in the last inventory of the Haydel plantation.
Source: SJB-178-1860/Inventory of the estate of Widow Marcelin Haydel; 10-12 November 1860.

Ancestors of Marc Morial

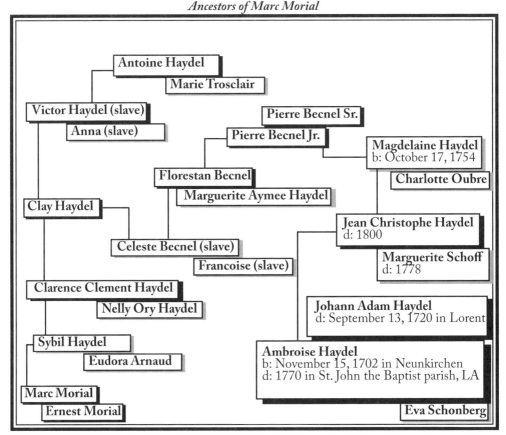

Fig. 5.5. The European and African connections of the Morial family of New Orleans.

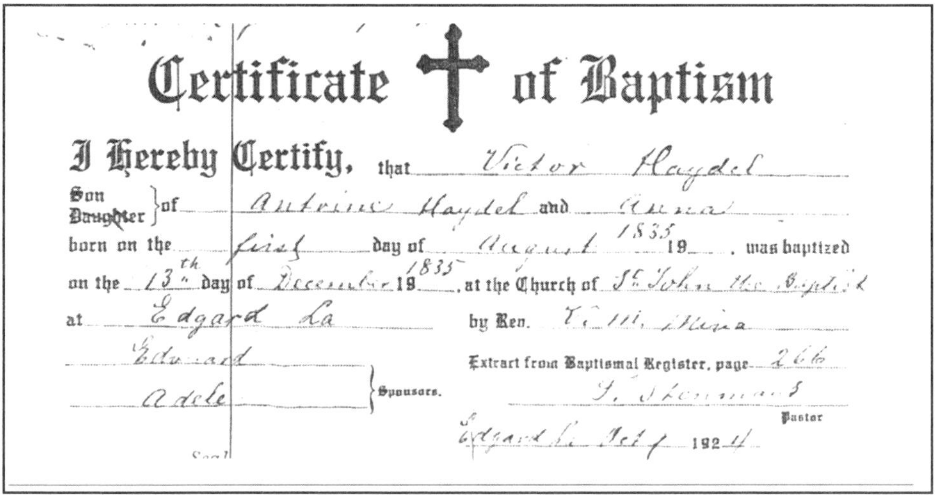

Certificate of Baptism

I Hereby Certify, that Victor Haydel

~~Daughter~~ Son of Antoine Haydel and Anna

born on the first day of August 1835 19__, was baptized

on the 13th day of December 1835 19__, at the Church of St. John the Baptist

at Edgard La by Rev. V. M. Mina

Edouard
Adele
Sponsors.

Extract from Baptismal Register, page 266

J. Stemmans
Pastor

Edgard La Oct 1 1924

Seal

Fig. 5.6. Baptism certificate of Victor Haydel. Courtesy of Belmont F. Haydel.

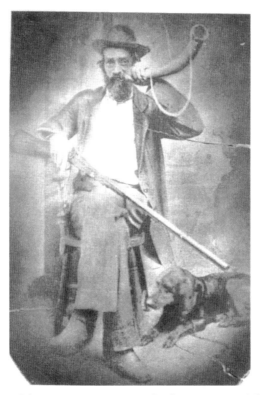

Fig 5.7. Victor Haydel (ca 1895). Courtesy of Belmont F. Haydel.

Fig. 5.8. Céleste Becnel (ca. 1880). Courtesy of Belmont F. Haydel.

Fig. 5.9. The Morial family after Ernest "Dutch" Morial was elected mayor of New Orleans (1978). From left to right: Jacques, Ernest "Dutch," Monique, Marc, Sybil Haydel Morial, Julie, Cheri. Courtesy of Sybil Haydel Morial.

EPILOGUE

Whitney Plantation: From Bradish Johnson to the Formosa controversy

The main plantation attached to the estate of Marie Azélie Haydel was sold to George W. Johnson, along with a smaller farm. Bradish Johnson was the real buyer behind these two sales. He made all the payments through the same agent and had the property officially registered under his name before Pierre Charles Cuvellier, notary public in New Orleans.[1] One source describes him as a Northerner and the one who named the old Habitation Haydel after his grandson, Harry Payne Whitney.[2] In fact he was a Southerner who turned the fallout from the Civil War to his advantage. Bradish Johnson (1811-1892) was born in the city of New Orleans and grew up downriver on the Magnolia plantation. At a later date, his father, William M. Johnson, Sr., moved to New York and engaged in the distilling business. Bradish Johnson was educated there and graduated from Columbia College. He was later successful in the distilling business himself. He soon became a millionaire and occupied a very prominent position in New York in commercial and social circles. Shortly before the war, he inherited from his brother, William M. Johnson Jr., the Woodland Plantation in Plaquemines Parish, where he erected the largest sugar mill in the state. After the war, he purchased many other plantations in the same parish in addition to the Haydel and Caroll plantations in St. John the Baptist Parish. He was one of the first members of the Louisiana Sugar Planters' Association and one of the founders of *The Louisiana Planter and Sugar Manufacturer*, a weekly newspaper devoted to the production of sugar, rice, and other agricultural industries of Louisiana.[3]

Bradish Johnson was married to Louisa Anna Lawrence, a member of New

---

1 SJB-107-1867. Partage de la succession de feu Dame Azélie Haydel veuve Marcelin Haydel. 18 July 1867. SJB-CB-1867-Ans-285. Succession Azélie Haydel to George W. Johnson. SJB-CB-1873-Cns-210. Johnson Bradish: Transfer of land to him by George W. Johnson. 13 May 1873.

2 The National Park Services [http://www.nps.gov/nr/travel/louisiana/whi.htm (accessed 6 October 2011)].

3 The Louisiana Planter and Sugar Manufacturer, Vol. IX, No. 20, New Orleans, 12 Nov. 1892, p.350. SJB-CB-1896-Lns-185. Succession of Bradish Johnson: 13 May 1896.

York's prominent merchant families. One of their daughters, Margaret Lawrence Johnson, married Stephen Whitney, the grandson of a New York millionaire. Their son, Harry Whitney, is the one after whom the Whitney plantation was named. Many sources confuse him with his much wealthier and better-known contemporary Harry Payne Whitney, but there was no relation between them.[4] Following the death of Johnson's wife in 1880, the Whitney plantation was sold to Pierre Edouard St. Martin and Théophile Perret. By that time, it was again thriving, producing 720 hogsheads of sugar.[5] In 1919, ten years after the death of Théophile Perret, the plantation was extended upstream with the purchase of the neighboring Aurelia plantation, better known then as the Mialaret plantation. By 1928, the property was totally controlled by Perret's daughter Mathilde and her husband, George Henri Tassin.[6] After the retirement of George Henri Tassin, his son George Sidney Tassin became the manager of the plantation. The latter was married to Léonie Granier, the daughter of the owner of Aurelia Plantation, Alovon

---

4 Stephen Whitney Lindsay 2008. Bradish Johnson (1811-1892), pp.7-9. Article accessed online on 5 December 2013 [http://stevelindsay.net/DickeyLindsay/BRADISH_JOHNSON_AND_ME.pdf]. The author is the great great-grandchild of Stephen Whitney and Margaret Lawrence Johnson. This article ends a long-lived confusion between the sportsman and Arctic explorer Harry Whitney (1873-1936) and the businessman Harry Whitney (1872-1930).

5 Johnson Bradish & heirs of Mrs. Bradish Johnson to P.E. St. Martin and T. Perret. 17 May 1880 [SJB-CB-1880-Fns-120]. US Agricultural Census 1880, quoted by Roberts 2005, p.24. Pierre Edouard St. Martin was born in St. John the Baptist parish in 1842. His paternal grandfather, Pierre B. Saint-Martin, was a planter and an attorney, who served during a number of years on the bench as judge of the district composed of St. John the Baptist, St. Charles and Jefferson parishes. The most famous case handled by the latter was the trial of the slaves involved in the 1811 uprising on the German Coast [*Biography of Pierre E. St. Martin: http://files.usgwarchives.org/la/orleans/bios/s-000037.txt. Submitted by Mike Miller July 1998. Accessed 18 October 2010*].

Théophile Perret (1834-1909), Edouard's half-brother and brother-in-law, lived at Whitney with his wife Mathilde St. Martin. Their daughter, Mathilde Louise Perret (1857-1936) married George Henri Tassin (1851–1929) in 1876. The latter was the plantation's overseer and his wife operated the plantation store. They also lived in the big house at Whitney Plantation. Their children were: Marie Henriette Tassin (1878-1960), Georges Sidney Tassin (1879-1950), Charles J. Tassin (1882-1972), George Henri Tassin Jr. (1884-1903), Albin Tassin (born July 1886), and Marie Amélie Tassin (1888-1973). All the information on the Tassins is from personal communication with Deanna Tassin Sexnayder (October 2010).

6 Succession of Théophile Perret, 7 June 1909 [SJB-CB-1909-Sns-82]. Genealogy Trails History Group [http://genealogytrails.com/lou/plantatons.html].

Granier.[7] George Sidney and his wife lived in the Mialaret house, but his mother and unmarried siblings continued to live in the big house on Whitney Plantation. Albin and Amélie, the youngest children of George Henri Tassin and Mathilde Louise Perret, were the ones who made most of the graffiti (height markings and signatures) on the walls of the loggia and adjoining bath on the second floor. They date back to the late 19th century and early 20th century and have survived time and restoration. Maybe nobody loved this house as much as Amélie did. In late October 1945, a New Orleans newspaper referred to her as "Tante Lili, living alone in the big house with a revolver under her pillow at night."[8]

Ownership shifted again in 1946 when Whitney was sold to Alfred Mason Barnes of New Orleans. Its fourteen-room two-story house, built of masonry and cypress, was then described as "one of the most interesting in the entire South" by Charles E. Peterson, senior landscape architect of the United States Department of the Interior. The plantation had at that time 1,200 acres of land in cultivation, and large sugar cane crops were harvested and transformed by a nearby co-operative sugarhouse. Rice was also cultivated for commercial purposes and enough corn, potatoes, and other small crops were produced for domestic use along with cattle and poultry.[9] A. M. Barnes kept the name Whitney and hired Maurice Tassin, the son of George Sidney Tassin, as the manager of the plantation. All the Tassins and St. Martins moved from the plantation, except for Maurice, his wife Gladys, and their children. The Barnes visited on weekends and for longer periods in the summer, but no one lived full-time in the big house. Maurice kept his job for nearly a quarter of a century. During the entire time, the plantation was profitable in all but a couple of years, due to hurricanes Hilda in 1964 and Betsy in 1965, winning several awards from the St. James Sugar Cooperative for the quality of the sugar cane crop, which translated to higher payments. The plantation store was still the gathering place of the laborers who enjoyed cold drinks after work. Besides food, it also

---

7 This plantation became the property of Mathias Roussel Sr. by 1785 when the latter went through an exchange of farms with Francois André. Roussel apparently extended the farm in the late 1790s with land acquired by his wife from the estate of her father Mathias Haydel. When Mathias Roussel died in 1818, the property was passed on to his widow Marie Charlotte Haydel. Between 1844 and 1846, the Roussel plantation fell under the control of Félix Becnel and his partner Drauzin R. Perret, the brother of Théophile Perret and half-brother of Pierre Edouard St. Martin. Drauzin sold his portion of the land to Marie Azélie Haydel in 1853, and Antonin Mialaret purchased the rest of the property in 1867. The Mialaret plantation became "Aurelia" when Alovon Granier bought it in 1895 and renamed it after his wife [Jean Jacques Haydel to André Portier: land sale (SJB-BR-8-1784); André Portier to Mathias Haydel: land sale (SJB-39-1785); Mathias Roussel père: Echange d'habitation avec Francois André (SJB-44-1785); Mathias Haydel: Acte d'abandon (SJB-10-1798); Mathias Roussel père: sale of estate (SJB-51-1818); Widow Roussel's succession (SJB-169-1846); D. Perret to Widow Marcellin Haydel: sale of land (SJB-36-1853); Dillard & als. 2005, p.29].

8 *The Times Picayune*, 29 October 1945.

9 Dillard & als. 2005, p.29. The Times Picayune, 29 October 1945.

contained various commodities, from nails to tooth brushes, but it was closed in 1968.[10]

Maurice Tassin retired in the early 1970s because of age and poor health, but he had permission from the Barnes to live on the plantation as long as he wished. At that time, he arranged for the plantation farmland to be leased to local farmers belonging to the Hymel family. He finally moved from Whitney in 1975, and the resident labor force did so around the same time. This was the real beginning of the downfall of the plantation since maintenance was not performed anymore on any of the buildings, and they deteriorated greatly. The Barnes' children did not have the same interest in the plantation that their father did, and they had no other plan but selling it. Steve Barnes, a grandson of A. M. Barnes, remembers, with a bit of anger, members of his family advocating the bulldozing of all the buildings on the site in order to sell it for a better price. The cypress slave cabins were still in a very good shape in the late 1970s when they were torn down and removed from the site in order to allow the big tractor-trailers to swing easily into the plantation from River Road and get loaded with cane, which was transported to the cooperative sugar mill located upriver near Oak Alley plantation. In 1991, when the widow of Maurice Tassin made her last trip to Whitney with several members of her family, she was totally shocked to see the condition of the site, but she was relieved that her husband, who died in 1980, never saw the place in such terrible shape.[11]

In 1990, the plantation was sold to the Formosa Chemicals and Fiber Corporation, which had the intention to build the world's largest rayon plant on the site. The company also envisioned buying the nearby Evergreen Plantation, but it had to face local activists concerned by the destruction of historic landmarks and the negative effects of the rayon plant, notably the "use of local bottomland hardwood in vast quantities, and substantial dioxin pollution from the pulp-bleaching process." The protest was undertaken by members of the Delta Chapter of the Sierra Club through its Hazardous Waste Committee. The claims of the environmentalists, echoed by the *Time-Picayune*, consisted of three points: a diversified approach to economic development along the River Road Corridor, the recruiting of clean industries, and the consideration of alternative land use and development plans.[12] Formosa apparently came to a compromise when it decided to turn the buildings on Whitney plantation into a museum (The Museum of Louisiana's Creole Culture) and commissioned a study from the Department of Geography and Anthropology at Louisiana State University. The idea came from anthropologist Jay Edwards and his colleagues at Louisiana State University. They were introduced to the plantation in 1981 by Deanna

---

10 Communicated by Deanna Tassin Schexnayder, the daughter of Maurice Tassin [October 2010].

11 Interviews with Steve Barnes and Deanna Tassin Schexnayder [October 2010]. Some of the information was taken from a short manuscript written by Mrs. Ann Wood Barnes, the mother of Steve Barnes.

12 Hal Dean, "In opposition to Formosa plant." Letter to the editor, *The Times-Picayune* (3 January 1991), p.B8. The Sierra Club is America's oldest, largest, and most influential grassroots environmental organization. The Delta Chapter supports the work of the Sierra Club in Louisiana [http://louisiana.sierraclub.org/].

Tassin Schexnayder who was also part of the faculty of this institution at that time. They immediately recognized the historic and archeological significance of the buildings at Whitney and conducted research on the property even before it was purchased by Formosa.[13]

The Whitney Plantation is a complex of buildings composed of a dozen historic structures. According to Jay Edwards, the Big House is one of the finest surviving examples of Spanish and French Creole architecture and one of the earliest and best preserved raised Creole cottages in Louisiana. It is clearly antedated only by the house on Destrehan plantation. It is one of the best preserved Creole plantation houses standing on the River Road. Sometime prior to 1815 the big house was rebuilt in its present configuration with seven rooms on each level, plus a full-length gallery across the front and an open loggia facing the rear. Moreover, it is one of the very few historic American houses known to have received decorative wall paintings on both its exterior and its interior. Whitney Plantation is also significant because of the number of its historic outbuildings which were added to the site over the years, thus providing a unique perspective on the evolution of the Louisiana working plantation. This is something which is impossible to find anywhere else on the river road since very few plantations preserve their early outbuildings. Even Evergreen Plantation, which preserves many of its early buildings, provides the visitor with a much distorted view of the historic Louisiana sugar plantation. Evergreen was carefully planned and laid out at one time (ca. 1840) according to a single plan. At Whitney, eleven outbuildings were recognized as worthy of National Register. These include: an original kitchen building, a saddle storage shed, a privy, a watering trough for mules, an overseer's house, a mule barn and feed storage building, a late 19th century plantation store, a pigeonnier, and the last surviving example of a true French Creole barn. The kitchen is believed to be the oldest detached kitchen in Louisiana.[14]

In 1992, the site was added to the National Register of Historic Places. Meanwhile the rayon business underwent depression, thus encouraging the Formosa Corporation to sell the site to the Cummings family of New Orleans in 1999. Urbain Alexandre Diagne, then the mayor of Gorée Island (Senegal), visited Whitney in May 2000 after presiding over the initiation of the African-American Museum in Saint-Martinville, in southwest Louisiana. It was then that this writer came in contact with the site for the first time as part of the large mayoral delegation composed of administrators, teachers, and business people. We found the plantation literally "wrapped" and awaiting badly needed restoration, but much brainstorming and consulting with local scholars was undertaken. Finally, it was decided to turn the site into a museum with a focus on the lives of the slaves and their legacies, a topic so far neglected by most of the old plantations inscribed on the flyers of the local tour operators. Whitney Plantation is a genuine landmark built by African slaves and their descendants. The site is now dedicated to the interpretation of slavery along River Road

---

13 Communicated by Deanna Tassin Schexnayder [October 2010].

14 Edwards J. 1991, p. 1-20. The house on Destrehan Plantation was erected between 1787 and 1790 by Charles Paquet, a free man of color (the same as in chapter 5). In the 19th century it also went through further phases of construction.

with the involvement of the local community. As a site of memory and consciousness, the Whitney Plantation Museum is meant to pay homage to all the slaves who lived on the plantation itself and to all of those who lived elsewhere in Louisiana. May those who reach this sacred ground meditate profoundly upon the fate of the forgotten ones who gave this part of the country most of its unique culture.

In opposition to Formosa plant

New Orleans

The Delta Chapter of the Sierra Club opposes the siting and construction of the proposed Formosa petrochemical complex on the west bank of St. John the Baptist Parish.

The Environmental Protection Agency plans to hold a public hearing on the matter today at 7 p.m. in the Edgard courthouse.

Formosa Chemical plans to build first a pulp/rayon plant, then a much larger polyvinyl chloride (PVC) facility.

State and parish officials have offered Formosa a total of $448 million in tax relief over 10 years to entice the company to come here to create jobs.

Formosa Chemical has bought the 1,800-acre Whitney Plantation and is contemplating purchase of Evergreen Plantation, much to the outrage of historic preservationists. The company is also buying out homes in Wallace, a small, low-income, black community, reminiscent of the buyouts of Reveilletown and Morrisonville, now ghost towns adjacent to Dow Chemical.

A totally unprecedented decision by the St. John Parish Council rezoned the Whitney tract from single-family residential to unrestricted-use industrial.

The local cheerleader for Formosa, Parish President Lester J. Millet Jr., has described the

rayon process as one with a raw material of wood chips and thus "very clean with no pollution. ... It's all clean jobs." In reality, the situation is quite the opposite.

Formosa's environmental history is notorious. It proposes to use local bottomland hardwood in vast quantities, and substantial dioxin pollution from the pulp-bleaching process is guaranteed.

The EPA is preparing an Environmental Impact Statement (EIS) on the social, economic and other broadly defined impact of the rayon plant. Shockingly, EPA has neglected to include in its EIS Formosa's PVC facility, which is three-quarters of the proposed complex.

In addition, EPA ought to include the expected impact of the Aristech Chemical phenol and cumene plant, on the drawing board for directly across the Mississippi River from Formosa's plot.

The Delta Chapter of the Sierra Club supports a diversified approach to economic development along the River Road Corridor by encouraging the recruiting of "clean industries" and supports the consideration of alternative land use and development plans.

Hal Dean
Hazardous Waste Committee,
Sierra Club,
Delta Chapter

Fig. 6.1. "In opposition to Formosa plant." Letter to the editor, by Hal Dean. Source: *Times Picayune* (3 January 1991), p.B8

Fig. 6.2. Aerial view of Whitney Plantation from the riverside. Only one pigeonnier is standing between the plantation store (front) and the main house. The second one was knocked down by a hurricane (1965), but it has been rebuilt to its original form since then. The plantation store, still in operation, was closed in 1968.
Source: Photography by Sam R. Sutton, October 1967. Courtesy of Steve Barnes.

Fig. 6.3. Aerial view of Whitney Plantation from the rear. The slave cabins that used to be downriver, to the right, were removed in the late 1970s.
Source: Photography by Sam R. Sutton, October 1967. Courtesy of Steve Barnes.

Fig. 6.4. Front view of Whitney's big house.
Source: Photography by Sam R. Sutton, October 1967. Courtesy of Steve Barnes.

Fig. 6.5. Rear view of Whitney's big house.
Source: Photography by Sam R. Sutton, October 1967. Courtesy of Steve Barnes.

Fig. 6.6. The Mialaret house under restoration on Whitney plantation [March 24, 2010]. Anthony Turducken's photo gallery : http://www.flickr.com/photos/anthonyturducken/4460187703/in/set-72157623562109041/ (Accessed 24 March 2010).

Fig. 6.7. Close-up of mantle – Initials "MH" on ceiling. Source: Erika Sabine Roberts 2005, p. 6.

Fig. 6.8. Front view of Evergreen's Big House.
Photograph by Belmont F. Haydel

Fig. 6.9. John & Donna Cummings.
Photograph by Tracy Smith.

Fig. 6.10. Mayor of Goree Island, Urbain Alexandre Diagne (middle of first row), and his delegation pausing with American hosts after a ride on paddlewheel boat Natchez.

Fig. 6.11. Whitney Plantation. Memorial dedicated to the people enslaved in Louisiana (107, 000 names retrieved from the Louisiana Slave Database).

Fig. 6.12. His excellency Mr. Amadou Niang, Ambassador of Senegal to the US, in front of the Wall of Honor dedicated to the slaves who lived on Whitney Plantation.

Fig. 6.13. Whitney Plantation: Ambassador Niang in the Field of Angels, a memorial dedicated to 2,200 slave children who died in St. John Parish between 1823 and 1863.

APPENDICES

Appendix I
Sale of slaves: community of Jean Jacques Haydel Père and his late wife, January 13, 1820

- Raphael, Kiamba nation, 60 years old, estimated 50 piastres.
- Lubin, Mandingo nation, 50 years old, afflicted with hernia, estimated 50 piastres.
- Mars, Kiamba nation, 60 years old, estimated 50 piastres.
- Augustin, Kiamba nation, 50 years old, good house Negro, estimated 400 piastres
- Francois, Creole "griffon" (Black and Indian), 50 years old, carpenter, barrel maker, and a good domestic, estimated 900 piastres.
- Alexandre, Bambara nation, 30 years old, for a long time in a sickly condition, estimated 50 piastres.
- Antoine, Creole, 20 years old, good cart man, ploughman, and a good cattle keeper, estimated 1600 piastres.
- Hilaire, Creole, 19 years old, good cart man, ploughman, and a good cattle keeper, estimated 1600 piastres.
- Etienne, Creole, 19 years old, good cart man, ploughman, and a good cattle keeper, estimated 1700 piastres.
- Azor, Creole, 19 years old, good cart man, ploughman, and a good cattle keeper, estimated 1700 piastres.
- Joseph, Creole, 20 years old, good cart man, ploughman, and a good cattle keeper, estimated 1700 piastres.
- Robin, Creole of America, 18 years old, good cart man, ploughman, and a good cattle keeper, estimated 1600 piastres.
- Dick, Creole of America, 25 years old, good cart man, ploughman, and a good cattle keeper, estimated 1600 piastres.
- Jean Pierre, Creole, 22 years old, good cart man, ploughman, and a good cattle keeper, estimated 1600 piastres.
- Reguine, Creole Negress of America, 18 years old, good house Negress, estimated 1100 piastres.
- Catherine, Creole Negress, 16 years old, good house Negress, estimated 1100 piastres.
- Julien, Creole, 16 years old, good house Negro, estimated 1200 piastres.
- Rene, Creole, 13 years old, good cattle keeper, estimated 1200 piastres.
- Claire, Creole Negress, 20 years old, domestic, seamstress, and child Ursin, 7 years old, estimated 1600 piastres.

Appendix II
Sale of slaves: community of Jean Jacques Haydel Père and his late wife, January 14, 1820

- Sam, Sozo (Soso) nation, 60 years old, blind, and wife Marguerite, Creole, 66 years old, estimated null, were not sold because of their age and were given the choice to live in any of the houses of the heirs. Marguerite had to take care of Sam.
- Marie Joseph, Creole, 50 years old, cook, and daughter Eleonore, 9 years old, estimated 950 piastres, sold together to Jean Jacques Haydel père for 1500 piastres.
- Marie, Creole Negress, 43 years old, cook, estimated 450 piastres, sold to Pierre Becnel fils for 800 piastres.
- Pauline, Creole Negress, 10 years old, estimated 500 piastres, sold to Pierre Becnel fils for 1155 piastres.
- Honoré, Canga nation, 30 years old, good house Negro, formerly afflicted with hernia, and estimated 1,200 piastres, sold at bidder's risk to Andre Hymel for 1205 piastres.
- Agathe, Creole Negress, 43 years old, and three children: Jean and Jeanne, twins, 4 yr; and Clemence, 18 months, estimated 1800 piastres, sold together to Pierre Becnel fils for 2115 piastres.
- Rosette, Creole Negress, 40 years old, good house Negress, estimated 750 piastres, sold to Jean Jacques Haydel fils for 905 piastres.
- Rose, Creole Negress, 14 years old, domestic, estimated 1200 piastres, sold to Florestan Becnel for 1605 piastres.
- Francoise, Creole Negress, 12 years old, estimated 750 piastres, sold to Daniel Caraby for 965 piastres.
- Eugenie, Creole Negress, 24 years old, good house Negress, and 2 children: Basile, 4 years old, and Syphorien, 1 year old, estimated 1700 piastres, sold to Pierre Becnel for 1730 piastres.
- Sila, Creole of America, 40 years old, and 2 children: Toussaint, 2 years old, and Moliere, 6 months, estimated 1200 piastres, sold to Louis le Bourgeois for 1305 piastres.
- Bernard, Kiamba nation, 50 years old, afflicted in the past by moments of dementia (*moments de démence*), estimated 100 piastres, sold to Pierre Becnel père for 210 piastres.
- Alexis, Bambara nation, 50 years old, sugar maker, estimated 250 piastres, sold to Jean Jacques Haydel fils for 300 piastres.
- Henry, Jamaican Creole, 50 years old, estimated 500 piastres, sold to Jean Jacques Haydel fils for 1000 piastres.
- Flore, Creole Negress of St. Domingue, 60 years old, estimated 250 piastres,

sold to Jean Jacques Haydel for 360 piastres.

- Sophie, Negress of the Congo nation, 35 years old, good house Negress, estimated 600 piastres, sold to Marcellin Haydel for 625 piastres.
- Barnabe, Bambara nation, 30 years old, sugar maker, sawyer, and good house Negro, estimated 1000 piastres, sold to Marcellin Haydel for 1850 piastres.
- Manuel, Creole, 23 years old, a thief and a maroon (*voleur et maronneur*), estimated 400 piastres, sold to Michel Simon for 600 piastres.
- Lucas, Soso nation, 35 years old, good house Negro, estimated 1200 piastres, sold to Marcellin Haydel for 1450 piastres.
- Hector, Sozo (Soso) nation, 50 years old, estimated 100 piastres, sold to Germain Ayme for 355 piastres.
- Michel, Canga nation, 30 years old, good house Negro, estimated 1500 piastres, sold to Georges Roussel for 2015 piastres.
- Valere, Canga nation, 25 years old, cartman, ploughman, and good house Negro, estimated 1600 piastres, sold to Georges Roussel for 2015 piastres.
- Achile, Mandingo nation, 22 years old, cartman, ploughman, and good house Negro, estimated 1600 piastres, sold to Jean Jacques Haydel fils for 1780 piastres.
- Philipe, Timiny (Temne) nation, cartman, good house Negro, estimated 1000 piastres, sold to Marcellin Haydel for 1,700 piastres.
- Isidore, Congo nation, 20 years old, cartman, good house Negro, afflicted with "the ring worm," estimated 500 piastres, sold to Louis le Bourgeois for 800 piastres.
- Gabriel, Congo nation, 25 years old, good house Negro, estimated 900 piastres, sold to Marcellin Haydel for 915 piastres (cf. succession Azelie Haydel/SJB-178-1860).
- Baptiste, Creole, 15 years old, good cattle keeper, estimated 1200 piastres, sold to Pierre Becnel père for 1,605 piastres.

Appendix III
Sale of slaves: estate of late Jean Jacques Haydel Père, March 10, 1827

- Augustin, Kiamba nation, 60 years old, estimated 50 piastres, sold to Jean Jacques Haydel for 200 piastres.
- Francois, negre Creole, 60 years old, estimated 100 piastres, sold to Marcellin Haydel for 410 piastres.
- Antoine, negre Creole, 30 years old, cart driver, and ploughman, estimated 700 piastres, sold to Marcellin Haydel for 1105 piastres.
- Hilaire, negre Creole, 28 years old, cart driver, and ploughman, estimated 700 piastres, sold to Marcellin Haydel for 1205 piastres.
- Joseph, negre Creole, 30 years old, cart driver, and ploughman, estimated 1000 piastres, sold to Becnel Freres & Brou for 1505 piastres.

- Azor, negre Creole, 29 years old, cart driver, and ploughman, estimated 1000 piastres, sold to Marcellin Haydel for 2055 piastres.
- Julien, negre Creole, 25 years old, cart driver, and ploughman, estimated 1000 piastres, sold to Marcellin Haydel for 1805 piastres.
- Rene, negre Creole, 23 years old, cart driver, and ploughman, estimated 1000 piastres, sold to Becnel Freres & Brou for 2130 piastres.
- Etienne, negre Creole, 29 years old, cart driver, and ploughman, estimated 1100 piastres, sold to Jean Jacques for 1600 piastres.
- Yorick, Negro from Virginia, 30 years old, cart driver, and ploughman, estimated 1000 piastres, sold to Marcellin Haydel for 2010 piastres.
- Robert, negre Creole, 28 years old, cart driver, and ploughman, estimated 700 piastres, sold to Jean Jacques Haydel fils for 1375 piastres.
- Ursin, negre Creole, 16 years old, cart driver, estimated 500 piastres, sold to Martian Belfort Haydel for 1670 piastres.
- Reguini, Negresse Creole, 28 years old, and child Jean Baptiste, 6 mo., estimated 550 piastres, sold to Marcellin Haydel for 1105 piastres.
- Joseph, orphan, 7 years old, estimated 100 piastres, sold to Marcellin Haydel for 330 piastres.
- Marie Joseph, Negresse Creole, 60 years old, cook, estimated 200 piastres, sold to Jean Jacques Haydel fils for 200 piastres. (Note: emancipated April 30, 1827 ; Ref. SJB-72-1827: Liberté par J. J. Haydel a la Négresse Marie Joseph).
- Claire, négresse Créole, 32 years old, estimated 400 piastres, sold to Jean Jacques Haydel fils for 400 piastres. (Note: emancipated April 30, 1827 ; Ref. SJB-71-1827 : Liberté par J. J. Haydel a la Négresse Claire).

Appendix IV
Auction of slaves attached to the estate of Jean Jacques Haydel, Jr. (April 30, 1840).

Sold at the Bath Saloon of the St. Louis Hotel, by Joseph Le Carpentier, Auctioneer, by virtue of an order from the Honorable the District Court for the First Judicial District of the State of Louisiana dated 24th March 1840, and at the request of the syndics of the creditors of Jean Jacques Haydel, after the advertisements required by law, to wit: In the Bee (State paper) in French and English, March 27th, April 13th, 20th & 30th, and in the Louisiana Courier in French and English, March 29th, April 13th, 20th & 29th, the following slaves. Terms: One half payable in March 1841 and one half in March 1842 in notes satisfactorily endorsed and bearing mortgage until final payment. Said notes must be made payable in New Orleans and in case of non payment when due will bear from the day of expiration an interest of 10% per annum until final payment. Said clause not to be taken advantage of to defer the payment of any note. The slaves will be delivered to the purchasers when the conditions of the sale will be fulfilled. The acts of sale to be passed at the cost of the purchasers before Felix Grima, Esq., notary public.

Negroes

1. Little Guim, 50 years, African, sold to Mr. Etienne Villere, f.c.m., $170.
2. Paul, 48 years, Congo, sold to Cyprien Tremoulet, $300.
3. Achille 48 years, carter & ploughman, sold to Achille Lorio, $800.
4. George, 48 years, American, sold to Edmond Fazende, $650.
5. Big John, 45 years, American, carter & ploughman, sold to Phi Lambert, $675.
6. Borel, 30 years, American, carter & ploughman, sold to Felix Garcia, $1,325.
7. Lewis, 34 years, American, engineer, carter & ploughman, sold to Felix Garcia, $1,400.
8. Maille, 32 years, American, carter & ploughman, sold to Felix Garcia, $1,425.
9. Diastone, 32 years, American, carter & ploughman, sold to Sosthene Roman, $950.
10. Andre Jackson 36 years, American, carter & ploughman, sold to Felix Garcia, $1,225.
11. Andrew King, 36 years, American, field hand, sold to Pascalis Labarre, $11,00.
12. Andrew Rolling, 32 years, American, carter & ploughman, sold to Marcelle Bienvenu, $1,275.
13. Moses, 32 years, American, carter & ploughman, sold to Mauge Quentin, $1000.
14. Patrice, 40 years, American, carter & ploughman, sold to Felix Garcia, $1,125.
15. Queto, 28 years, Creole, maimed in one arm, carter and ploughman, sold to Widow Choppin, $350.
16. Roffine, 24 years, American, carter & ploughman, sold to Widow Louis Bourgeois, $1,025.
17. William, 32 years, American, carter & ploughman, sold to Felix Garcia, $1,225.
18. Steeving, 36 years, American, sold Joseph Labarre, $1,050.
19. Guimilas, 32 years, American, carter & ploughman, sold to Philip Young, $1,025.
20. Charles, 32 years, American, carter & ploughman, sold to Marcelle Bienvenu, $1,375.
21. Guiribraia, 36 years, American, carter & ploughman, sold to Felix Garcia, $1,275.

22. Maurice, 12 years, Creole, coachman, sold to Nicolas Bertoli, $1,200.

23. Andrew, 36 years, American, blacksmith, sold to Pascalis Labarre, 1,225.

24. Denis, 40 years, American, carter & ploughman, sold to Belford Haydel, $800.

25. Jacques, 65 years, African, sold to Louis Charbonnet, $525.

26. Guilbert, years, American, carter & ploughman, sold to Felix Garcia, $1,175.

27. Dick Nouveau, 26 years, American, carter & ploughman, sold to Widow Arnaud, $1,100.

28. François, 65 years, African, has an hernia, sold to Pascalis Labarre, $225.

29. Plaisant, 40 years, American, has an hernia, sold to Antoine Bienvenu, $500.

30. Gairie, 20 years, American, carter & ploughman, sold to Drausin Gaudet, $1,450.

31. Ned, 34 years, American, good cooper, sold to Samuel Mc Cutchon fils, $1,500.

32. Grand Dick, 30 years, American, carter & ploughman, sold to Marcelle Bienvenu, $1,400.

33. Dick Gros, American, good carter, sold to Antoine Bienvenu, $1050.

34. Gueret, 30 years, American, carter & ploughman, has a swollen leg, sold to Melicourt Bienvenu, $1,200.

35. Gurine Luta, 36 years, American, carter & ploughman, sold to Felix Garcia, $ 1525.

36. Rasumud, 34 years, American, carter & ploughman, sold to Felix Garcia, $1,325.

37. Davis, 30 years, American, field hand, sold to Felix Garcia, $1,325.

38. Alexander, 65 years, African, field hand, sold to A.P. Lanaux, $325.

39. Gaspard, 50 years, African, field hand, attacked with the piles, sold to Felix Garcia, $450.

40. Charlot, 30 years, Creole, carter and ploughman, sold to Felix Garcia, $1375.

41. Jacob, 70 years, African, has an hernia, sold to Lucien Wells, $175.

42. Paul, 51 years, African, distiller, sold to George Haydel, $475.

43. Azor, 11 years, house servant, sold to Lucien Wells, $725.

Negresses

44. Marianne, 56 years, Congo, field hand, sold to Etienne Villeré, $300.

45. Suzanne, 51 years, Congo, field hand, sold to John Hoover, $350.

46. Helene, 50 years, American, field hand, sold to J.B. Lotorez, $400.

47. Victoire, 58 years, Congo, field hand, attacked with the piles and her child Hilaire, 10 years, sold to Achille Lorio, $975.

48. Celeste, 28 years, Creole. Seamstress & her child Eve, 4 years, sold to Edouard Planchard, $925.

49. Marguerite, 28 years, somewhat of a servant, sold to William Knight, $800.

50. Marie Jeanne, 18 years, Creole, servant, sold to Douradon Bringier, $700.

51. Lucy, 18 years, Creole, servant, sold to Jose Marti, $925.

52. Corine, 16 years, Creole, servant, sold to Samuel Mac Cutchon fils, $950.

53. Fanchonnette, 14 years, Creole, sold to Etienne Doleze, $1000.

54. Marguerite, 30 years, American, good servant, seamstress, washer & cook, sold to Theophile Verloin, $1,225.

55. Peguy, 65 years, African, field hand, sold to Pascal Labarre, $225.

56. Anne, 38 years, field hand, sold to A. Degruis, $550.

57. Cloe, 65 years, American, attacked with the asthma, sold to Lucien Wells, $175.

58. Clemence, 30 years, Creole, field hand, sold to Mauge Quentin, $900.

59. Lady, 30 years, American, field hand, with 5 children: Fitsus Negro 8 years, Arthur 6 years, Lucy 3 years, Celeste and Celestine twins of two years, sold to Felix Garcia, $2,650.

60. Liza, 28 years, field hand with a child aged 4 years, sold to Omer Fortier, $1000.

61. Sery, 25 years, idiot, sold to Omer Fortier, $105.

62. Suzette, 16 years, Creole, servant, sold to Emile Verloin, $1,125.

Total: $57,075
New Orleans, April 30th 1840
Signed. J.L. Carpentier
Source: NONA, Felix Grima, Vol. 30, Act 462. June 27, 1840.

Appendix V
A digest about our Haydel family

By Belmont F. Haydel, Ph.D
December 8, 2013

Ref: My research and book about "Our Haydel Family" — the descendants of Victor Haydel (Pépère) and Céleste Becnel. (See my book, *The Victor Haydel Creole Family: Whitney (Haydel) Plantation — Plantation Beginnings And Early Descendants*, 3rd ed. 2009, Copyright 2009. Warminster, PA: Cooke Publishing Company. Throughout my digest here, I refer to it as my "book." In my digest, whenever I write "Our Family," I am referring to direct descendants of Victor and Céleste Haydel...

About Anna: for years, Our Family has heard various versions about Anna's ethnic and racial background, and most of us have struggled to find the facts about her ancestry and from where she came (See my book, pp. 34-36). We cannot agree with census reports that she was black, for many reasons (too much to elaborate here). One clear reason is that census-taking clerks found it more convenient to simply accept information from families, whether true or not. I know that such was the case with material about Anna. There are many variations that it is almost impossible today to consider any *one* belief or even any official one as factual. Sadie Haydel Woods, Anna's grandchild (through Victorin) said that "Anna was pure Indian with no racial mix" (See my book, p. 36, second column), despite your claim that she was black. It appears that your viewpoint came from official sources, such as census records, and also from someone with whom you may have been in contact about Our Family ancestry.

As of now, I have not found any *definitive* facts in my research about my great, great grandmother Anna's racial background, that consider her to be other than Indian; Indians were given their freedom by 1820 in Louisiana, before Anna was born, circa 1821. Clearly, if Anna had any Indian blood when Pépère was born in 1835, she was supposed to have been legally free, thus not a slave... When Pépère's death certificate was signed in 1924, by Elphège (Anna's grandson), he wrote in the place provided on the form requiring the origin of the deceased's mother, Elphège wrote "Ind," which could be interpreted either that Anna came from the state of Indiana or she was an Indian. (I am inclined to believe that Elphège meant that his father's mother, Anna, was an Indian, since there was no indication, from any source, she came from Indiana. Elphège and his siblings were closer to reality than anyone else in oral history that claims that Anna had come from Indiana; I note that you wrote: "she [Anna] came from the East coast, probably Virginia." As a child, I had always heard that Anna was from Virginia. Also, one only needs to look at Anna's grandchildren and some offspring thereafter, to safely determine their Indian ancestry. I invite you to review my book, p. 37, bottom of left column:

From "the numerous accounts…about Anna's ancestry" perhaps a clue might be uncovered when we look closely at the appearance of Victor and Céleste's eight adult children and their subsequent offspring that we can identify their Indian features, as I describe below. That Anna was either a pure Indian or mixed Indian should undeniably be biologically known, by simply observing Anna's offspring. Their physical appearance could not be an accident of nature, but rather a genetic truism; nature and biology do not contradict each other (we are biologically what our foreparents were). That Victor and Céleste's children may have had Indian blood has been noted by their reddish-tone pigmentation, straight black hair, and high cheekbones. Numerous accounts corroborate the claim that Anna had Indian blood. I point out that Victor and Céleste's first grandchild, Norma, had reddish color skin, and she had high cheekbones (See p. 88, photo of Norma, who was Victor Jr.'s daughter, whom I personally knew). Surely, many of Victor and Céleste's descendants still have Caucasian and/ or Negroid features. Today, Our Family acknowledges that we have black (Negroid), white (Caucasian), and red (Indian) blood. Numerous times, then as today, our physical appearance reflects these racial mixtures. (See photos in my book of Victor's children, pp. 46 – 66; and later their offspring, all Victor's direct descendants on pp. 95, 130, 133, 134, 137, 138). I am not overly concerned that certain family members insist that Anna was purely black; much of this behavior is motivated by personal reasons. To the best of knowledge, few, if anybody, today, could tell you much about Anna's true ancestry. Likewise, she seemed to have vanished into the "unknown" shortly after Victor's birth. I have not examined when her name was no longer recorded on any census report...

Victor was dearly cared for by his aunt, Antoine's sister, Marie Azélie Haydel, who also raised one of her sister's children, Alphonse Becnel; both Victor and Alphonse were born in the same year, 1835. The two boys most likely were playmates (from reliable oral history). Likewise, Victor and Céleste Becnel, who lived on the Haydel Plantation for several years after their cohabitation, were not treated as slaves, although they lived during the end of slavery time. Baby Victor was baptized "Victor Haydel" in the Catholic Church, on Dec 13, 1835, an occasion that was probably orchestrated by Azélie (See my book, p. 85, "Victor's Certificate of Baptism"). At that time, slaves were not usually baptized. This act might also show that Azélie cared much for baby Victor, perhaps equally with her nephew Alphonse. We know, too, that Azélie considered Anna a "companion" servant, not a slave, perhaps...because Azélie was barren. (From oral history: ever since I was knee-high to a duck, I have heard about Anna's unique position in the Haydel Plantation at that time, despite census records that listed her as a slave and a black.)

Appendix VI
African names retrieved from Louisiana Slave Database

Aba, Abba Gender: female. Name explanation: Akan female born on Thursday.
Abbey, Abby Gender: female. Name explanation: common name among Fulbe and Wolof.
Achem Gender: male. Name explanation: from Hashim, ancestor of Prophet Mohammed. Inventory of plantation at Point-la-Hache.
Agata Gender: female. Birthplace: Congo.
Alcindor, Alsindor, Alzindor Gender: male.
Ama, Amada Gender: female. Birthplace: Coromanti.

Amadis Gender: male. Birthplace: Fulbe/Pular.

Aoussa Gender: both male and female. Birthplace: Hausa.

Arada Gender: both male and female. Birthplace: Aja/Fon/Arada.

Aram Gender: female. Wolof.

Ayda Gender: female. Wolof. Birthplace: St. Domingue.

Aysou Gender: male. Birthplace: Imputed African based on age.

Aza Gender: male. Birthplace: Congo.

Babila Gender: male. Birthplace: Fulbe/Pular.

Babilasse Gender: male. Birthplace: Fulbe/Pular.

Bacara Gender: male. Moor/Nar?

Baco Gender: male. Birthplace: Manding.

Badan Gender: male. Birthplace: Nago/Yoruba.

Badand Gender: male. Birthplace: Nago/Yoruba.

Bala Gender: male. Wolof?

Bamba Gender: male. Birthplace: Bamana.

Bambara Gender: male. Birthplace: Bamana.

Banga Gender: male. Birthplace: Africa.

Banjo Gender: male. Birthplace: Manding?

Banny Gender: male. Birthplace: Africa.

Bara/Barra Gender: male. Birthplace: Bamana/Wolof/Kanga.

Baraca Gender: male. Birthplace: Fulbe/Pular.

Barre Gender: male. Birthplace: Moor/Nar.

Barry Gender: male. Birthplace: Fulbe/Pular.

Bausson Gender: male. Birthplace: Congo.

Bayda Gender: male. Birthplace: Fulbe/Pular.

Belali Gender: male. Birthplace: Fulbe/Pular.

Beli/Belly Gender: male. Birthplace: Fulbe/Pular.

Bella Gender: male. Birthplace: Fulbe/Pular.

Bella Gender: female. Birthplace: Congo.

Biram/Birame Gender: male. Birthplace: Sénégal/Wolof.

Bobo Gender: male. Birthplace: Fulbe/Pular.

Bocary/Boucary Gender: male. Birthplace: Fulbe/Pular.

Bocham Gender: male. Birthplace: Kanga.

Bony Gender: male. Birthplace: East Nigeria?

Barka/Borca Gender: male. Birthplace: Fulbe/Pular.

Bosal (Maria) Gender: female. Bosal or Brut/Bruto means a slave born in Africa.

Bossal (Jean) Gender: male. Birthplace: Congo.

Bougman/ Bougouman Gender: female. Birthplace: Sénégal/Wolof.

Boulari Gender: male. Birthplace: Fulbe/Pular?

Bouqui Gender: male/female. Birthplace: Sénégal/Wolof. Bouqui is the Wolof name for Hyena.

Bram, Braman, Brahman Gender: male. Different versions of biblical name Ibrahim/Abraham.

Cadis/Caadian? Kakia (reads Kacha) Gender: female. Probably Cadia/Kajah, Fulbe dimunitive of Khadijah, first wife of the prophet of Islam.

Cabel Gender: female. Birthplace: Congo.

Cacamba/Cacambo Gender: male. Birthplace: Wolof.

Cachy Gender: female. Birthplace: Imputed African based on age.

Cacroco Gariem Gender: male. Birthplace: Imputed African based on age.

Cago Gender: female. Birthplace: Imputed African based on age.

Cahiou Gender: male. Birthplace: Imputed African based on age.

Caifas Gender: male. Birthplace: Manding.

Caledon Gender: male.

Camina Gender: male. Birthplace: Mina.

Candian Gender: male. Birthplace: Mina.

Canga Gender: male/female. Birthplace: Kanga.

Cani/Caniba Gender: female. Birthplace: probably Manding.

Caraba Gender: male. Birthplace: Congo.

Caromanbi Gender: male. Birthplace: Nation Unidentified.

Cassa/Cassova Gender: female. Birthplace: Mina.

Chalou Gender: female. Birthplace: Congo.

Chamba Gender: male. Birthplace: Konkomba.

Choucoura Gender: male. Birthplace: Imputed African based on age; probably Bamana.

Ciba Gender: male/female. Akan name.

Cinigal Gender: male. Birthplace: Wolof.

Ciry Gender: male. Probably from Fulbe name Ciré.

Coacou, Couacou, Coucou, Cok Gender: male. Akan name for male born on Wednesday.

Coco Gender: female. Birthplace: Konkomba.

Cocomina Gender: male. Birthplace: Native American.

Cocoquo Gender: male. Birthplace: Imputed African based on age.

Cocoro Gender: male. Birthplace: Guinea/Guinea Coast.

Coefi, Coffe, Coffee, Coffey, Coffi, Coffy, Cofi, Cofie, Cofy, Cophie, Cuff, Cuffy Gender: male. Male born on Friday; Akan or Ewe name. A Mandingo and a Bambara also bore this name. Their godfathers were probably Akan.

Caissy, Coissy, Cochi, Kessy Gender: male. Akan name for male born on Sunday.

Cassy/Kesiah/Kisiah Gender: female. Akan name for female male born on

Sunday.

Cola Gender: male. Birthplace: Bamana.

Cole Gender: female. Probably from Wolof name Kollé.

Colly Gender: male. Widespread among the Mande people.

Comba, Couba, Combas Gender: female. From Kumba, second born female among Fulbe/Pulaar. The first one was identified as a Sereer (West Senegal).

Congo, Congot Gender: male. Birthplace: Congo.

Conni Gender: male. Birthplace: Soso.

Cory, Corry Gender: male. Birthplace: Kanga.

Coura (Jean Louis) Gender: male. Birthplace: Corri, Cories.

Coura (Jean Louis) Gender: male. Birthplace: Atoyo/Atyo/Auda.

Codio, Cudjo, Cudjoe, Cuyo Gender: male. Name for male born on Monday. Birthplace: Brut.

Diaca Gender: male/female. Probably Fulbe or Manding.

Dimanche Gender: male. Birthplace: Louisiana Creole.

Dimba Gender: male. Birthplace: Manding.

Dimba Gender: male. Birthplace: Fulbe/Pular. Third born male.

Dina, Dinah Gender: female. Birthplace: Fulbe/Pular.

Ebo Adam Gender: male. Birthplace: Igbo.

Ebo Wile Gender: male. Birthplace: Igbo.

Ecara Gender: male. Birthplace: Mina.

Eloy Gender: male. Birthplace: Kisi.

Enganga Gender: male. Birthplace: Congo.

Engnaga Gender: male. Birthplace: Congo.

Esther Gollan Gender: female. Birthplace: Congo.

Eulalia Gender: female. Birthplace: Kanga.

Eulalie Gender: female. Birthplace: Kisi.

Eulalie Gender: female. Birthplace: Manding.

Evom Gender: male. Birthplace: Nago/Yoruba.

Fa, Fha Gender: male. Birthplace: Bamana.

Facon Gender: male. Birthplace: Africa.

Fadoua/Fadouat Gender: male. Birthplace: Bamana/Manding.

Falgout Gender: male. Birthplace: Wolof.

Famacoussi Gender: male. Birthplace: Bamana/Manding.

Famonza Gender: male. Sounds like a Bamana name/e.g. Da Monzon, King of Segou.

Famsa Gender: male. Birthplace: Manding.

Famsa Gender: male. Birthplace: Bamana.

Fani Gender: female. Birthplace: Guinea/Guinea Coast.

Fania Gender: female. Birthplace: Jamaica.

Fatima/Fatime Gender: female. Name of the daughter of the Prophet of Islam.

Febey/Febi/Febie/Feby/Fibie/Fiby Variant of Afi, Afia, Akan; Gender: female. Name for a female born on Friday.

February, Fevrier Gender: male. Birthplace: Congo.

Fina Gender: female. Birthplace: Manding. Diminutive of Islamic name Nafisatu.

Firmin Gender: male. Probably Bambara.

Fon, Fond (Martain) Gender: male. Birthplace: Aja/Fon/Arada.

Foula Gender: female. Birthplace: Fulbe/Pular.

Fourlourou Gender: male. Birthplace: Guinea/Guinea Coast.

Foy (Louis dit) Gender: male. Birthplace: Bamana.

Gabla Gender: male. Birthplace: Bamana.

Ganga Gender: female. Birthplace: Igbo.

Gay Gender: male. Birthplace: Wolof.

Gaye Gender: male. Birthplace: Kanga.

Giaur Gender: male. Birthplace: Portuguese America.

Gola (Maria) Gender: female. Birthplace: Gola.

Hibou Gender: female. Birthplace: Igbo.

Ifa Gender: male. Birthplace: Bamana.

Indigo Gender: male. Birthplace: Imputed African based on age.

Jaco Gender: male. Birthplace: Mina.

Jaco Gender: female. Birthplace: Fulbe/Pular. This is very likely a misspelling of Taco.[1]

January/Janvier Gender: male.

Jasmin Gender: male. Birthplace: Aja/Fon/Arada.

Jasmin Gender: male. Birthplace: Bamana.

Jasmin Gender: male. Birthplace: Manding.

Jasmin Gender: male. Birthplace: Wolof.

Jasmin Gender: male. Birthplace: Nago/Yoruba.

Jasmin Gender: male. Birthplace: Congo.

Jasmine Gender: female.

---

1 Many misspellings in the database are obviously related to errors of transcription made by some of the collectors who were unfamiliar with African naming traditions and some aspects of the calligraphy on the manuscripts.

Kaco Gender: male. See Quaco.

Kango Valere Gender: male. Birthplace: Kanga.

Kato Gender: male. Birthplace: Brut.

Kemby Gender: unidentified. Birthplace: Congo.

Kiakia Gender: female. Birthplace: Imputed African based on age.

Kiam Baptista Gender: male.

Kiamba (Alexandre) Gender: male. Birthplace: Konkomba.

Kiamba (Louis) Gender: male. Birthplace: Louisiana Creole.

Kinga Gender: female. Birthplace: Congo.

Kissy/Kizey/Kizy/Kizzy Gender: male/female. Birthplace: Kisi (Guinea/Sierra Leone).

Koua Gender: unidentified. Birthplace: Congo.

Koukoubala Gender: unidentified. Birthplace: Congo.

Lagany Gender: male. Birthplace: Imputed African based on age.

Lagouin Gender: male. Birthplace: Nago/Yoruba.

Laisere Gender: female. Birthplace: Congo.

Laiza Gender: female. Birthplace: St. Domingue.

Lassa Gender: female. Birthplace: Bamana.

Lasty Gender: male. Birthplace: Mina.

Latorin Gender: male. Birthplace: Nago/Yoruba.

Lindor Gender: male. Birthplace: Sénégal/Wolof.

Linion Gender: unidentified. Birthplace: Congo.

Lisbie Gender: female. Birthplace: Manding.

Loco Gender: male. Birthplace: Manding.

Louis Congo Gender: male. Birthplace: Congo.

Louis Phon Gender: male. Birthplace: Aja/Fon/Arada.

Louma Gender: male. Birthplace: Konkomba.

Luban Gender: male. Birthplace: Duguri.

Lubas Gender: male. Birthplace: Louba.

Lubin Gender: male.

Lundi (Monday in French) Gender: male. Birthplace: Mina.

Lundi Pierre Louis dit Gender: male. Birthplace: St. Domingue.

Luscute Gender: female. Birthplace: Edo.

Lusse Gender: female. Birthplace: Congo.

Maca Gender: male. Birthplace: male names among the Makwa (East Coast of Africa).

Macaqui (Mardi dit) Gender: male. Birthplace: Congo.

Macaya Gender: female. Birthplace: Brut (very likely Congo).

Macouta Gender: male. Birthplace: Congo.

Madou Gender: female. Birthplace: Manding.

Madoure Gender: male. Birthplace: Wolof.

Madrus Gender: male. Birthplace: Kisi.

Maga Gender: male. Birthplace: Bamana.

Maham Gender: male. Birthplace: Moor/Nar.

Mahomet Gender: male. Birthplace: many men from Guinea/Guinea Coast were named after the prophet of Islam.

Malaga Gender: male.

Malambo Gender: male.

Malbo Gender: male. Birthplace: Nago/Yoruba.

Malbouro Gender: male. Birthplace: Manding.

Malbrong Gender: male. Birthplace: Bamana.

Malbrouck Gender: male. Birthplace: Manding.

Malimbe Gender: male. Birthplace: Congo. Malimbe was one of the slave harbors of Central Africa.

Maly, Mely Gender: female. Frequent name among the Fulbe/Pulaar.

Mamarie Gender: female. Birthplace: Sacoulé (Soninkeh), Upper Senegal River.

Mamourou Gender: male. Name explanation: means Mohammed.

Mande Gender: male. Birthplace: Coast of Senegal (Mandingo).

Mandela Gender: female. Probably Wolof (Ma Ndela means "the child of Ndela").

Mandinga/Maniga/Manega/Maninga Gender: male. Birthplace: Manding.

Manel Gender: male. Birthplace: Manding.

Mantouga Gender: male. Muntaqa (Islamic name).

Mapon or Mapou Gender: female. Birthplace: St. Domingue.

Mapougue Gender: male. Birthplace: Congo.

Maquilas Gender: male. Birthplace: Congo.

Marabou Gender: female. Name for a woman born from a quadroon and a negress (Moreau de St. Méry, description de St. Domingue). Name given to Muslim clerics in French.

Marant, Marante, Maranthe Gender: female.

Maratte Gender: female. Birthplace: Congo.

Mardi Gender: male. Birthplace: Congo.

Marezan Gender: male. Birthplace: Manding.

Mars Gender: male. Birthplace: Bamana.

Marzo Gender: male. Birthplace: Brut.

Masa Gender: male. Birthplace: Manding.

Matoumba (pelagie in 1818) Gender: female. Birthplace: Congo.

Matouta Gender: unidentified. Birthplace: Congo.

May Gender: male. Birthplace: Louisiana Creole.

Maya or Maga Gender: male. Birthplace: Bamana.

Mayala Gender: unidentified. Birthplace: Congo.

Mayambo Gender: female. Birthplace: Mayombe (one of the slave harbors of Central Africa).

Medi Gender: male. Moor/Naar?

Memba Gender: female. Congo?

Mercredi Gender: male. Birthplace: Manding.

Migalo Gender: male. Birthplace: Bamana.

Milado Gender: female. Birthplace: Moor/Nar.

Mimba Gender: female. Birthplace: Jamaica.

Mina/Minan Gender: male/female. Birthplace: Mina (Gold Coast/Bight of Bénin).

Mingo Gender: 100% male. Birthplace: Wolof; also Congo, Hausa.

Minia, Minta, Minty Gender: female. From Arabic Mint (daugter of) or Aminata (mother of the prophet of Islam).

Mirsa/Mirza Gender: 100% female. Birthplace: Wolof, Igbo.

Moca/Moco Gender: male. Birthplace: Ibibio/Moko.

Monday Gender: male. Birthplace: Louisiana Creole.

Mondes Gender: male. Birthplace: Soso.

Mondor Gender: male. Very likely Sereer (Senegal).

Morican, Moricau, Morico, Moro Listed under birthplace Nar, code 104. Morico means Moor in Spanish.

Mory Gender: male. Marabout (Muslim cleric in Mandingo).

Mota Gender: male. Birthplace: Imputed African based on age.

Moto Gender: male. Means child in Bantu languages.

Moussa Gender: male. Birthplace: Imputed African based on age. Arabic version of Moses.

Moya Gender: male. Birthplace: Brut.

Muna Gender: female. Birthplace: very likely Central Africa.

Nacis Gender: male. Birthplace: Edo.

Naco Gender: male.

Nadaeu Gender: male. Birthplace: Native American.

Nade Gender: male.

Nade Gender: male.

Nadi Gender: female.

Nado Gender: male.

Nagaud, Nago, Nagos, Nagot, Nagu, Nango Gender: male/female. Birthplace: Nago/Yoruba.

Naicu Santiago Gender: male. Birthplace: Manding.

Naide Gender: male. Birthplace: Mina.

Naier Gender: male. Birthplace: Louisiana Creole.

Nalu Gender: male. Birthplace: Nalo (Guinea Bissau).

Naly Gender: female. Birthplace: Louisiana Creole.

Nambre Gender: female.

Namerod Gender: male.

Nana Gender: female. Birthplace: Konkomba.

Nanei Gender: female. Birthplace: Brut.

Nanine Gender: female.

Nanni Gender: female.

Nannu Gender: female.

Nanny Gender: female. Birthplace: Virginia.

Nanny Gender: female. Birthplace: Guinea/Guinea Coast.

Nanny Gender: female. Birthplace: Carolinas.

Nany Gender: female. Birthplace: Louisiana Creole.

Napinapi Gender: male. Wolof?

Napis Gender: male. Birthplace: Imputed African based on age.

Naquion? Gender: male. Birthplace: Africa.

Narcisse Morlo Gender: male. Birthplace: Congo.

Nase Gender: male. Birthplace: Africa.

Naserre Gender: male. Islamic name (Nasr).

Nasse Gender: male.

Nasy Gender: male.

Natigau (Pierre alias) Gender: male. Birthplace: Wolof.

Nayde Gender: male. Birthplace: British Mainland Creole.

Neangu Gender: male. Birthplace: Imputed African based on age.

Ned, Net, Nete, Nette, Nettle Gender: male. Ned has been retained as a last name in Southwest Louisiana.

Nedo, Nedor Gender: male. See Ned.

Nelfar Gender: male. Birthplace: Maryland.

Nemy, Nenny Gender: female. Birthplace: Guinea/Guinea Coast.

Nenon Gender: male. Birthplace: British Mainland Creole.

Nensis Gender: female. Nancy?

Neo Gender: male. Birthplace: Louisiana Creole.

Nepruno Gender: male. Neptuno?

Nequi Gender: male. Birthplace: Manding.

Neurod dit Francois Gender: male.

Nianga Gender: male. Birthplace: Africa.

Nigna Gender: female.

Nima Gender: male. Birthplace: Guinea/Guinea Coast (very likely Fulbe/Pulaar).

Nincumba Gender: unidentified.

Ningo Gender: male.

Ninguet Gender: female.

Nini, Ninine Gender: male. Birthplace: Louisiana Creole.

Nion/Rion Gender: male. Birthplace: Africa.

Nionion/Niouguion Francoise Gender: female.

Nis, Nish Gender: male. Birthplace: British Mainland Creole.

Nishy Gender: female.

Nizaque Gender: male. Birthplace: British Mainland Creole.

Nole Gender: male.

Nomaque Gender: male.

Nonfoun Gender: male.

Nongonitte Marie Jeanne dit Gender: female.

Nory Gender: male.

Noubean Gender: male.

Novembre, November Gender: male.

Nowell Gender: male.

Nuame Gender: male.

Nucgek Gender: male.

Nue? Gender: male. Birthplace: Congo.

Numa Gender: male.

Obana Gender: female. Akan name for female born on Tuesday (Abena).

Obe (Pedro) Gender: male. Birthplace: Nago/Yoruba.

Obediah Gender: male. Birthplace: British Mainland Creole.

Obiny Gender: female.

Oby Gender: male.

Oce Gender: male.

Ocole Gender: male. Birthplace: Manding.

Octobre/October Gender: male.

Ocurru Gender: male.

Odahia Gender: male.

Oerlequin Gender: male. Birthplace: Fulbe/Pular. Or, Harlequin?

Ofazi Gender: female.

Ogam Gender: female. Birthplace: Imputed African based on age.

Ogou Gender: male. Birthplace: Congo.

Oharu Gender: male.

Oizde Gender: male.

Olancho? Gender: male. Birthplace: Jamaica.

Olick Gender: male. Birthplace: Ibibio/Moko.

Olivier dit Pitchon Gender: male.

Oloferme Gender: male. Birthplace: Imputed African based on age.

Omar Gender: male. Name of second Kalif (leader) of Islam after the death of Mohamet.

Omey Gender: female. Very likely Wolof.

Omset Gender: male. Birthplace: Mina.

Onadalie Gender: male.

Ondona Gender: male. Birthplace: Imputed African based on age.

Onequin Gender: male. Birthplace: Louisiana Creole.

Onesime, Onesime, Onesine, Onesinne, Onezim, Onezime, Onezine, Onezinie, Onezinne, Onzienne Gender: male. Birthplace: Louisiana Creole/Calabar/ Igbo. Onzième (11th in French).

Oney, Oni Gender: female. See Oumey.

Onora Gender: unidentified. See Onore.

Onore Gender: male. Honoré?

Onova Gender: male. Birthplace: Kanga.

Opta dit Toby Gender: male.

Orcanille Gender: male. Birthplace: Cuba.

Ordia Gender: male. Birthplace: Imputed African based on age.

Orue Gender: unidentified. Birthplace: Brut.

Orusso Gender: male. Birthplace: Fulbe/Pular.

Ose Gender: male. Birthplace: Mande/Maecaye (Marka).

Osmano Gender: male. Osman (fourth Kalif/leader of Islam).

Osse Gender: female. Birthplace: St. Domingue.

Osse Gender: male.

Ossie Gender: male.

Osson Gender: male. Diminutive of Osman?

Othon Gender: male. Birthplace: Hausa. Diminutive of Osman?

Otimpie Pauline Gender: female.

Ouana, Sem Gender: male. Birthplace: Virginia.

Ouatio Gender: male. Birthplace: Imputed African based on age.

Oudallon/Oudalley Gender: male.

Ouegnes Gender: male. Birthplace: Imputed African based on age.

Ouelle Gender: male. Birthplace: Igbo.

Ouetiste Gender: male.

Ouignan Gender: male. Birthplace: Africa.

Ouliam Gender: male. Birthplace: Coromanti.

Oulice Gender: male. Birthplace: Fanti.

Oulou Gender: male. Birthplace: Imputed African based on age.

Ourou Gender: male. Birthplace: Mina.

Ouyet Gender: female. Birthplace: Imputed African based on age.

Oved Gender: male. Birthplace: Louisiana Creole.

Oyon Gender: male.

Oysee Gender: male. Birthplace: Louisiana Creole.

Ozaville Gender: male.

Ozee Gender: female.

Ozezime Gender: unidentified.

Ozie Gender: male.

Ozioell Gender: male.

Ozite Gender: male.

Ozite, Ozitte Gender: female. Birthplace: Manding.

Paka Gender: male.

Palao Gender: male. Birthplace: Brut.

Palas (Jean Palas?) Gender: male. Birthplace: Kisi.

Palee Gender: female. Birthplace: British Mainland Creole.

Palemon Gender: male.

Paley Gender: female.

Pallas Gender: female.

Pallie, Pally, Paly Gender: female. Birthplace: Louisiana Creole.

Palmon Gender: male. Birthplace: Congo.

Palsie Gender: male. Birthplace: Congo.

Paly Gender: female. Birthplace: Manding.

Pambou Gender: unidentified. Birthplace: Congo.

Panga Gender: male. Birthplace: Guinea/Guinea Coast.

Pange Gender: male. Birthplace: Congo.

Panjon/Panjou Gender: male. Birthplace: Congo.

Pans Gender: unidentified. Birthplace: Brut.

Panti Gender: male. Birthplace: Mina.

Panzo Panzu', Panzudo Gender: male. Birthplace: Congo.

Papaje--- or Basil Gender: male. Birthplace: Imputed African based on age.

Parada Gender: male. Birthplace: Louisiana Creole.

Paran Gender: male. Birthplace: Kanga.

Pasquin Gender: male. Birthplace: Hausa.

Pasy Gender: female.

Pate Gender: male. Birthplace: Louisiana Creole. Name of 5th male born among Fulbe/Pulaar.

Patera Gender: female.

Patonca Gender: male. Birthplace: Imputed African based on age.

Pattagouna Gender: female.

Payna Gender: female. Birthplace: Konkomba.

Pebaja Gender: female. Birthplace: Louisiana Creole.

Pelebes Gender: male. Birthplace: Bamana.

Pella Gender: female. Birthplace: Barary.

Pemba Gender: unidentified. Birthplace: Congo.

Penda Gender: female. Birthplace: Imputed African based on age. Name of third-born female among Fulbe/Pulaar.

Peram Gender: male. Birthplace: Kanga.

Perigond Gender: male. Birthplace: Manding.

Pety Gender: male. Birthplace: Imputed African based on age.

Phabe/Pheobe Gender: female. Probably a corruption of Akan name Afiba.

Phatiman Gender: female. Birthplace: Imputed African based on age. See Fatima.

Phaton Gender: unidentified. Fatou ? > Fatima.

Philbie Gender: female. Birthplace: Guinea/Guinea Coast.

Philbus Gender: male. Birthplace: Bamana.

Phile Gender: male. Birthplace: Virginia.

Philledine? Gender: male. Birthplace: Africa.

Phitosaphor Gender: male. Birthplace: Congo.

Phocine Gender: female. Birthplace: Louisiana Creole.

Piache/Piachy Gender: female. Birthplace: Virginia.

Piemba Gender: female. See Pemba or Penda.

Pigi Gender: female. Birthplace: British Mainland Creole.

Pilikale Gender: female. Birthplace: British Mainland Creole.

Pimba Gender: female. Birthplace: Congo. See Pemba.

Pimba Gender: female. See Pemba.

Pin Gender: male. Birthplace: Cuba.

Pinda/Pinder Gender: female. See Penda.

Pinedy (Antoine dit) Gender: male. Birthplace: Congo.

Piram/Pirame/Pirome See Biram, Abraham in Arabic. Gender: male.

Pirance Gender: female. Birthplace: Wolof.

Pita Gender: male/female. Fulbe?

Pitta Gender: male. Birthplace: Kanga.

Pity Gender: unidentified. Birthplace: Ibibio/Moko.

Podesi Gender: male. Birthplace: Mina.

Pognon Gender: female. Birthplace: New Orleans Creole.

Poinnas Gender: female. Birthplace: Konkomba.

Poitzail Gender: male. Birthplace: Jamaica.

Pol/Polay/Poll/Polley Gender: male/female. Pël/Fulbe?

Pongy Gender: male. Birthplace: Congo.

Ponosscinte Gender: male. Birthplace: Guinea/Guinea Coast.

Pontom? Gender: female. Birthplace: St. Domingue.

Pool Gender: male. Birthplace: Virginia. Pël/Fulbe?

Poona Gender: male. Birthplace: Congo.

Pope Gender: male. From Pape? (father in Wolof)

Porreau Gender: male. Birthplace: Guinea/Guinea Coast.

Porus Gender: male. Birthplace: Konkomba.

Possy Gender: female.

Potopo Gender: female. Birthplace: Mina.

Poulard Gender: male. Birthplace: Guinea/Guinea Coast. Fulbe/Pulaar.

Poulard Joseph Gender: male. Birthplace: Fulbe/Pular.

Poutane Gender: female. Birthplace: St. Domingue.

Pumba Gender: unidentified. Birthplace: Congo.

Pumbo Gender: male. Congo?

Qiumba Francois Gender: male. Birthplace: Konkomba.

Quachee See **Caissy, Coissy, Cochi, Kessy**. Gender: male. Akan male born on Sunday.

Quaco, Quako See **Coacou, Couacou, Coucou, Cok, Quau?** Akan male born on Wednesday.

Quadsin Gender: female. Birthplace: Africa. See **Cassy/Kesiah/Kisiah.** Gender: female.

Qualmley, Quamina Gender: male. Akan male born on Tuesday (Komlá, Kwabena).

Qualpien, Queble, Quebra Gender: male. See **Qualmley**.

Queda, Quedor Gender: male. Birthplace: Konkomba.

Quedore Gender: male. Birthplace: Hausa.

Queesy Gender: female. See **Caissy, Coissy, Cochi, Kessy**.

Quefer Gender: male. Birthplace: Imputed African based on age. See **Coefi, Coffe, Coffee, Coffey, Coffi, Coffy, Cofi, Cofie, Cofy, Cophie, Cuff, Cuffy**. Akan male born on Friday.

Quelot Gender: male. Birthplace: Hausa.

Quembris Gender: male.

Quen Gender: male. Birthplace: Imputed African based on age.

Quenot Gender: female.

Quentet Gender: female.

Quequay Gender: female. Birthplace: Imputed African based on age.

Querry Gender: male.

Queteau Gender: male. Birthplace: Manding.

Queteaur Gender: male. See **Quedore**.

Quetelle Gender: female.

Quetne Gender: male.

Quetous Gender: male. See **Queteau**.

Quette Gender: male. See **Queteau**.

Quevalu Gender: male.

Queyroi Gender: male. Birthplace: Imputed African based on age.

Quiamaba Gender: male. Birthplace: Congo.

Quiamba Gender: male/female. Birthplace: Konkomba.

Quiamba Gender: male. Birthplace: Congo.

Quiame Gender: female. Birthplace: Imputed African based on age.

Quiato Gender: male. Birthplace: Louisiana Creole.

Quibio Gender: male.

Quicou See **Quaco**. Gender: male. Birthplace: Guinea/Guinea Coast.

Quieto Gender: male. See **Quiato**.

Quietty Gender: female. Birthplace: Carolinas.

Quilder Gender: male.

Quince Gender: male. Birthplace: Louisiana Creole.

Quinguet Gender: female.

Quinque Gender: male. Birthplace: Guinea/Guinea Coast.

Quintale Gender: male. Birthplace: Louisiana Creole.

Quinton Gender: male.

Quiom or Granjean Gender: male. Birthplace: Imputed African based on age.

Quiquile? Gender: female. Birthplace: Louisiana Creole.

Quiquo Gender: male. See **Quicou**.

Quiquya Gender: male.

Quisso Gender: male. Birthplace: Creole Mobile.

Quisy Gender: male. Birthplace: Kisi.

Quite Gender: female. Birthplace: Louisiana Creole.

Quito, Quiton Gender: male.

Quivet Forte Gender: male. Birthplace: Louisiana Creole.

Qulbu or Gulby Gender: male.

Quoalou Gender: male.

Qurcia Gender: female.

Raba Gender: male. Birthplace: Igbo.

Raban Gender: male. Birthplace: Imputed African based on age.

Rabar Gender: male. Birthplace: Brut.

Rabas, Rabat Gender: male. Birthplace: Igbo.

Rada Gender: male. Birthplace: Aja/Fon/Arada.

Radia Gender: male. Birthplace: Africa.

Rady Gender: male.

Rael Gender: male. Birthplace: St. Domingue.

Rafin Gender: male.

Ragnia Gender: unidentified. Birthplace: Manding.

Ragoude Gender: female. Birthplace: Imputed African based on age.

Raguin Gender: female.

Rah Gender: male. Birthplace: Louisiana Creole.

Raizno Gender: male. Birthplace: Bamana.

Ramguiat Gender: female. Birthplace: Wolof.

Ramone Gender: male. Birthplace: Manding.

Ranaule Gender: male. Birthplace: Kanga.

Ratti Gender: male. Birthplace: Louisiana Creole.

Reguine, Reguina Gender: female. Birthplace: Louisiana Creole.

Reiny Gender: male. Birthplace: Louisiana Creole.

Renty Gender: female. Birthplace: Louisiana Creole.

Riquette Gender: female. Birthplace: Ibibio/Moko.

Roclor Gender: male. Birthplace: Hyban/Ibani (Ibo?)

Rodias Gender: male. Birthplace: Imputed African based on age.

Rofe Gender: female. Birthplace: Manding.

Roque Gender: male. Birthplace: Manding/Congo.

Rosina dit Penny Gender: female. Birthplace: Africa.

Rouam Gender: female. Birthplace: Brut.

Saba Gender: female.

Sabary Gender: male. Manding?

Sabina Gender: female. Birthplace: Angola.

Sacambele Gender: male.

Sacka Gender: female. Birthplace: Congo.

Sacony Gender: male.

Safrona Gender: female.

Sagoin Gender: male. Birthplace: Nago/Yoruba.

Saguoin Gender: male. Birthplace: Bamana.

Sahra Gender: female. Birthplace: Fulbe/Pular.

Sailla Gender: male. Birthplace: Bamana.

Saipan Gender: male. Birthplace: Fulbe/Pular.

Saire Gender: female. Birthplace: Congo.

Saiute Gender: female. Birthplace: St. Domingue.

Saladin Gender: male. Birthplace: Manding.

Saladin Gender: male. Birthplace: Moor/Nar.

Salic (Salie?) Gender: female. Birthplace: Brut.

Salidin Gender: male. Birthplace: Manding.

Salmonie Gender: female. Birthplace: Wolof.

Samb, Samba, Sanbat, Sambo, Semba Gender: male. Second born male among Fulbe/Pulaar and Hawsa. Widespread in West Africa.

Samedi, Samedy (Saturday) Gender: male.

Sanas Gender: male. Birthplace: Manding.

San Sonoy, Sancrisy (mispelling of Sans Souci/worriless) Gender: male.

Birthplace: Congo.

Sancantie, Sancartie, Sancartie, Sancatoe, Sarcondier, Sencartie, Sercandier, Soinquatie Misspelling of "Sans Quartier" ("Merciless").

Sanco Gender: male. Birthplace: Manding.

Sande Gender: male. Name explanation: Sande may be diminutive of Sandene, a Serer name. Birthplace: Guinea/Guinea Coast.

Sandey Gender: female. Birthplace: Imputed African based on age.

Sandigue Gender: male. Birthplace: Imputed African based on age.

Sango Gender: male. Birthplace: Sango.

Sango Gender: male. Birthplace: Manding.

Sangonan Gender: male. Birthplace: Sango.

Sangot Gender: male. Birthplace: Manding.

Sanite Gender: female. Birthplace: St. Domingue.

Sanite Gender: male. Birthplace: Moor/Nar.

Sannom, Sans nom (nameless) Gender: male/female.

Sanoy Gender: male. Birthplace: Kisi.

Sara Gender: male. Firstborn son among Fulbe/Pulaar.

Satio Gender: male. Birthplace: Bamana.

Saturday Gender: male. See **Samedi**.

Sauqi Gender: male. Birthplace: Mina.

Savory Gender: male. Misspelling of Favori (the favored one).

Schougie Gender: unidentified. Birthplace: Congo.

Secabane Gender: female. Birthplace: Imputed African based on age.

Sefino Gender: male. Birthplace: Guinea/Guinea Coast.

Segol? Gender: male. Birthplace: Imputed African based on age.

Seguy Gender: male. Birthplace: Imputed African based on age.

Seingy Gender: male. Birthplace: Angola.

Seira Gender: male. Birthplace: Congo.

Sellah, Seller, Serry Gender: female. Possible misspelling of Selli, a Fulbe name meaning someone in good health.

Sem Gender: male. Birthplace: British Mainland Creole. Biblical name.

Sem Gender: male. Birthplace: Mina.

Sena Gender: female. Birthplace: Calabar (East Nigeria).

Senegal Gender: male/female. Birthplace: Wolof.

Senfont Gender: male. Birthplace: Fulbe/Pular.

Sephir Gender: male. Birthplace: Congo.

Septembre, September Gender: male.

Serard Gender: male. Birthplace: Guinea/Guinea Coast.

Serata now Arsena Gender: female. Birthplace: Guinea/Guinea Coast.

Sernie Gender: female. Birthplace: Edo.

Seros Gender: male. Birthplace: Congo.

Serry, Sery Gender: female. See Sellah.

Sesar Gender: male. Birthplace: Toma, Bamana.

Sésé Gender: male. Birthplace: Kisi.

Sibby Gender: female.

Sierre Gender: male. Birthplace: Konkomba.

Sigy Gender: male. Birthplace: Bamana.

Sina, Sinah Gender: female.

Siza (Sira) Gender: male. Birthplace: Wolof.

Soileau Gender: male. Birthplace: Imputed African based on age.

Soizy Gender: male. Birthplace: Congo.

Soliman, Solimant, Solimon Biblical name (Suliman/Solomon).

Solime Gender: female. Very likely Moor/Naar.

Solline Gender: female. Birthplace: Congo.

Solon Gender: male. Birthplace: Guinea/Guinea Coast.

Somba Gender: female. Birthplace: Imputed African based on age.

Somiman Gender: male. Birthplace: Congo.

Somma Gender: male. Very likely Fulbe/Pulaar.

Sonami Gender: male. Birthplace: Manding.

Sondan (Soudan?) Gender: male. Birthplace: Guinea/Guinea Coast.

Sonday Gender: male. See **Dimanche**.

Sondo Gender: female. Birthplace: Imputed African based on age.

Sonris or Sonni Gender: male.

Sontipoly Gender: male. Birthplace: Congo.

Sosie Gender: male. Birthplace: Congo.

Soso Albert Gender: male. Birthplace: Manding.

Sosso Gender: male/female. Birthplace: Susu (Upper Guinea Coast).

Souguy Gender: female. Birthplace: Igbo.

Souman, Soumat, Soumay Gender: male. Birthplace: African.

Sourday (Sunday?) Gender: male. Birthplace: Manding.

Sourie (female), Souris (male). Mouse in French.

Sozy Gender: female. Birthplace: Congo.

Subana Gender: female. Birthplace: Louisiana Creole.

Soqui, Suck, Suckey, Sucky, Sukey Gender: female. Diminutive of Arabic name Sukeyna.

Suicou Gender: male. Birthplace: Hausa.

Sulicie Gender: female. Birthplace: Manding.

Sully Gender: male. Birthplace: Congo.

Sultan Gender: male.

Sumedy or Fumedy? Samedi? See **Samedi**. Gender: male.

Sunday, Sunney Gender: male. See **Dimanche**.

Surart Gender: male. Birthplace: Angola.

Suri, Surit, Surray (Sori ?) Gender: male. Birthplace: Guinea/Guinea Coast.

Suron Gender: female. Birthplace: Native American.

Surry Gender: male. Birthplace: Congo.

Surya Gender: male. Birthplace: Africa.

Swarow Gender: male. Birthplace: Igbo.

Syres Gender: unidentified. Birthplace: Native American.

Ta or La or Sa Gender: male. Birthplace: Guinea/Guinea Coast.

Tabby, Tabey, Tabie, Taby Gender: female.

Tabeau Gender: male.

Taca Gender: female.

Tache Gender: unidentified. Birthplace: Igbo.

Taco Gender: female. Fourth born female among Fulbe/Pular.

Taf Gender: male. Birthplace: Africa.

Tain Gender: male. Birthplace: Calabar.

Taira, Taire Gender: unidentified.

Tairaisse Gender: unidentified. Corruption of Thérèze.

Taison Gender: male. Birthplace: Mina.

Tala Gender: male. Birthplace: Nago/Yoruba.

Tally Gender: male.

Tam Gender: male. Birthplace: Brut.

Tamba Common among Mande. Gender: male. Birthplace: Guinea/Guinea Coast.

Tame? Gender: male. Birthplace: Congo.

Tami Gender: male. Birthplace: Manding.

Tasis Gender: female. Birthplace: Guinea/Guinea Coast.

Tasmin Gender: male. See Yasmin.

Tata Gender: female. Birthplace: Brut.

Tatine Gender: male. Birthplace: Wolof.

Tauine Gender: male. Birthplace: Konkomba.

Tchamba Jacques dit Gender: male. Birthplace: Konkomba.

Tehamba Gender: unidentified. Birthplace: Konkomba.

Telo, Teloue Gender: female. Birthplace: Congo.

Tenda Gender: female. Birthplace: Congo.

Tene, Tenne Gender: female. Birthplace: Imputed African based on age.

Teneriffe Gender: male. Birthplace: Wolof. May have transited through Canary Islands.

Tenny Gender: male. Birthplace: Brut.

Terci Gender: male. Birthplace: Edo.

Tereme Gender: male. Birthplace: Fulbe/Pular.

Terion Gender: female. Birthplace: Guinea/Guinea Coast.

Terresse Gender: female. Birthplace: Native American. Corruption of Thérèze.

Tertangues Gender: male. Birthplace: Africa.

Tessandico Gender: male. Birthplace: Bamana.

Teton Gender: male. Birthplace: Brut.

Themarr, Themire, Themire Gender: female. Birthplace: Congo.

Thiamba Marie Therese Gender: female. Birthplace: Konkomba.

Thiedor Gender: male. Birthplace: Manding.

Thiedor Gender: male. Birthplace: Congo.

Tholo Gender: male. Birthplace: very likely Upper Guinea Coast.

Thos Gender: male. Birthplace: Igbo.

Thyamba Gender: male. Birthplace: Konkomba.

Tiamba Gender: male. Birthplace: Konkomba.

Tiando Gender: male.

Tiasy Gender: male. Birthplace: Brut.

Tibel Gender: female.

Tibere Gender: male. Birthplace: Mina.

Tiembre Gender: male. Birthplace: Timbo (capitale of Futa Jalon, Upper Guinea Coast.

Tienis Gender: male. Birthplace: Guinea/Guinea Coast.

Tigo Gender: male. Birthplace: Bamana.

Timar Gender: male. Birthplace: Mandongo.

Timate Gender: male. Birthplace: St. Domingue.

Timba Gender: male. Birthplace: Manding.

Timban Gender: male. Birthplace: Calabar.

Timbas Gender: female.

Time Gender: male. Birthplace: Louisiana Creole.

Timno Gender: male.

Timrick Gender: male. Birthplace: Guinea/Guinea Coast.

Tinor Gender: female.

Tircis Gender: male. Birthplace: Edo.

Tirsis Gender: male. Birthplace: Fulbe/Pular.

Tisba? Gender: unidentified. Birthplace: Manding.

Titemba Gender: female. Birthplace: Imputed African based on age.

Titi Gender: female. Birthplace: Martinique.

Titom Gender: unidentified.

Tivee? Gender: male. Birthplace: Imputed African based on age.

Tolly Gender: male. Birthplace: Imputed African based on age.

Tone Gender: male. Birthplace: Kanga.

Tonelit Gender: male. Birthplace: Africa.

Tonnau Gender: male. Birthplace: Congo.

Tons Gender: male. Birthplace: Brut.

Toroc Gender: male. Birthplace: Kanga.

Toto Gender: female.

Toupanit Gender: male. Birthplace: St. Domingue.

Toussane Gender: male. Birthplace: Manding.

Tout Tato Gender: male. Birthplace: Congo.

Trape Santiago Gender: male. Birthplace: Wolof.

Trim Gender: male. Birthplace: Brut.

Tubon Gender: male. Birthplace: Manding.

Tunque Gender: male. Birthplace: Imputed African based on age.

Tyamba Gender: male. Birthplace: Konkomba.

Usebi Joseph Gender: male. Birthplace: South America.

Usin Gender: male. Birthplace: Louisiana Creole.

Vendredi, Vendredy, Vendridy, Vendudy Gender: male. Means Friday.

Warika Gender: female. Moor/Naar?

Yaba Gender: female. Birthplace: Nago/Yoruba.

Yabou Gender: female.

Yaca Marie Louise dite Gender: female.

Yacine, Yasine Gender: female. Very likely Wolof.

Yacko Gender: male. Birthplace: Kanga.

Yama Gender: male. Birthplace: Imputed African based on age.

Yaman Gender: female. Birthplace: Imputed African based on age.

Yamba Gender: male. Birthplace: Imputed African based on age.

Yambo' Gender: male.

Yanga Louis dit Gender: male.

Yara Gender: male. Birthplace: Manding.

Yarra Gender: male. Birthplace: Kanga.

Yo Gender: male.

Yarrow, Yerah Gender: male. Probable version of Yéro, fourth-born male among the Fulbe/Pulaar.

Yasmin Gender: male. See **Jasmin**.

Yassa Gender: female. Birthplace: Imputed African based on age.

Yata Gender: male.

Yinah, Yini Gender: female. Birthplace: Brut.

Youla Bill Gender: male. Birthplace: Diola.

Zair, Zaire, Zayre Gender: female. Birthplace: Moor/Nar.

BIBLIOGRAPHY

Archives

National Archives of Sénégal: Sous-série K2, "Traite des Noirs-saisie de navires qui se livrent à la traite des Noirs (1818-1830)."

National Archives, Washington DC: Records of the Field Offices for the State of Louisiana, Bureau of Refugees, Freedmen, and Abandoned Lands 1863-1872.

New Orleans Notarial Archives, New Orleans, City Hall.

New Orleans Public Library, Louisiana Division, Microfilms section.

St. John the Baptist Parish Court House Archives, Edgard, Louisiana.

St. John the Baptist Parish Colonial Archives, Baton Rouge, State Archives.

St. Charles Parish Court House Archives, Hahnville, Louisiana.

St. James Parish Court House Archives, Convent, Louisiana.

Source Books

Adanson, Michel. *Histoire naturelle du Sénégal. Coquillages. Avec la Relation abrégée d'un voyage fait en ce pays.* Paris: Chez C. J.-B. Bauche, 1762.

Baudry des Lozières, Louis-Narcisse. *Second Voyage à la Louisiane, 1794 à 1798.* Paris, 1934.

Beauvais-Raseau, M. de. *Art de l'Indigotier.* Paris: L.F. Delatour, 1770.

Biographical and Historical Memoires of Louisiana. Chicago: Goodspeed Publishing Company, 1892.

Boilat, Abbé David. *Esquisses sénégalaises.* 1853. Reprint, Paris: Karthala, 1984.

Champomier, P.A. *Statement of the Sugar Crop Made in Louisiana.* New Orleans: Cook, Young, & Co., 1844, 1845-45, and 1849-50 to 1858-59.

Christian, Marcus B. *A Black History of Louisiana.* Unpublished manuscript, Earl Kong Library, Special Collections, University of New Orleans.

Collot, Victor. *A journey in North America, volume 2.* Paris: Arthus Bertrand, 1826.

Conrad, G. R. *Saint-Jean-Baptiste des Allemands, Abstracts of the Civil Records of St. John the Baptist Parish with Genealogy and Index (1753-1803).* Lafayette: The Center for Louisiana Studies, University of Southwestern Louisiana, 1972.

Cultru, Prosper. *Premier voyage du Sieur de la Courbe fait à la Coste d'Afrique en 1685.* Paris: Champion et Larose, 1913.

Cuoq, J. *Recueil des sources arabes concernant l'Afrique Occidentale, VIIIe-XVIe siècle-Bilâd al-Sudân.* Paris: CNRS, 1975.

Daget, Serge. *Répertoire des Expéditions Négrières Françaises à la Traite Illégale*

(1814-1850). Nantes: Comité Nantais d'Etudes en Sciences Humaines, 1988.

Donnan, Elizabeth. *Documents Illustrative of the Slave Trade to America, vol IV, the Border Colonies and the Southern Colonies.* New York: Octagon Book, 1969.

Drake, Philip. *Revelations of a slave smuggler: being the autobiography of Capt. Rich`d [i.e. Philip] Drake, an African trader for fifty years, from 1807 to 1857.* New York: R. M. DeWitt, 1860.

DuTertre, Jean Baptiste. *Histoire Générale des Antilles Habitées par les François,* 4 vols. Paris, 1776.

Early Census Tables of Louisiana, Hill Memorial Library, Louisiana State University.

Edwards, Jay D. and Nicolas Pecquet du Bellay de Verton. *A Creole Lexicon, Architecture, Landscape, People.* Baton Rouge: Louisiana State University Press, 2004.

Fortier, Alcée. *Louisiana Folktales.* Boston, MA: American Folklore Society, 1895.

---. "Bits of Louisiana Folklore." *Transactions and Proceedings of the Modern Language Association* 3 (1887): 100-168.

French, B. F. *Historical Collections of Louisiana: Embracing Translations of Many Rare and Valuable Documents Relating to the Natural, Civil, and Political History of that State.* New York: D. Appleton, 1851.

King, Edward. *The Great South; A Record of Journeys in Louisiana, Texas, the Indian Territory, Missouri, Arkansas, Mississippi, Alabama, Georgia, Florida, South Carolina, North Carolina, Kentucky, Tennessee, Virginia, West Virginia, and Maryland.* Hartford, Conn: American Publishing Co., 1875.

Le Maire, J.J. *Les Voyages du sieur Le Maire aux îles Canaries, Cap-Verd, Sénégal et Gambie.* Paris: J. Collombat, 1695.

Le Page du Pratz. *Histoire de la Louisiane.* 3 vols. Paris: De Bure, 1758.

Lowrie W., ed. *American State papers, Documents, Legislative and executive, of the Congress of the United States in relation to the public lands.* 2d vol. Washington, D.C., 1834.

Michelet, Madame J. *The Story of my Childhood*; translated from the French by M.F. Curtis. Boston: Little, Brown, and Company and London: Sampson Law, Son, and Company, 1868.

---. *Mémoires d'une Enfant.* Paris: Hachette & Cie, 1867.

Moreau de Saint-Mery. *Description physique et topographique de la partie française de l'Isle de Saint-Domingue.* Revised and expanded edition. Edited by B. Maurel and E. Taillemite. 3 vols. Paris: Société de l'histoire des Colonies Françaises et Librairie Larose, 1958.

Niane D.T. *Soundjata ou l'épopée mandingue.* Paris: Présence africaine, 1960.

Nolan, Charles et al, eds. Sacramental Records of the Roman Catholic Church of the Archdiocese of New Orleans, several volumes in progress. New Orleans.

Northrup, Solomon. *Twelve years a slave*. London: Sampson Low, Son & Company, 1853.

Nougaret, Pierre J.B. *Voyages Intéressans dans différentes colonies françaises, espagnoles, anglaises, etc.* Londres-Paris, 1788.

Ollier, Edmund. *Cassell's History of the United States*. 3 vols. London, 1874-77.

Pelletan de Caplon. *Mémoire sur la colonie du Sénégal, par le citoyen Pelletan, ancien administrateur et ancien directeur de la Compagnie du Sénégal.* Paris, An IX, 1802.

Persac, A. *Norman's Chart of the Lower Mississippi River.* New Orleans: B.M. Norman, 1858.

Pruneau de Pommegorge. *Description de la Nigritie.* Amsterdam-Paris: Maradan, 1789.

Raffenel A. *Nouveau voyage dans le pays des Nègres.* Paris: Imprimerie et Librairie Centrales des Chemins de Fer, 1856.

Ripley, Eliza. *Social life in Old New Orleans: Being Recollections of my Girlhood.* New York and London: Appleton and Company, 1912.

Rowland, D. and A.G. Sanders, eds. *Mississippi Provincial Archives 1701-1729, French Dominion*, volume 2. Jackson: Press of the Mississippi Department of Archives and History, 1929.

Saugnier. *Relations de plusieurs voyages à la côte d'Afrique, à Maroc, au Sénégal, à Gorée, à Galam, etc.* Paris: Roux et Compagnie, 1792.

Villiers du Terrage, Bon Marc de. *Les dernieres années de la Louisiane française.* Edited by E. Guilmoto. Paris: Librairie Orientale & Americaine, 1903.

Waller, H. *The last journals of David Livingstone in Central Africa, from 1865 to his death.* 2 vols. London: John Murray, 1875.

Weld, Theodore D. *Slavery and the internal slave Trade in the United States.* New York: Arno Press & the New York Times, 1969.

Books, Theses, Periodicals, and Articles

Agyekum, Kofi. "The Sociolinguistic of Akan Personal Names." *Nordic Journal of African Studies* 15.2 (2006): 206–235.

Alford, Terry. *Prince among Slaves.* New York: Oxford University Press, 1977.

Ancelet, Barry Jean. *Cajun and Creole Folktales, the French Oral Tradition of South Louisiana.* Jackson: University Press of Mississippi, 1994.

Arthur, Stanley C. *Jean Laffite-Gentleman Rover.* New Orleans: Harmanson, 1952.

Awoonor, Kofi. *Guardians of the sacred word: Ewe poetry.* New York: Nok Publishers Ltd, 1974.

Barry, Boubacar. *Senegambia and the Atlantic slave trade.* Cambridge: Cambridge

University Press, 1998.

Bathily, A. *Les portes de l'or. Le royaume de Galam (Sénégal) de l'ère des musulmans au temps des négriers (VIIIe-XVIIIe siècle)*. Paris: L'Harmattan, 1989.

Beckwith, Martha W. *Jamaica Anansi Stories*, Memoirs of the American Folk-Lore Society, vol. 17. New York: American Folklore Society, 1924.

Blair, Dorothy S. *African Literature in French*. Cambridge University Press, 1976.

Blume, Helmut. *The German Coast during the Colonial Era 1722-1803*. Translated, edited and annotated by Ellen C. Merrill. Originally published in 1956 as *Die Entwicklung der Kulturlandschaft des Mississippideltas in Kolonialer Zeit, unter Besonderer Berücksichtigung der Deutchen Siedlung*. Destrehan, LA: The German-Acadian Coast Historical and Genealogical Society, 1990.

Bolland, Rita. *Tellem Textiles. Archaeological finds from burial caves in Mali's Bandiagara Cliff*. Amsterdam: Royal Tropical Institute, 1991.

Brandon, Elizabeth. "Les moeurs de la paroisse Vermilion en Louisiane." *Le Bayou* 64 (1955).

Brockett, Charles D. *Land, Power, and Poverty: Agrarian Transformation and Political Conflict in Central America*. Westview Press, 1988.

Brockway, William. *The preservation and restoration of the Whitney Plantation. Volume III: Specifications for Restoration and Preservation of the Existing Structures and Specifications for the Proposed Visitor's Center*. Submitted to the Fred B. Kniffen Cultural Ressources Laboratory, Department of Geography and Anthropology (LSU), for the Formosa Plastics Corporation of Louisiana, 15 November 1991.

Brown, Christopher Leslie. *Moral Capital: Foundations of British Abolitionism*. Chapel Hill, NC: University of North Carolina Press, 2006.

Byfield, Judith A. *The bluest hands: a social and economic history of women dyers in Abeokuta (Nigeria), 1890-1940*. Portsmouth, NH: Heinemann, 2002.

Cable, George W. *Creoles and Cajuns. Stories of Old Louisiana*. Edited by Arlin Turner. New York: Doubleday Anchor, 1959.

Canu, Gaston, ed. *Contes du Zaïre, Contes des montagnes, de la savane et de la forêt au pays du fleuve Zaïre*. Paris: EDICEF, 1975.

Carney, J.A. and R. N. Rosomoff. *In the shadow of slavery: Africa's botanical legacy in the Atlantic world*. Berkeley, Los Angeles, and London: University of California Press, 2009.

Caron, Peter. "Of a nation which the others don't understand: Bambara slaves and African ethnicity in Louisiana, 1718-60." In *Routes to slavery. Direction, ethnicity and mortality in the Transatlantic slave trade*, edited by David Eltis and David Richardson, 98-121. London-Portland: Frank Cass, 1997.

Centre de Recherches Littéraires et Sociales. *Contes et Légendes d'Haïti*. Port-au-Prince, Haiti: Editions Christophe, 1993.

Chambers, Douglas B. "Slave trade merchants of Spanish New Orleans, 1763-

1803: Clarifying the colonial slave trade to Louisiana in Atlantic perspective."
Atlantic Studies 5.3 (2008): 335-346.

---. *Murder at Montpelier: Igbo Africans in Virginia.* Jackson: University Press
of Mississippi, 2005.

Chastanet M. "Le « sanglé », histoire d'un plat sahélien (Sénégal, Mali,
Mauritanie)." In *Cuisine et société en Afrique, histoire, saveurs, savoir-faire*,
edited by M. Chastanet, F.X. Fauvelle-Aymar & D. Juhe-Beaulaton, 173-90.
Paris: Karthala, 2002.

---. 1991. "La cueillette de plantes alimentaires en pays soninké (Sénégal)
depuis la fin du XIXe siècle: histoire et devenir d'un savoir-faire." In *Savoirs
paysans et développement*, edited by G. Dupré, 253-287. Paris: Karthala-
ORSTOM, 1991.

Chrétien J.-P. "L'histoire de longue durée de la consommation alimentaire
en Afrique. Perspectives de recherches." In *Les changements des habitudes et
des politiques alimentaires en Afrique: aspects des sciences humaines, naturelles et
sociales*, edited by I. De Garine, 63-83. Paris: Publisud, 1991.

Cissoko, Sékéné Mody. *Histoire de l'Afrique occidentale. Moyen Age et Temps
modernes, VIIe siècle-1850.* Paris: Présence Africaine, 1971.

Clark, Andrew F. "Environmental decline and ecological response in the upper
Senegal valley, West Africa, from the late nineteenth century to World War I."
Journal of African History 36.2 (1995): 197-218.

Comhaire-Sylvain, Suzanne. *Le roman de Bouqui.* Port-au-Prince, Haiti:
Imprimerie du Collège Vertières, 1940.

Cooper, W. and T. Terrill. *The American South, a History*, vol. 1. New York:
MacGraw-Hill, 1991.

Courlander, Harold. *The Drum and The Hoe: Life and Lore of the Haitian People.*
Berkeley: University of California Press, 1960.

Curtin, Philip. *Economic Change in Precolonial Africa: S enegambia in the Era of
the Slave Trade.* Madison: University of Wisconsin Press, 1975.

---. *The Atlantic slave trade: A Census.* Madison: University of Wisconsin Press,
1969.

Dadié, Bernard B. *Le Pagne Noir.* Paris: Présence Africaine, 1955.

Darrac, Pierre-Paul and Willem Van Schendel. *Global Blue: Indigo and Espionage
in Colonial Bengal.* Dhaka, India: University Press Limited, 2006.

Dart, Henry P. "The career of Dubreuil in French Louisiana." *Louisiana
Historical Quarterly* 18 (1935): 291-331.

Debien, Gabriel. "Marronage in the French Caribbean." In *Maroon Societies,
Rebel Slave Communities in the Americas*, edited by Richard Price, 107-134.
Baltimore and London: Johns Hopkins University Press, 1996.

Delafosse, Maurice. *Haut-Sénégal-Niger.* 2 vols. Paris: Maisonneuve et Larose,
1972.

Delcourt André. *La France et les Etablissements Français au Sénégal entre 1713 et 1763.* Dakar, Senegal: Mémoires IFAN, 1952.

Diagne, Pathé. *Bakari II (1392) et Christophe Colomb (1492) à la rencontre de l'Amérique.* Dakar: Editions Sankoré, [n.d.].

Deiler, J.H. *The settlements of the German Coast of Louisiana and the Creoles of German descent.* Philadelphia: Americana Germanicana Press, 1909.

Diarassouba, Marcelle. *Le lièvre et l'araignée, deux animaux des contes de l'Ouest africain.* Thèse de 3e cycle, Universités de Lille et d'Abidjan, 1970.

Dieterlen, G. and Y. Cissé Y. *Les fondements de la société d'initiation du Komo.* Paris-La Haye: Mouton & Co., 1972.

Dillard et al. "Whitney and Evergreen Plantation." In *River Road Preservation and Promotion*, 28-29. Tulane University, School of Architecture: Preservation Studies, Spring 2005.

Diop, Abdoulaye Bara. *La Société Wolof, Tradition et Changement: Les systèmes d'inégalité et de domination.* Paris: Karthala, 1981.

Diop, Birago. *Les contes d'Amadou Koumba.* Paris, Présence Africaine, 1947.

Dorson, Richard M. *American Negro Folktales.* Greenwich, CT: Fawcett Premier Book, 1967.

Edwards, Jay. 1991. *The Preservation and Restoration of the Whitney Plantation, St. John the Baptist Parish, Louisiana. Volume I: Historic Structures Report.* Department of Geography and Anthropology, Louisiana State University, Baton Rouge, LA, 15 November 1991.

Ellis, Colonel A. B. "Evolution in Folklore: Some West African prototypes of the Uncle Remus Stories." *Appleton's Popular Science Monthly* 48 (Nov. 1895 – April 1896): 93-104.

Emerson, Jon and Associates. *The preservation and restoration of the Whitney Plantation. Volume II: Landscape and Site Planning.* Submitted to the Fred B. Kniffen Cultural Ressources Laboratory, Department of Geography and Anthropology (LSU), for the Formosa Plastics Corporation of Louisiana, 15 August 1991.

---. *The preservation and restoration of the Whitney Plantation. Volume IV: Museum of Louisiana's Creole Culture.* Submitted to the Fred B. Kniffen Cultural Ressources Laboratory, Department of Geography and Anthropology (LSU), for the Formosa Plastics Corporation of Louisiana, 1 November 1991.

Faye, Stanley. "Privateers of Guadeloupe and their Establishment in Bartataria." *Louisiana Historical Quarterly* 23 (1940).

Fletcher, Richard. *Moorish Spain.* Berkeley: University of California Press, 1992.

Follett, Richard. *The sugar masters: Planters and slaves in Louisiana's cane world, 1820-1860.* Baton Rouge: Louisiana State University Press, 2005.

Fontenot W. *Secret Doctors - Ethnomedecine of African-Americans.* Westport and

London: Bergin & Garvey, 1994.

Fortier, Alcée. *Louisiana Folk-Tales, In French Dialect and English Translation.* Memoirs of the American Folk-Lore Society, Vol.II. Boston, MA: Houghton, Mifflin and Co., 1895.

---. "Bits of Louisiana Folklore." *Transactions and Proceedings of the Modern Language Association* 3 (1887): 100-168.

Foubert, Bernard. "Le marronnage sur les habitations Laborde à Saint-Domingue dans la seconde moitié du XVIIIe siècle." *Annales de Bretagne et des pays de l'Ouest* 95.3 (1988): 277-310.

Gayarré, Charles. "A Louisiana Sugar Plantation of the Old Regime." *Harper's Magazine* 74 (1887): 442.

---. *History of Louisiana.* 2d ed. 4 vols., vol. 1. New Orleans: James A. Gresham Publisher, 1879.

Genovese, Eugene D. *Roll, Jordan, Roll: The World the Slaves Made.* New York: Vintage Books, 1974.

Gerber, A. "Uncle Remus traced to the Old World." *Journal of American Folk-Lore* 6.23 (1893): 245-257.

Giraud, Marcel. *Histoire de la Louisiane Française,* tome III, *L'Epoque John Law, 1717-1720.* Paris: PUF, 1966.

---. *Histoire de la Louisiane Française,* tome 1, *Le Règne de Louis XIV, 1698-1715.* Paris: P.U.F, 1953.

Gomez, Michael A. *Black Crescent: The experience and legacy of African Muslims in the Americas.* New York: Cambridge University Press, 2005.

Hall, Gwendolyn Midlo. *Slavery and African Ethnicities in the Americas: Restoring the Links.* Chapel Hill: University of North Carolina Press, 2005.

---. *Africans in Colonial Louisiana: The Development of Afro-Creole Culture in Eighteenth Century Louisiana.* Baton Rouge: Louisiana State University Press, 1992.

Harris, Jessica B. *High on the hog. A culinary journey from Africa to America.* New York, Berlin, London, Sydney: Bloomsbury, 2011.

Harris, Joel Chandler. *Nights with Uncle Remus, Myths and Legends of the Old Plantation.* New York: McKinley, Stone & Mackenzie, 1883.

---. *Uncle Remus: His Songs and Saying.* New York: D. Appleton and Company, 1880.

Hawthorne, Walter. *Planting Rice and Harvesting Slaves: Transformations Along the Guinea-Bissau Coast, 1400-1900.* Portsmouth, NH: Heinemann, 2003.

Haydel, Belmont F. *The Victor Haydel Creole Family: Whitney (Haydel) Plantation — Plantation Beginnings And Early Descendants.* 3d ed. Warminster, PA: Cooke Publishing Company, 2009.

Hébrard, Jean M. and Rebecca J. Scott. *Freedom Papers: An Atlantic Odyssey in the Age of Emancipation.* Cambridge: Harvard University Press, 2012.

Heinrich, Pierre. *La Louisiane sous la Compagnie des Indes (1717-1731)*. New York: Burt Franklin, 1908.

Herskovits, Melville J. and Frances S. Herskovits. *Suriname Folk-Lore*. New York: Columbia University Press, 1936.

Hien, Ansomwin Ignace. *Le Conte de la Volta Noire-Contes Dagara*, Corpus II. Ouagadougou, Burkina Faso: Editions G.T.I., 1995.

Hirsch A. and Logsdon J., eds. *Creole New Orleans: Race and Americanization*. Baton Rouge: Louisiana State University Press, 1992.

Holloway, J. and W. Vass. *The African Heritage of American English*. Bloomington: Indiana University Press, 1993.

Holmes, Jack D.L. "Indigo in Colonial Louisiana and the Floridas." *Louisiana History* 8.4 (1967): 329 - 349.

Howard P.L. "Women and the plant world: An exploration." In *Women and Plants: Gender Relations in Biodiversity Management and Conservation*, edited by Patricia L. Howard. London: Zed, 2003.

Hunter et al. *Whitney Plantation: Archeology on the German Coast. Cultural Resources Investigations in St. John the Baptist Parish, Louisiana*. Prepared under contract with Walk, Haydel & Associates, Inc. for the Formosa Plastics Corporation of Louisiana, 2 volumes, 1 Nov. 1991.

Hurston, Zora Neale. 1935. *Mules and Men*. Reprint, New York: Harper & Row, 1990.

Ingersoll, Thomas N. *Mammon and Manon in Early New Orleans: The First Slave Society in the Deep South, 1718-1819*. Knoxville: University of Tennessee Press, 1999.

---. "The Slave Trade and the Ethnic Diversity of Louisiana's Slave Community." *Louisiana History* 37.2 (1996): 135-42.

Inikori, Joseph E. "Africa in world history: the exports slave trade from Africa and the emergence of the Atlantic economic order." In UNESCO *General History of Africa*, vol 5, edited by B.A. Ogot, 74-112. Paris: UNESCO, 1992.

F.R. Irvine. "The edible cultivated and semi-cultivated leaves of West Africa." *Qualitas Plantarum et Materiae Vegetabiles* 2 (1956): 35-42.

Johnson, Walter. *Soul by soul. Life inside the antebellum slave market*. Cambridge, Massachusetts and London, England: Harvard University Press, 1999.

Juhe-Beaulaton, Dominique. "Alimentation des hommes, des *vodoun* et des ancêtres. Une histoire de créales dans le golfe de Guinée." In *Cuisine et société en Afrique, histoire, saveurs, savoir-faire*. Monique Chastanet, François-Xavier Fauvelle-Aymar and Dominique Juhe-Beaulaton, 53-66. Paris: Karthala, 2002.

Kane, Oumar. *La Première Hégémonie Peule. Le Fuuta-Tooro de Koli Tenella à Almaami Abdul*. Dakar: Karthala-Paris, PUD, 2004.

Karenga, Maulana. *Introduction to Black Studies*, 2d ed. Los Angeles: The

University of Sankore Press, 1993.

Kilpatrick, Thaddeus Roger III. *A Conservation Study of the Decorative Paintings at Whitney Plantation, St. John the Baptist Parish, Louisiana.* A Thesis in the Graduate Program in Historic Preservation. Presented to the Faculties of the University of Pennsylvania in Partial Fulfillment of the Requirements for the Degree of Master of Science, University of Pennsylvania, 1992.

Kilpatrick et al. *The preservation and restoration of the Whitney Plantation, volume V Historic paints analyses.* Submitted to the Fred B. Kniffen Cultural Ressources Laboratory, Department of Geography and Anthropology (LSU), for the Formosa Plastics Corporation of Louisiana, 5 Nov. 1992.

Kolb, Carolyn. "Beyond Gumbo: The Secret Life of Okra." *Reckon, The Magazine of Southern Culture,* vol. 1, Première Issue (1995): 1-2.

Landers, Jane G. *Atlantic Creoles in the Age of Revolutions.* Cambridge, Massachussetts and London, England: Harvard University Press, 2010.

Levine, Lawrence W. *Black Culture and Black Consciousness: Afro-American Folk Thought From Slavery to Freedom.* Oxford: Oxford University Press, 1977.

Lewicki T. & Johnson M. *West African Food in the Middle Ages according to Arabic Sources.* London: Cambridge University Press, 1974.

Lovejoy, Paul E. *Transformations in Slavery.* Cambridge: Cambridge University Press, 2000.

---. "Forgotten Colony in Africa: The British Province of Senegambia (1765-83)." In S*lavery, Abolition and the Transition to Colonialism in Sierra Leone,* edited by Paul E. Lovejoy and Suzanne Schwarz. The Harriet Tubman Series on the African Diaspora. Trenton, NJ: Africa World Press (forthcoming).

Lowery, Charles D. "The Great Migration to the Mississippi Territory." *Journal of Mississippi History* 30.3 (1968): 173–192.

Lucas, Rafael. "Marronnage et marronnages." *Cahiers d'histoire. Revue d'histoire critique* 89: *Les enjeux de la mémoire.* (2002): 8. Accessed 5 September 2013. URL: http://chrhc.revues.org/1527.

Menn, Joseph K. *The large slaveholders of Louisiana-1860.* New Orleans: Pelican Publishing Company, 1964.

Merrill, E.C. *Germans of Louisiana.* Gretna, LA: Pelican Publishing Company, 2005.

Miller & Smith. *Dictionary of Afro-American Slavery.* New York: Greenwood Press, 1988.

Miller, Surrey. *The commerce of Louisiana during the French Régime, 1699-1763.* Doctoral dissertation, University of Columbia, Faculty of Political Science, New York, 1916.

Nast, Heidi J. *Concubines and Power: Five Hundred Years in a Northern Nigerian Palace.* Minneapolis: University of Minnesota Press, 2005.

Pélissier, Paul. *Les paysans du Sénégal.* Saint-Yrieux, France: Fabrègue, 1966.

Philips, Ulrich B. 1918. *American Negro Slavery*. Reprint, New York: Appleton-Century Inc., 1936.

Portères, R. "Géographie alimentaire, berceaux agricoles et migrations des plantes cultivées en Afrique intertropicale." *Société de biogéographie* 239 (1951).

Pluchon, Pierre. *Vaudou-Sorciers-Empoisonneurs, de Saint-Domingue à Haïti*. Paris: Karthala, 1987.

Price, Richard. *First Time: The Historical Vision of an Afro-American People*. Baltimore: Johns Hopkins University Press, 1983.

Rasmussen, Daniel. *American uprising. The untold story of America's largest slave revolt*. New York: HarperCollins Publishers, 2011.

Rehder, John B. *Delta Sugar: Louisiana's Vanishing Plantation Landscape*. Baltimore: John Hopkins University Press, 1999.

Roberts, Erika Sabine. *Digging through discarded identity: archaeological investigations around the kitchen and the overseer's house at Whitney plantation, Louisiana*. Thesis submitted to the Graduate Faculty of the Louisiana State University and Agricultural and Mechanical College in partial fulfillment of the requirements for the degree of Master of Arts in the Department of Geography and Anthropology, May 2005.

Robichaux, Albert J., Jr. *German Coast Families, European Origins and Settlement in Colonial Louisiana*. Hebert Publications, Copyright by A. Robichaux, 1997.

Roger, Baron Jacques-François. *Fables Sénégalaises recueillies de l'ouolof et mises en vers Français : avec des notes destinées à faire connaître la Sénégambie, son climat, ses principales productions, la civilisation et les moeurs de ses habitants*. Paris: Nepveu, Firmin Didot, Ponthieu, 1828.

Rolph, George M. *Something about sugar. Its history, growth, manufacture, and distribution*. San Francisco: John J. Newbegin, 1917.

SALL (Ibrahima Abou). 2002. "Les céréales et le lait au Fuuta Tooro (Mauritanie, Sénégal): un métissage culinaire." In *Cuisine et société en Afrique, histoire, saveurs, savoir-faire*, by M. Chastanet, F.X. Fauvelle-Aymar & D. Juhe-Beaulaton, 191-204. Paris: Karthala, 2002.

Schafer, Judith K. *Slavery, the Civil Law, and the Supreme Court of Louisiana*. Baton Rouge: Louisiana State University Press, 1994.

See, Alva B. III. "Whitney Plantation." Architectural Thesis, Tulane School of Architecture. November 1982.

Senghor, L. and Sadji A. *La Belle Histoire de Leuk-le-Lièvre*. Paris: Hachette, 1953.

Simpson G.W., ed. *The Photographic News. A weekly record of the progress of photography* 10.898 (20 April 1866). Printed and published in London by Thomas Piper.

Stein, Robert L. *The French sugar business in the eighteenth century*. Baton Rouge: Louisiana State University Press, 1988.

Sternberg, M.A. *Along the River Road. Past and Present on Louisiana's Historic Byway*. Rev. ed. Baton Rouge: Louisiana State University Press, 2001.

Teas, Thomas S. "A Trading Trip to Natchez and New Orleans: Diary of Thomas S. Teas." *Journal of Southern History* 7.3 (1941): 378-99.

Thomas, Hugh. *The Slave Trade*. New York: Simon and Schuster, 1997.

Thrasher, Albert. *On to New Orleans: Louisiana's Heroic 1811 Slave Revolt*. 2d ed. Monterey, CA: Cypress Press, 1996.

Usner, Jr., Daniel H. *Indians, Settlers, & slaves in a frontier exchange economy. The Lower Mississippi Valley before 1783*. Chapel Hill and London: The University of North Carolina Press, 1992.

List of illustrations

Tables

Maps, Graphs, and Pictures

INDEX